THE END GAME

The End Game

HOW INEQUALITY SHAPES OUR FINAL YEARS

Corey M. Abramson

Harvard University Press   Cambridge, Massachusetts · London, England   2015

First printing

Library of Congress Cataloging-in-Publication Data

Abramson, Corey M., 1980–

The end game : how inequality shapes our final years / Corey M. Abramson.

   pages cm

 Includes bibliographical references and index.

 ISBN 978-0-674-74395-3

1. Older people—United States—Social conditions. 2. Aging—Social aspects—United States. 3. Ageism—United States. 4. Discrimination—United States. I. Title.

HQ1064.U5A223 2015

305.260973—dc23   2014043464

To my father,
who spent his years in toil to provide his family with a better life,
but perished before getting the chance to grow old.

CONTENTS

An Old Workman
Warped . . . gland-dry . . .
With spine askew
And body shrunken into half its space . . .
Well-used as some cracked paving-stone . . .
Bearing on his grimed and pitted front
A stamp . . . as of innumerable feet.

—Lola Ridge

THE END GAME

INTRODUCTION

The End Game

You can't win,
You can't break even,
And you can't get out of the game.
People keep sayin',
Things are gonna change,
But they look just like they're staying the same.

—William Brown, *The Wiz,* 1978

On a brisk October afternoon in 2010, Bernard and I were listening to a radio broadcast of the San Francisco Giants game. The commentary blared out over a cheap plastic radio in the musty backroom of a senior center in Rockport, a predominantly poor, multiethnic, urban neighborhood in the greater San Francisco Bay area. Small groups of African American men were listening to the radio while playing pool, chess, and dominoes. Although Bernard was only in his early sixties, he could no longer stand up long enough to play a game of pool. The self-proclaimed former hustler was also consistently frustrated by the way his chess game had gone downhill. He felt he was now too "fuzzy-headed" to hang with the other guys in the senior center, so he mostly resigned himself to dominoes. On this particular day, however, Big B (as Bernard was known to his friends) was fixated on the baseball game. Like many of the other seniors involved in my ethnographic study of how American inequality shapes later life, Big B was a huge baseball fan. He took slow sips from a small Styrofoam cup containing sugar, cream, and a bit of coffee, while patiently trying to explain the nuances of baseball to me. He pointed out that it wasn't just the athletic movements that made the game gripping, but also the connections between the players, team dynamics, rules, strategies, and individual backstories. I nodded. The truth, though, is that while I understood each of these parts in isolation, I had only a superficial understanding of the game. What I eventually learned from Big B and the other seniors in my study is that explaining how inequality shapes our final years, like understanding baseball, requires understanding how the pieces fit together. It necessitates charting the larger underlying connections that constitute what sociologist Pierre Bourdieu calls the "logic of the game." This book explains what I found.[1]

The chapters that follow show that while seniors from across the social spectrum face a set of common challenges associated with growing old, they do not do so on equal footing. It will quickly become apparent that the disparities that structure our lives from our first breath onward do not end with the promise of Medicare and a Social Security check. When the challenges of "old age" present themselves to us, what they mean and how we can respond are contingent on inequalities both past and present. Some of us ultimately confront common difficulties in later life—such as increasing physical problems or watching friends and loved ones perish—with access to substantial wealth, social support, and education. Others will face the same problems, but do so alone with few resources. The larger implication is that how we grow old, and the options available to us as we do, often depend on whether we are rich or poor, male or female, black or white. In other words, aging is a stratified process.[2]

Throughout this book, I extend the analogy of the game to help explain how inequality shapes later life. The comparison is analytically useful, because social life, like games, consists of active players, organizing mechanics, temporal phases (e.g., innings, periods, quarters) and different styles and strategies of approaching challenges. Further, games quite often thrive on the illusion of being fair even when they are not. In a similar vein, some mistakenly equate the shared experiences of old age with the dissolution of other social divisions. While looking at the presence of certain shared experiences in later life is essential to understanding the *end game* an increasing number of us will play, the reality is that the score does not revert to zero, nor do the inequalities that existed throughout the game vanish. Socioeconomic, racial, and gender divides still determine who steps onto the field, the equipment they bring with them, the score they start with, and the strategies they can ultimately deploy.[3]

The goal of this book is to show how key mechanisms of social stratification—such as, health disparities, structural inequality, culture, and networks—structure everyday life in old age, and, conversely, how the unique practical and symbolic aspects of old age make it an important axis of American inequality. In doing so, this book explains why the opportunities and outcomes of the end game remain stratified, and what its players and rules tell us about inequality more generally.[4]

Why the End Game?

I have often been asked why, as a scholar of stratification and inequality, I chose to study old age. After all, the saying goes, "The children are our future," so why not just study inequality in the early years? The answer is straightforward: later life is both central to understanding the shifting contours of American society, *and* it provides a particularly rich location for charting how key mechanisms of stratification operate in everyday life.

First, while youth is an obsession for many Americans (social scientists being no exception), the simple fact is that more of us will live to be old than at any other point in human history. In 1900, the average life expectancy for an American child coming into the world was just over forty-seven years. In contrast, a newborn in the United States in 2011 could expect to live to be almost seventy-nine. Some wager that as the twenty-first century progresses, the majority of children born in affluent nations will live to be over one hundred. This shift is part of a larger historical trend toward a longer, more secure, and more predictable life course that has radically altered the social landscape in America and elsewhere. Consequently, seniors now make up a larger portion of the US population than at any other point in history. Although several groups of racial minorities and those subject to socioeconomic disadvantage still have shorter lives than their peers on average, their life expectancy has increased drastically as well.[5]

While substantial differences and disparities in life expectancy remain, Americans are living an average of three decades longer than they were at the outset of the previous century, and the group of Americans that survives to "grow old" is more diverse than ever before. This is a major demographic transformation that is already affecting the shape of American society. Many Americans will now spend a larger portion of their lives engaged with elderly parents or ill spouses than with small children. As medical technologies advance and baby boomers transition into old age, these trends are expected to accelerate. Examining the lives of seniors is not only timely, but also it has never been more important to understanding the changing contours of the American social order.[6]

Second, the later years provide a unique and underutilized lens for understanding the operation and persistence of social stratification and inequality. Most of us will grow old and all of us will die. These simple facts provide tremendous and often underutilized leverage for understanding how key mechanisms of stratification operate. Unlike most challenges that people are called on to solve in their lives, the shared physical and social difficulties of advanced age confront all who survive to meet them. Consequently, people from different backgrounds face what Bourdieu refers to as a set of "similarly shaped problems." In later life, Americans from divergent backgrounds come to face common predicaments such as declining mobility, health problems, and the deaths of friends and loved ones.[7]

Like childhood, the site of myriad studies of social stratification and inequality, old age is analytically powerful because it involves certain convergent experiences that facilitate comparisons that are harder to make in the middle of the life course. Examining the different (and sometimes similar) responses of individuals and groups provides a powerful vantage point for seeing how inequalities past and present shape experience and behavior. Further, old age and childhood are particularly important in the American context, given that they provide rare acknowledgments of, and support for, government interventions into inequality—via the promise of schooling in youth and the delivery of entitlements such as Social Security and Medicare in old age. Social scientists know a great deal about how inequality, social mobility, and policy interventions work in the early years of life, but we know less about how these influence everyday existence at the end. Examining the lives of seniors from different backgrounds, in real-world contexts, is therefore key to expanding our understandings of how stratification and inequality operate in America.[8]

Approach

To examine how inequalities past and present shape the lives of older Americans, this book presents data collected during two and a half years of comparative ethnographic fieldwork in four urban neighborhoods along with sixty in-depth interviews with older Americans from diverse ethnic, racial, and socioeconomic backgrounds. Throughout, I use embedded observations in people's homes, hospitals, senior centers, nursing facilities, and related settings to illustrate how key mechanisms of stratification continue to shape the everyday lives of American seniors. By combining and integrating these observations with seniors' own accounts and understandings, the chapters that follow outline the complexities and contradictions of the end game as well as what it can tell us about stratification and inequality more broadly.

Each chapter advances toward this overall goal by showing how women and men from different backgrounds approach everyday life in old age—often in ways that present puzzles for both popular and social-scientific accounts of inequality. For instance, this book will explain why Jane, a middle-class white woman, regularly skips chemotherapy for breast cancer, while her neighbor Laney, another middle-class white woman living down the block, attends treatment religiously for the same condition. It will clarify why Tim, a middle-class white man, goes to a doctor every time he develops a cough, whereas James, a middle-class African American man around the same age, will delay until an ambulance drags him to the emergency room. It will illuminate why Donald, a Chinese immigrant in a middle-class community, responds to his aging body by trying to maximize longevity, while Ray, an African American man living in a poor neighborhood, tries to have as much fun as possible before his body breaks down. This book will also address a puzzle that runs throughout the data: Despite their very different backgrounds and circumstances, why do seniors like Ray, Donald, Jane, and Laney *all* use similar language to describe what it means to grow old in America? As I will show, unraveling these puzzles and the many parallels observed during field research reveals how intricate and powerful relationships between inequality, social life, and the human body stratify our experiences and opportunities in later life.[9]

What will become most apparent as I present data about how Jane, Donald, Ray, and others approach their everyday lives is that explanations that attempt to attribute stratification in later life to one catchall pathway—for example, structural disparities, biology, networks, or culture—cannot adequately explain the diversity of responses and outcomes seen among American seniors. Like other researchers who operate in the tradition sometimes referred to as analytical sociology, I take a different tack. Rather than attempting to determine which factor provides *the* key link between inequality and social life in old age, each chapter focuses on comparative observations of everyday social life and seniors' understandings of it to explain *when* and *how* interconnected mechanisms of stratification systemically shape action and outcomes.

While analytical distinctions between different mechanisms of stratification are central to understanding the causes of different outcomes (e.g., Is it a lack of money that leads Jane to skipping chemotherapy, or her orientations to the human body?), explaining variation in later life also requires understanding how mechanisms work in concert. In charting the patterns observed during fieldwork, this book shows how the elements of the end game fit together, why the end game remains unequal, and what this means for the players involved. The remainder of this introduction sets the stage by situating this book's contributions to social science, introducing the methodology underlying the study, and providing a brief road map of the book.[10]

Situating the End Game

The Changing Life Course and the Persistence of American Inequality

While Americans can expect to live longer than in the past, race, class, and gender divisions continue to profoundly shape the length and trajectory of our lives. A recent examination of vital statistics by a number of prominent public health scholars puts this into stark relief:

> In 2008 US adult men and women with fewer than 12 years of education had life expectancies not much better than those of all adults in the 1950s and 1960s. When race and education are combined, the disparity is even more striking. In 2008 white US men and women with 16 years or more of schooling had life expectancies far greater than black Americans with fewer than 12 years of education—14.2 years more for white men than black men, and 10.3 years more for white women than black women. These gaps have widened over time [between 1990 and 2008].[11]

In practice, this means many of America's most disadvantaged simply die before they ever receive Medicare or a Social Security check, a process demographers refer to as "selective mortality." Put simply, those with fewer socioeconomic resources, and those from marginalized groups, tend to be less healthy and consequently die younger than their peers on average. Likewise, when and how the physical challenges of later life present themselves varies along these same lines. This is part of an even broader pattern whereby social divisions translate into health disparities from birth onward. While recognizing the fact that we are living three decades longer than those born a century earlier is essential for understanding the structure of American society, it does not mean we have reached the end of inequality.[12]

The continuation of stark disparities in aging and health not only raises important questions about equity, but also it highlights analytical puzzles that are central to understanding social stratification. Below I outline some of the questions that are most relevant to understanding the end game that shapes the lives of millions of older Americans.

If a key component of the relationship between inequality and aging plays out prior to old age by determining who dies before they get old (i.e., selective mortality), what happens to the pool of "survivors"? Do interventions such as Social Security and Medicare serve to even the playing field? According to one line of reasoning, the answer is yes. The argument goes that the combination of survivors' "robustness" with social insurance programs makes old age a time when the inequalities that structure the earlier part of the life course are mitigated, resulting in a form of "leveling." Classically, this was evidenced in part by what is known as the "crossover effect"—the observation that whites have sub-stantially lower mortality rates than African Americans until about age seventy-five, where the pattern narrows then shifts. Likewise, scholars sometimes point to the "paradox" that Latinos typically fare better in later life than would be predicted by their socioeconomic status.[13]

A competing line of argument suggests that old age is better under-stood in terms of "cumulative advantage" and disadvantage, where inequalities that shape earlier life continue to matter and converge. Scholars who embrace this line of argumentation point to an expanding body of data that shows that for any given individual, the advantages conferred by factors such as education accumulate over the life course, despite the aggregate appearance of leveling at the population level associated with "selective mortality." There is evidence of the "rising importance" of factors such as education across cohorts that suggest the gap is not closing. Further, some have argued the presence of the black/white crossover effects is largely an artifact of measurement issues and the failure to disentangle age, period, and cohort effects. Poor seniors, those with less education, and members of certain racial minority groups are worse off than their surviving peers, when all else is equal. Rather than being leveled away, inequalities in material, bodily, and cultural resources continue to structure our opportunities until our deaths.[14]

While progress has been made in understanding these patterns in aggregate, and there are rich ethnographic accounts suggesting that later life is filled with challenges, there is a relative dearth of cross-site ethnographic studies showing what all this means in the everyday lives

of seniors from different backgrounds living in different neighborhoods. This book aims to help address this issue.[15]

Is Age Just a Number?

The relationship between inequality and aging leads to another set of
questions. If the length and trajectories of our lives vary radically based
on our social position, does the notion of "old age" even make sense? If
so, what defines it? Is age "just a number," or is it something more? Is it
a social fact or a stereotype? Is it defined by its biological, chronological,
or social components?

Old age is notoriously difficult to conceptualize. While aging and
death are comparatively universal, the paradigms we use to understand
and explain them vary widely. Aging in modern societies is a complex
phenomenon that resides at the intersection of linked biological and
social forces. Yet in practice, biomedical, sociological, psychological,
and folk theories are placed in competition with one another. Discussions
about later life are cast in terms of contradictory dualisms. Aging is
simultaneously treated as social *or* biological, physiologically natural *or*
pathological, a monolithic life phase *or* an artificial construction (i.e.,
"just a number"), a time of psychological continuity *or* disruption and
disengagement. The issue is further complicated demographically by
the fact that the various effects of old age are not as easy to separate and
measure as one might imagine. Markers of "chronological age" reflect
not only the number of years lived but also the cohort to which a person
belongs (i.e., when that person was born) and when the observations
take place.[16]

The everyday reality, as the seniors in this book attest, is complex.
Reductionist frameworks are often inadequate for explaining the commonalities and differences that shape the end game. Still, it is necessary
to outline basic assumptions to clarify the object of empirical investiga-
tion. This study was guided by three basic propositions about aging and
"old age" drawn from findings in the existing biological and social science literatures:

First, aging involves intertwined physiological and social processes.
Social circumstances affect who lives to grow old and the degree of

physiological challenges they face once there. Likewise, the aging body, and what it signifies in an age-stratified society, affects seniors' circumstances and options in a particular historical period.[17]

Second, "old age" is not just a number but also a cultural category with shared characteristics, challenges, expectations, and prejudices that are connected to (but not reducible to) demographic and biological markers. That is, while the speed and manifestation of biological *aging* varies substantially, *old age* can be fruitfully conceived of as a durable cultural category that stratifies our lives.[18]

Third, while age itself can be an important axis of inequality, it exists alongside and intersects other persistent lines of American inequality such as race, socioeconomic status, and gender.[19]

Do the Mechanisms of Social Stratification Change in Later Life?

If we accept the growing body of evidence suggesting that inequality continues into later life, and the proposition that old age can be a category of inequality, we are faced with another question: Do the mechanisms of stratification that matter earlier in life remain the same, or do they change? If so, how?

A multitude of studies have documented that American society is characterized by unequal contexts, opportunities, and outcomes. Where we go to school, how much money we will earn, the professions we select, who we befriend, and how long we are likely to live are often closely linked to our social circumstances at birth. These patterns reflect and help reproduce historical ethno-racial, socioeconomic, and gender inequalities that are central to patterns of social stratification in America. A related body of research has examined how potential sources of social mobility, such as education, might serve to mitigate or exacerbate these forces in youth and middle age. Yet, how and why specific aspects of American stratification continue to shape, or cease shaping, everyday life in old age is murkier. This book addresses this issue by showing the continuities and differences in how key mechanisms of inequality—health disparities, structural inequalities, culture and social networks—continue to stratify experiences and opportunities in later life.[20]

HEALTH DISPARITIES

In addition to well-documented disparities in education, wealth, and life-chances, inequality powerfully shapes health and well-being. Biomedical researchers and social scientists alike have repeatedly shown that being poor and socially marginalized contributes to stress and illness from birth into adulthood. The consequence is that the poor and members of many racial minority groups are both more likely to die young and suffer from debilitating illness. Increasingly, socioeconomic and racial inequalities are being recognized as one of the fundamental causes of health disparities. In their work building upon this literature, sociologists Freese and Lutfey summarize this profound and durable relationship in unambiguous terms when they note, "The lower status people are, the sooner they die, and the worse health they have while alive."[21]

Disparities in health and illness do more than reflect historical patterns of inequality, however. They actively contribute to its persistence over time and across generations. Social scientists know that being ill limits opportunities for socioeconomic mobility. Recent research shows that even childhood experiences with health problems can powerfully shape life trajectories and mobility. Numerous studies have established that gaps in access to information, uneven material resources, unequal treatment in medical institutions, toxic environments, and differences in social networks constitute mechanisms that link social inequalities to observable disparities in morbidity, mortality, and health behaviors over the life course.[22]

However, despite our knowing that macrostructural and institutional factors *predict* disparities in health, and that poor health limits our options for mobility, we know less about *when* and *how* these key mechanisms shape everyday life among the different groups of Americans that survive to old age. Understanding how the relationship between social inequality and the human body operates is central to this book. Doing so requires moving beyond reductionist accounts to explain how the physical and symbolic aspects of the end game are connected—the subject of Chapter 1.[23]

STRUCTURAL INEQUALITIES

Social scientists have long shown that structural inequalities such as unequal material resources and differential treatment by institutions such as schools and hospitals affect the life chances, trajectories, and well-being of individuals and communities. Gaps in wealth, institutional discrimination, and disparities in health care limit both socioeconomic mobility and opportunities for maintaining well-being over the life course. Regardless of their beliefs or desires, it is likely that access to resources and opportunities affects how people respond to challenges such as growing older. But, specifically, which facets structure later life, and how?[24]

In the American case, structural issues associated with patterns of physical isolation and an unequal distribution of resources across neighborhoods are well documented. Limited opportunities in the job market and housing market throughout the life course, often associated with a legacy of racial discrimination, have frequently concentrated families with lower incomes in the same locale. In addition to the challenges this creates for mobility, concentrated poverty produces skewed access to the medical services that become increasingly salient in later life. A body of research has charted the unequal spatial distribution of hospitals and other health resources, showing that greater resources of higher quality are often clustered in more affluent white areas. Further, racially segregated neighborhoods with concentrations of lower-income populations tend to have higher levels of violence that may discourage local inhabitants, particularly older people, from leaving their places of residence. This can lead to increased isolation and potentially shape how seniors manage challenges, physical or otherwise. Further, there is some evidence that living in environments with concentrated poverty and violence increases mental, as well as physical, health problems. The available data continually reaffirm a classical sociological insight: the "context" of the neighborhood itself is still vital for understanding inequality in general and viable responses to biosocial challenges—aging in particular.[25]

While social scientists have made great inroads in showing how structural factors impact inequality in the aggregate, there is less systematic ethnographic data showing how the mechanisms by which these factors differentially affect (or cease to affect) the everyday experiences and behaviors of different groups in later life—the topic of Chapter 2.

CULTURE

Examining the connection between culture and inequality is often contentious in both contemporary social science and public discourse. Since the "culture of poverty" debate, connecting collective meanings, motivations, and practices of people to broader systems of social stratification has often been framed (in varying degrees) as "blaming the victim." Further, although many social scientists have long recognized that culture and structure are intertwined, "cultural explanations" for behavioral differences are still cast as being in direct competition with "structural" explanations. As this book shows, culture is key to understanding important behavioral differences that simply cannot be explained in only structural terms. Attempting to do so misconstrues how the persistent effects of inequality shape experience and outcomes.[26]

In their attempts to explain differences that are not reducible to material resources, researchers from across the social sciences are returning to an insight central to both classical and contemporary sociology: culture matters for inequality—and it can do so without acting as a monolithic "culture of poverty." In other words, while difficult to measure, unparsimonious, and loaded with baggage dating back to Oscar Lewis's *Five Families* and the Moynihan report, examining culture is empirically necessary. Beliefs, motivations, and strategies shape the ends people pursue, and how. These facets of culture reflect prior experiences and inequalities and are necessary to explain key behavioral differences in the present (particularly when people have similar resources but respond differently). Further, in the last three decades, the notion of culture has also been fruitfully expanded to capture differences in the collectively available cultural resources, tools, and strategies different groups deploy to interact with important institutions such as the educational system, labor markets, or complexes of medical care. A growing number of scholars are coming to recognize that understanding individual and communal responses to concrete and complex biosocial issues such as aging requires a serious examination of culture. [27]

How various aspects of culture (e.g., motivations, orientations, and resources) shape later life, and how these are connected to prior experiences and present inequalities, is the topic of Chapter 3. As the reader will see, whether seniors are motivated by a desire to *maximize enjoyment* or *preserve the body,* whether they understand aging through a *medical body* or *natural body frameworks,* and whether they have the "cultural capital" and "repertoires" to navigate formal and informal organizations shapes behavior and stratifies outcomes.

SOCIAL CONNECTEDNESS

Sociologists have long recognized the importance of social ties, networks, and community in explaining the reproduction of inequality. Work on aging, health, and inequality in particular has also continually pointed to the importance of social connectedness, which is often contrasted to disengagement and isolation. For instance, Eric Klinenberg's well-known work *Heat Wave* explains the life-and-death outcomes of the 1995 Chicago heat wave in these terms. Klinenberg shows that those seniors who lived alone, socially isolated from the community and networks outside, were more likely to die—and they died alone in droves. Klinenberg argues that compared to Latino elders, a disproportionate number of African Americans died because, even though their economic circumstances were otherwise quite similar, the African American seniors were more isolated. Recent work by ethnographers such as Elena Portacolone has shown that the "precariousness" of isolated seniors is not unique to Chicago, but remains a pressing social problem across the country. [28]

In addition to recognizing the importance of isolation versus connectedness, there is a growing move to acknowledging how the effects of social connectedness are contingent on other cultural and structural factors. That is, social connectedness does not universally produce "positive" or "negative" outcomes—even among the aged. Social connectedness does not mean the same thing to everyone. As I will show, "seeing friends within the last week," one common measure used on surveys, can mean very different things for different people. It can mean friends drove a senior to the clinic, or that they discouraged one from going to the doctor in favor of drinking alcohol at the local pub. Similarly, noting whether or not a senior "visits with family members" says nothing about whether that visit was one that provided food, an emotionally supportive encounter, or a stressful and aggressive exchange regarding finances. In short, more sweeping accounts often neglect the importance of variability in the quality, realization, and resources provided by social ties. There is a saying popular in some circles that goes, "Friends can be good medicine," but, as this book shows, they can also cause unwanted side effects.[29]

While we know that measures of social connectedness are linked to differences in aggregate behavior and outcomes, with a few important exceptions there is less work explaining the complex way these links work out across concrete contexts in the everyday lives of older Americans—the fourth major theme of this book.[30]

Study Design and Methodology

Like much social scientific research, this project began with an empirical question that had an uncertain answer: How do key mechanisms of inequality (i.e., health disparities, structural inequalities, culture and social connectedness) shape the way in which Americans from different backgrounds manage and make sense of growing old in everyday life? This section provides a brief overview of how I approached this topic (additional detail is provided in the methodological appendix).

In an attempt to answer the question above, I conducted field research at various field sites in four urban neighborhoods in Northern California. Two of the neighborhoods were largely poor, and two were mostly middle-class. Each of the neighborhoods contained racial, ethnic and gender variation. The findings I present in this book are drawn largely from two-and-a-half years of participant observation conducted in communal contexts populated by older Americans, such as senior centers, hair salons, bars, and shared spaces in housing developments, as well as more private settings such as people's homes, hospital rooms, and doctors' offices. Although I made a decision early on to focus on manifestations of inequality among neighborhood-dwelling seniors, I also conducted regular observations in two assisted-living facilities, one in a poor neighborhood and one in a middle-class neighborhood. I also occasionally visited other facilities of this type as I accompanied seniors on their visits to friends and family. In addition to fieldwork, I collected sixty in-depth interviews with neighborhood residents ranging from sixty-one to ninety-nine years of age, which provided additional life-history data and revealed how seniors made sense of growing older and the challenges they faced in their specific neighborhoods. Each of the seniors described in this book was informed of my research and consented to participate. The methodological appendix at the end of this book provides more information on my entrance into the field, how I interacted with seniors during data collection, how neighborhoods and sites were selected, and how I organized and analyzed my data.[31]

It is important to note that while my observations take place *in* different neighborhoods, this is not a study *of* neighborhoods per se. My focus is more narrowly on how mechanisms of inequality shape the lives of individuals and groups. This differs substantially from classic ethnographies that aim to reveal the "social order" of urban communities. Still, since charting the effect of unequal contexts both earlier in the life course and in later life is a key theme of this study, selecting a single neighborhood would have been insufficient. Social scientists have long shown that neighborhoods matter for the form and reproduction of inequality, so focusing on sites within a single neighborhood could potentially mean missing the way different neighborhood contexts shape seniors' survival strategies. In other words, since neighborhood differences are potentially key to explaining the inequalities in the end game, focusing on only one neighborhood would have removed a crucial comparative aspect of the research design. Ultimately, the diversity of individuals from different class, racial, and ethnic groups within the four neighborhoods in this study, while not exhaustive, allowed me to examine when and how various aspects of inequality shaped the end game. While this comparative sampling strategy (including seniors from different social strata occupying different neighborhoods) does not *directly* tell us how seniors came to be in their present condition, it does provide leverage in understanding how they make sense of their situations and how they behaved once there. A brief description of each of the neighborhoods in which I conducted field research is provided below.[32]

Poor Neighborhood 1 (racially mixed): "Rockport." Rockport was located in the center of a predominantly poor urban area and contained many African Americans and Latinos, as well as some whites. Many of the seniors lived in public or subsidized senior housing units, and the majority had been poor for much of their lives.

Poor Neighborhood 2 (more racially homogenous): "Elm Flats." Elm Flats was also in a predominantly poor urban area. Most of the residents were African Americans who had been poor for much of their lives. Some lived in public or subsidized housing.

Middle-Class Neighborhood 1 (racially mixed): "Cedar Hills." Cedar Hills was located in a mostly middle-class area. The majority of its residents were white, but there was substantial racial and ethnic diversity. The seniors in this area generally did not live in public housing, though some received assistance or government subsidies. Most had been middle-class for most of their lives, although some were now on a fixed income.

Middle-Class Neighborhood 2 (more racially homogenous): "Baygardens." Baygardens was in another middle-class urban district. Most of Baygardens' seniors were white, but there were also smaller numbers of African Americans, Latinos, and Asian Pacific Islanders living there. Many seniors were on a fixed income but had been middle class for most of their lives. As in Rockport, many lived in public or subsidized senior-housing.

Organization of This Book

In order to explain how social inequalities past and present shape later life in America and what this tells us about social stratification and inequality more generally, this book focuses on connecting five aspects of the end game: (1) who gets to play, (2) the rules of the game, (3) the shape of the playing field, (4) the strategies of the players, and (5) team dynamics.

The first two chapters examine how present circumstances shape the lives of those who survive to old age. Chapter 1 shows that among those who survive, seniors from diverse backgrounds face convergent issues and experiences in a way rarely seen earlier in the life course. Further, this chapter explains how and why old age becomes an important form of inequality, why it is linked to unequal resources for social action, and how this creates similar predicaments (i.e., the rules of the game). Chapter 2 explains that although seniors face shared predicaments, the playing field remains uneven. This chapter shows that in later life, Americans continue to inhabit unequal social contexts and possess vastly different resources on the individual and neighborhood level that structure how they can approach the end game.

The next two chapters connect past experiences, present inequalities, and seniors' diverse approaches to the end game. Chapter 3 shows that the everyday strategies seniors employ in the present reflect ways of understanding and acting in the world that have been shaped over a lifetime of past experiences, many of which were structured by the contours of American inequality. This affects which strategies for approaching the end game they see as desirable, reasonable, and possible, given their circumstances. Chapter 4 turns to the central importance of seniors' networks in explaining how seniors respond to later life. This chapter shows that it is not just "who you know," but what these relationships mean in concrete contexts across the life course that shape approaches to old age. That is to say, it shows how team dynamics continue to matter and how they can be a source of inequality.

The final chapter places the everyday lives of seniors back into the context of American inequality more broadly. This chapter returns to the fundamental analytical task of this book—clarifying how inequalities past and present shape the lives of aging Americans. This chapter concludes by summarizing key lessons about the broader operation of inequality in America, as well as what might be done by those interested in changing the game.

1

"OLD IS A DIFFERENT ANIMAL ALTOGETHER"

The Shared Predicaments of the End Game

All would live long, but none would grow old.

—Benjamin Franklin

Americans from different backgrounds face a set of shared predicaments, and often come to shared realizations, as they reach their later years. Consider the experiences of James and Lila.[1]

James and Lila Describe Aging in Similar Terms

Though they live but a short car ride away, James and Lila have never met and appear to have little in common. James is an African American man who lives in a public housing development in Rockport. Lila is a white woman who lives in a single-family home that she owns in Baygardens. Despite their geographical proximity, they have been separated by an immense social distance for much of their lives—a chasm created by the racial, socioeconomic, and gender inequalities that have historically shaped, and continue to shape, American society. Consequently, James and Lila have lived very different lives. James was born in the 1930s and raised in the South during the era of legal racial segregation. Although Lila was born around the same time, she was raised in Northern California. James moved to the West Coast as soon as he was able, where he carved out a living doing manual labor and taking odd jobs. He never married. Lila stayed in California her whole life. She went to college, where she met her husband. She got married, raised children, and spent her middle years working as a homemaker.[2]

Although the earlier parts of their lives were quite different, James and Lila (like most of the elders in this study) described shared experiences and challenges when discussing growing older in contemporary America. James eloquently summed up sentiments common among seniors in this study when he stated,

> What you don't really understand about seniors is the way they feel. You can never understand the way they feel because you from another generation, and with that you have different ideas on the way that older people are supposed to fit into a category. The whole world is in that position. *No one understands being old but old people.* That's just an event that happens and it's catastrophic. You can't change it. It's like a tree out there. When it's young it's growing, when it gets to a certain age, it spreads out, but it don't grow any more. It's just, branches come back and they fall off, but you still the same. And when you get old, everything is a chore. Everything you do is a chore. Just getting up in the morning is a chore. Because you can't sleep the same, you can't eat the same, you can't walk the same. And you don't have the same dreams. *Everything changes. Old is a different animal all together.* And the only way you can understand it is you have to get there. [emphasis added][3]

Lila, who was a bit less talkative, made a similar point to a friend over lunch at a senior center when she commented, "When you get old things change. How you think and feel." Her comment was met with knowing nods.

James and Lila's convergent descriptions of the end game are not coincidental. As the reader will see in the pages that follow, like their peers in each of the four neighborhoods in this study, James and Lila faced a set of common practical and symbolic challenges associated with growing old in America. This chapter charts how these challenges shaped everyday life for seniors in this study and how they led to shared realizations about predicaments that often crossed racial, socioeconomic, and gender divides. In doing so, it will show how the practical and symbolic challenges associated with the aging body organized experiences and stratified opportunities for those in this study.

"My Body Won't Let Me":
Physical Changes and the Organization
of Everyday Life in Old Age

As noted in the introduction of this book, a large component of the connection between inequality and aging plays out through selective mortality; that is, who survives long enough to "grow old." Nonetheless, the practical and symbolic challenges associated with aging presented even the most differently positioned seniors in this study with shared challenges and experiences. While uneven in timing, the eventual degeneration of the aging body creates shared challenges that shape how seniors engage with the world around them. For those in this study, the physical aspects of aging were inseparable from their lived experience and in many cases became a structuring force in their lives.[4]

As our bodies reach advanced age, we undergo numerous physiological changes. Tissues break down. The cardiovascular system and heart become less efficient, and blood vessels become less elastic. Bones shrink and muscles atrophy. The immune system weakens, and the ability to fight off disease decreases. While ample resources, good fortune, strong social networks, and robust genes can delay and soften the onslaught of these processes (an essential issue charted through this book), all who live long enough have to face these issues.[5]

In accordance with these physical aspects of aging, public health researchers and medical practitioners have sometimes referred to the elderly as a "medically engaged population": a category of people subject to increased health needs and consequently a "biological imperative" to seek care. Anthropologists and medical sociologists have criticized such characterizations as resulting from processes of medicalization or biomedicalization that extend technologically reified systems of expertise, knowledge, and control. On the ground the reality is a bit less ambiguous—physical challenges, and their implications for social action, were a vivid aspect of lived experience, a structuring force in seniors' lives, and a very real axis of stratification that shaped the end game across neighborhoods. As subsequent chapters will show, the shared predicaments that set the basis of the game are essential to tracing how other mechanisms of inequality differentially shape later life for those from different backgrounds.[6]

I now turn to those physical issues that I observed to be central to shaping the everyday lives of seniors across neighborhoods: declining stamina, health problems, mobility, and cognitive and sensory changes.

"I'm a Ferrari, but I Can't Get out of Third Gear": The Social Significance of Declining Stamina

When we reach our later years, most of us will have to deal with the consequences of having less available energy. Confronting declining stamina and what it meant for social life was an ubiquitous concern within all four neighborhoods in this study. The extent of this, and the magnitude of the corresponding social ramifications, caught many of the seniors in this study off guard. For others, fatigue deeply limited what they could do and became a structuring aspect of everyday life. Even when it was more of an annoyance, however, declining stamina necessitated a response. The comments of Eleanor, a seventy-three-year-old retired white woman, provide a common description of how physical slowdown and declining energy can shape life even for relatively healthy individuals. She noted,

> Well, the main part [of getting old] is that you're actually surprised that you're physically not able to do what you could do before. Before it's, well, eight hours on end that I could do things, you know, if I had a big task in the yard that I wanted to do . . . I love gardening. I could spend three, four, hours without stopping and do it. When you're older it's part of the immobility that's bothering you. And, you know, you compensate for it, but in the main, it's either aches or pains, or not having the stamina.

Even the most active seniors in my study admitted that they do not have the stamina they did when they were younger. Although the timing, severity, and response of losing stamina varied, it was something with which all of them eventually had to come to terms.[7]

In more extreme cases, a lack of stamina profoundly limited how seniors could live their lives. Put another way, fatigue created problems of social action that became a major structuring force in the lives of older Americans. The experiences of Dave, a poor white man in his early sixties living in Elm Flats, provide a representative example. Dave prided himself on his mental acuity, but physical problems from numerous diseases and a general lack of energy limited his ability to go out and do things. On my visits I would always ask Dave how he was doing, to which he would often quip, "I've so many problems, my problems have problems." Despite his quick wit and sense of humor, Dave was extremely anxious. He was particularly afraid of falling due to overexertion or lack of energy. Dave told me falling was just about the worst thing that could happen to a senior like him, because in many cases (including his own), it would result in a loss of independence. Without children or close family members, Dave felt he was particularly vulnerable and was afraid of spending his final days in a nursing facility. He often talked about the importance of keeping enough "energy in reserve" to avoid such an incident.

Dave confessed that the disjuncture between what his mind wanted to do and what his energy levels allowed him to do was deeply upsetting. He explained the predicament by analogy: "I think I'm a Ferrari but I can't get out of third gear . . . I get about two hours of good energy a day, where it is safe for me to move around and do things." I once naïvely commented that the free time of retirement must have provided Dave, who always enjoyed reading, with the opportunity to read new books. He responded, "Well, keep in mind this is in the context of having lots of health problems and very little energy. I can't do a lot of things." On the occasions when we would go out together, simply walking down the stairs to the car placed a noticeable strain on Dave. His range for physical and social action was limited by his physical issues and lack of stamina.

For many seniors like Dave, the predicament created by the convergence of fatigue and various health problems was a major factor that shaped how they could organize their lives. Meals, visits with friends, and doctors' appointments had to be scheduled to accommodate physical limitations. In Dave's case, what he could eat, with whom he could visit, and where he could go were determined in large part by his physical limitations. The problem of fatigue became more salient even for healthy seniors as they age or younger seniors as they became sick. For instance, Sandy, an eighty-nine-year-old former nurse who occupied an apartment for independently living seniors in Baygardens, stated the problem clearly in one of our many informal conversations. She told me the hardest part of growing older was that as one ages, "Your body just doesn't do what you want it to do. You are tired all the time and you get confused." For Sandy, the decline became most noticeable in her eighties. For others who were less fortunate, the challenge came earlier, but the shape of the predicaments were similar. In each case the social possibilities and experiences of growing old were inseparable from their physical dimension.[8]

"A Full-Time Job":
Health Problems, Death, and the Organization of Activity

In addition to having less energy, most individuals in this study encountered physical health problems (i.e., observable physiological changes that affected everyday life in a way that seniors found undesirable) with greater frequency in their later years. Once again, this had a major effect on how they approached everyday life.[9]

Many seniors in this study spent a good portion of their week, and much of their limited energy, in medical settings. Dave, for instance, often quipped that if he went to see medical providers every time he was supposed to, he would spend his entire life in the hospital. For those with conditions requiring ongoing treatment (e.g., cancer, diabetes, wounds), this effect was magnified. A comment made by Jane, a sixty-five-year-old white woman with breast cancer, articulates a typical frustration: "I feel like having cancer is a full-time job. It has just been a really fucked-up week. The house is a wreck, dishes are piled up, I have all these appointments, and my car is broken . . . I haven't even checked my e-mail in three days. It has been a fucked-up week."

For many of the people in this study, following a treatment regimen limited time, energy, and the ability to do the things they enjoyed. In Jane's case, between the tiredness, constant medical tests, doctor appointments, chemotherapy infusions, trips to the pharmacy, and side effects, the logistical demands of dealing with physical conditions could easily take up most of her time. She also lamented the effect of her recent physical issues and the corresponding decline in energy on her social life, noting, "I can't do the things I want to do. I am tired and depressed." As with other people in these circumstances, her health problems shaped both how she acted and how others acted toward her. This often led to the exclusion of other more desirable aspects of life and created new challenges in maintaining previous identity (i.e., when she followed medical advice, a topic I return to in Chapter 3).[10]

Further, dealing with the pain associated with common health problems such as arthritis was an omnipresent issue among the seniors in my study. The presence of (often constant and sometimes excruciating) pain became a salient aspect of everyday life as people grew older or sicker (often together), and the need to address it in some way crossed neighborhoods. Even for younger participants (i.e., those seventy-four and under), many of whom were active and had experienced comparatively minor physical problems, the issue of managing "aches and pains" was a key part of their everyday experience. The subjective meaning of pain and the way people responded varied widely between (and even within) different groups, a topic that I address in depth in Chapter 3. Some seniors saw pain as a challenge, others an injustice. Many took narcotic pain pills; others tried holistic approaches to minimize discomfort. However, for seniors across neighborhoods, pain shaped how they experienced and approached everyday life. An eighty-year-old white woman with arthritis provided a typical example when she noted to friends, "Everything hurts. I want to go out and have all these new experiences, but my body just won't let me." The medications seniors were prescribed for pain could also compound issues with stamina. Those who did not enjoy narcotic pain medications but needed them to cope would often have less energy and be less alert than they were previously.[11]

Health problems also forced seniors to grapple with issues of mortality—both their own and that of others. For seniors in all four neighborhoods, growing old was associated with confronting the deaths of others such as friends, loved ones, and acquaintances. The loss of people through death (or permanent institutionalization) produced concrete challenges in both the instrumental and psychosocial arenas. One issue for seniors was acknowledging and developing strategies for facing the inevitable prospect of their own death. As seniors watched friends and family die, and they recognized that their own bodies were not as strong as they once were, they were presented with the inevitability of death. Further, the death of those in seniors' networks meant watching existing networks shrink (even if new ones were built). As Chapter 4 will show, while network change affected seniors from all four neighborhoods, it did not do so equally. However, just as widespread changes in physical capacities created shared predicaments across neighborhoods, so too did changes in social ties connected to the physical changes, health problems, and deaths of others.[12]

"We're All One Fall away from the Home": Mobility, Sociability, and Vulnerability

Problems of declining physical mobility also traversed the neighborhoods in this study. How well seniors could get around the urban environs affected their ability to pursue essential tasks (e.g., getting food, seeing a doctor), their options for recreation, and how they were viewed by others within their community. Almost without exception, the seniors in this study experienced a decline in physical mobility that limited their ability to participate in activities they found meaningful earlier in their lives. Sandy, the eighty-nine-year-old former nurse, articulated common problems faced by even comparatively healthy seniors when she noted, "Luckily my heart is good, but my legs and arms hurt, and are tired. I can't walk very far anymore. My legs get tired, and I have to sit down. That happens to a lot of people." In another instance, upon introducing my project as a study of aging in communities, a retired dentist in Cedar Hills noted, "That is interesting. One of the key issues is whether they are ambulatory or not."[13]

Seniors consistently noted that they could not walk as far, stand as long, or navigate the same sorts of physical environments (e.g., buildings with steps or sidewalks with lots of cracks) as when they were younger. Many seniors had trouble engaging in physical activities they once enjoyed (e.g., playing pool, dancing, bowling) because they lacked the capacity to coordinate their movements or stay standing for a long time. The ability to navigate the environment was not only a shared problem, but also a gradient of inequality between seniors that affected

their ability to construct identities. Mobility was a particularly important axis of distinction among seniors because it shaped the sorts of
activities in which seniors could participate. Comments like those of
Beatrice were common: "She can't even move around, and I am older
than her!" For Beatrice and other seniors within each of the neighborhoods I studied, the confluence of pain, fatigue, and injury affected
their physical mobility.

General mobility issues associated with physical breakdown were
closely related to the very serious problem of falls. Many seniors feared
falling, as this was a potentially catastrophic event that could substantially transform their everyday lives. Seniors in public spaces often joked
about being "one fall away from the home" (i.e., one accident away from
being placed in assisted living)—although, as one senior commented to
me in an aside, "We joke about that, but it's true." Even under the best of
circumstances, a fall typically resulted in increased pain and physical
problems. This can be seen in the experiences of Donald. When I met
him, Donald was already using a walker. He explained that previously he
could get around fine with a cane, but he had experienced several falls in
the last year. After his last fall, he noted that walking was harder, and he
began to move more slowly. During the years I followed him, Donald's
physical problems progressed. The falls, the increased pain, and his
declining stamina greatly reduced the distance Donald could walk.
Although he loved to walk, and enjoyed the independence of not having
to ask for help, he had to rely increasingly on his family to transport
him, which was challenging, given his former identity as a breadwinner.

Among those seniors who sustained serious damage during a
falling episode, the end result was typically hospitalization (even for
those who generally avoided medical settings). Even if the senior recov-
ered, the fall often involved prolonged rehabilitation (frequently in a
nursing home), which was generally regarded as undesirable across communities as it was associated with a sense of lost independence and even
competence. Such falls do not occur in a social vacuum, of course,
but in real world locations like homes, streets, doctors' offices, nursing
facilities, and senior centers. These environments often reflect social
inequalities in surprising ways that can render some seniors more vulnerable than others, a topic to which I return in the next chapter.
Likewise, how seniors deal with falls is a function of the cultural tools,

material resources, social networks, and understandings about the body that influence their actions (as discussed in Chapters 2, 3, and 4). Still, a point of commonality among seniors across social and geographical terrains was the potential of having to deal with falls and their potentially serious ramifications for everyday life.[14]

"My Head's All Fuzzy Now":
Cognitive and Sensory Change

Issues of cognitive changes and memory loss also affected seniors across all four neighborhoods. For some, memory lapses were an occasional annoyance. For others, severe cognitive degeneration made living alone unviable, and in some cases resulted in placements in "total institutions" such as nursing homes. Even in less serious cases, memory issues translated into problems managing medications, keeping track of doctors' appointments, finding important documents, paying bills, and even remembering to eat and drink. In extreme institutional cases, memory loss could be tantamount to a loss of identity. Even in minor cases however, it necessitated a behavioral response.[15]

Jokes about "senior moments" and "dementia" were common in public places where seniors congregated, such as barbershops, beauty salons, senior centers, diners, and clinics. Seniors acknowledged that one of the reasons they joked was to make light of issues that were a real source of concern. In nursing homes, the loss of memory was a concern as well, but because of the institutional implications of "losing your mind," it was used more frequently as an insult between seniors, and the "jokes" took on a more sinister tone.

Seniors from all neighborhoods, even individuals who kept a generally upbeat attitude about aging, exhibited frustration with forgetting things, the need to rely on others, and the way forgetting reminded them of growing old. When describing her problems during a visit to her home, Sandy simply commented that when you get old, "you get confused." During an interview, Tommy, a sixty-seven-year-old Chinese man from Elm Flats, stated more bluntly, "The thing about getting older is your memory is fucked!" Memory problems were often exacerbated by medication or treatment for other health problems. For instance, when I went to visit Jane's home at a time we had arranged, she seemed first surprised to see me and then flustered. She explained, "I am having a hard time with scheduling now because of 'chemo brain.'" The extent to which her cancer treatment led to her forgetfulness, versus her age, is impossible to discern. In all likelihood, both were contributing factors.

For seniors who prided themselves on being quick-witted, or whose identities were bound up with activities that required memory and concentration, this could be a significant loss and a challenge to their identity. Bernard, an African American man living in Rockport, explained that it was difficult for him to acknowledge that he could not "hang" with other seniors in chess anymore. Bernard described how he used to travel around to take part in chess tournaments. He explained that it was exhilarating and people looked up to him for his skill, but some of the younger men now were just too good. He noted, "I used to be really good, but my head's all fuzzy now. I can't concentrate like I used to, and they [are] competitive. They play with clocks and all." Bernard also said he could no longer hustle or gamble on games, an activity he enjoyed during his youth.

In addition to problems with memory, as people age they experience a host of sensory changes. Hearing, taste, smell, and touch become less acute. Many seniors talked about getting "a sweet tooth" as their sense of taste dulled. Others talked about tactile numbness and neuropathy, which led to accidents around the house and difficulties with basic tasks, such as opening jars. Many complained that they could no longer smell as well as they used to. In some cases, the degeneration of the senses had profound ramifications for everyday life, especially in the case of hearing and eyesight loss. Hearing difficulties affecting communication often required special equipment such as hearing aids and modified phones. Problems with sight affected seniors' ability to read, recognize other people at a distance, and drive. The older seniors in my study frequently talked about how declining vision required them to give up driving, which was generally experienced as a major loss of independence. In some cases their families convinced them they were a danger, and in other cases outside authorities intervened. Either way, the result was a set of profound symbolic and practical changes.[16]

The decline of hearing and sight were doubly difficult as they not only eroded a seniors' capacity to perform instrumental tasks like driving, but also signaled the loss of this capacity to others and themselves. For instance, many seniors talked about getting depressed when they had to give up their cars, because of what this entailed (lost mobility) and what it implied (lost independence and status). When the seniors in my study talked about the dulling of the senses, they never did so in a positive way. The divergent ways seniors from different groups responded to these changes, and how their responses were shaped by the continuation of inequality, is discussed in subsequent chapters. However, first it is necessary to elaborate how the predicaments of growing old translate into problems of social action and shared experiences.

"Becoming One of the Old People": The Practical and Symbolic Predicaments of the Aging Body

For many in this study, "becoming one of the old people" was intrinsically linked with losing prized and socially validated characteristics that are connected to the body, such as strength, beauty, stamina, and wit. Even when the shared predicaments of aging did not physically impede the basic ability of elders to act "independently" in the world (via institutionalization, death, or debilitating illness), changes in physical and cognitive capacities carried symbolic ramifications that profoundly shaped their experiences. As discussed above, seniors across neighborhoods had to contend with practical issues created by illness, mobility problems, pain, declining sight, touch, hearing, and smell. However, they also had to contend with what this meant for social life. While some adaptations may seem comparatively minor (e.g., having to ask people to speak up), others carried existential weight because of their implications for personhood and independence (e.g., when to give up driving). Although issues did not manifest identically, the symbolic predicaments associated with growing old affected seniors across communities.[17]

Being old became a salient aspect of seniors' experiences, and being treated as one of the "old people" was seen as a categorical form of inequality. There were important differences by gender and socioeconomic status. Men often talked of losing their physical presence. Women talked about developing wrinkles, and how this change in appearance affected the way they were treated. As one woman put it, "They [young people] treat you like you are from another planet." Another noted, "All they see is wrinkles." Seniors (particularly women) continually noted the way they were overlooked in interactions with service providers, retailers, and other people and commented that this was a source of irritation. I saw this in the numerous instances when people would address me instead of the senior I was following. Seniors often commented on this, with the following response being a typical example: "If it's at the restaurant it really bothers me because it almost feels like they don't think I can read the menu and make up my own mind because they always ask the other person." The issue of a newfound "invisibility" was difficult for many to deal with, particularly those from wealthier backgrounds or from racial groups unaccustomed to dealing with stigma rooted in their appearance.[18]

Those from comparatively disadvantaged backgrounds often had greater cultural tools for dealing with problems of invisibility, which many experienced earlier in life (see Chapter 3), but the social consequences of the physical losses could be more profound. For poor individuals with scarce material resources, social status is often closely connected to aspects of "physical capital." Losing the strength, beauty, wit, or stamina that were central to their identity earlier in life was often particularly difficult. For seniors who prided themselves on their ability to conduct manual work, the lack of the physical capacity to do so was difficult to deal with. Poor men in particular often talked about how the degenerating body signaled vulnerability in a way they found undesirable. It also created challenges in their ability to carry prior identities (often associated with independence and rugged individualism) into later life. Commenting on his increased need for medical care, an elderly African American man from Rockport noted, "A man has a certain image to project. And that image, it don't include doctors." This feeling of dependence was often associated with a sense of shame. The decreased physical deterrent and ability to ward off crime and predation were a concern as well. Resource disparities affected how people could respond within and across neighborhoods, but the fundamental predicament of dealing with the practical and symbolic issues associated with lost physical capacities was widely shared.[19]

The health problems and pain discussed in previous sections also affected the ability of seniors to work and participate in recreational activities that were a key part of their identity earlier in life. Seniors often described specific physical traumas such as strokes, injuries, heart attacks, cancer, the advancement of arthritis, and so on, as major turning points that required them to change how they behaved and engaged with the world. Eventually, many seniors were forced to give up physical activities such as dancing, hiking, gardening, bowling, or pool. Similarly, health problems also led to some individuals having to give up work even when this was against their wishes. This was a major challenge, not just financially, but psychologically. For many Americans, work is a key aspect of identity. For some, it is almost tantamount to personhood. Leaving the workforce was a major transition, and a challenge to their sense of self, particularly when seniors felt they had little choice in the matter. The experiences of Donald are representative. When I went to spend the day at the senior center he frequented, Donald was holding court and lamenting having lost his warehouse job to his friend (even though this was years earlier). I asked if he still worked. He said no and explained his trajectory: "I was forced to retire. Too many surgeries. I had nine surgeries." I asked what for. He said, "Aneurysm, blood clot in my leg. See here"—he showed me mismatched skin on his leg—"they had to graft skin from my thigh, which is why it looks ugly now. I also have diabetes which complicates things." Donald's health problems made his previous occupation, social role, and identity (as a hard worker and provider) much less viable.[20]

As the previous sections showed, changes in physical characteristics affected seniors' abilities to interact with the world in ways many younger people take for granted; things as simple as opening a jar or going up a curb could be difficult and fraught with peril. In extreme cases, declining physical capacities created predicaments where people felt trapped and profoundly limited by their bodies. Jason, a 76-year-old white male, provides an extreme example. While watching daytime television in a nursing home, Jason shook his head and said, "I'm an action man, and there's no action there." He raised his voice and repeated, "I'm an *action man*. I raced cars and flew planes." During my visit the following week, I asked how things were going. He shrugged and said, "I just sit around all week dying, and watching others waiting to die. I'm a fucking cripple, and I can't go out." Here the degeneration of the body, in this case produced by rheumatoid arthritis and a host of other physical problems, was understood as largely (and literally) taking away his capacity to act. The issue was complicated by the fact that he was living in a nursing facility, which in many cases served as a "total institution" that residents could not leave at will. However, his body would have been a profoundly limiting factor even if he were able to live independently. The fact was that Jason could not walk, could not bathe without assistance, and could not dress alone. His modest social security income could not cover a private aide to help him in everyday life, and even if he had such an aide, his ability to do what he wanted would be limited by his pain and physical degeneration. He poignantly noted, "You depend on them [the nurses] for everything. They control your biology." Although some actions, such as lamenting his lost "independence" to a sociologist, were available to Jason, his diminished physical resources limited his capacities for pursuing lines of action he found desirable. It is hard to continue to identify as an "action man" when the most fundamental physical resources for action are stripped away.[21]

"I Don't Want to Play the Cripple Card Yet":
Convergent Practical Predicaments and Symbolic Challenges

The way the degenerating body created interconnected practical and symbolic predicaments is exemplified by a set of interactions I observed at a senior center in Baygardens. During a health fair put on by local community organizations, Geronimo, an elderly Latino man, was standing in line for free food and medical supplies. The line was substantial. There were about twenty seniors waiting and the queue was moving slowly. After a few minutes, Geronimo grimaced then left. An elderly white woman commented to me, "He has a problem standing up, because of his hips." Upon returning, Geronimo commented to me, "It is hard for me to stand for a long time. They should have some chairs." An elderly Asian woman told me, "Please tell them to have chairs." The man shook his head and said, "I already told [the director]." I asked him, "Have you ever thought about one of those portable folding chairs?" Geronimo responded, shaking his head, "I don't want to play the cripple card yet. It's only six months since it got bad. Already I can tell my wife doesn't want to go out with me." His physical issues not only affected his ability to perform instrumental tasks, but had ramifications for his sense of identity and self-presentation as well. Geronimo, like many seniors, wanted to project an image of physical and social independence for as long as possible, a major theme in Chapter 3, although his declining health made this more and more difficult. In his case, as with other seniors, it led to a gradual withdrawal from public settings.[22]

As with many seniors, "presence" and a sense of self sufficiency were important to Geronimo. They were an aspect of his identity, tied to his masculinity (e.g., "a man's got a certain image to project"), and, in his understanding, inseparable from physical attributes. Even those who had historically constructed a sense of self around less clearly obvious "physical" capacities were forced to acknowledge how key aspects of their identity (e.g., intellectualism, ability to work, position in the labor market) were affected by their aging bodies. A financier visiting a middle-class senior center commented on this as well, noting that not only was his memory worse, but also that he had less energy, and even though he wanted to work, no one wanted to hire someone who "looked old." His comments were representative of a common frustration: "They just totally think we're all old, feeble people with no brains. And it is very upsetting. It's a really tough way to be treated."

A seemingly less physical aspect of identity, the ability to work in a nonmanual profession and produce income, was eroded with the changes in the aging body (energy), the capacities dependent on that body (cognition), and, perhaps most salient here, what age and the body signify to potential employers (lack of youthfulness and competence, etc.). As Erving Goffman noted in his work on stigma, the body can act as a point of signification. Certain types of bodies, or other visible attributes, can lead to individuals being placed in a "discredited" category that is tied to assumptions about competence, proficiency, and morality. This can be true even in the absence of diminished capacities. Ironically, as seen in the distinctions seniors draw, this was true among seniors themselves as well.[23]

Shared Experiences in Later Life:
Old Age as a Structural Dilemma

The sections above demonstrate how the physical issues associated with growing old created shared predicaments for seniors across the four neighborhoods in this study. As the example with James and Lila at the beginning of this chapter illustrated, elders confronted issues such as lost mobility, declining energy, and death, with different life histories and material, social, and cultural resources. Yet despite different backgrounds, they came to describe and focus up a shared set of circumstances. Although rooted in biosocial rather than purely institutional forces, the predicaments faced by the seniors in this study formed what sociologist Ann Swidler refers to as "structural dilemmas." These dilemmas create "tasks or practical difficulties of action, to which the wider culture generates many different, sometimes competing, and always only partially satisfactory solutions." For all of the observable variation in the motivations, behavior, and strategies of the seniors I studied, there were substantial points of congruence in how they made sense of aging. The shared experiences of those in this study result from a recognition of the symbolic and practical importance of the aging body in everyday life. Their convergent understandings are a cultural by-product of the shared dilemmas faced by those who make it to the end game.[24]

One theme that came up consistently in both observations and interviews was the centrality of the body in the experience of old age. Seniors across the board discussed aging in terms of a breakdown in biological function. Even those who would make public proclamations about feeling young—such as "Age is just a number," or "I feel thirty-five"—would often privately confide that they were experiencing some physical problems or "getting up there." Many worried about the implications this had for their futures in general and how this would affect their opportunities for independence, typically defined as living alone. Declining health and growing old were also largely linked in the minds of seniors across all communities.

A representative example occurred as I was spending the day with Jessica, a ninety-two-year-old white woman who lives alone in an apartment in Baygardens. On this particular day we were going to see her ophthalmologist. Jessica mentioned that her friend, who was recently hospitalized, was having a hard time. I asked what was wrong with her. Jessica laughed then said, "She's old. That's what's wrong with her. I can tell you what's wrong with me." She began to count on her fingers and said,

> I've got a slipped disk and a bad back, I got arthritis all over. I have a bad leg on the one side. I have glaucoma, a hurt ankle, and I can't hear too well. If I stand up too long I get dizzy, and my legs get tired. *That's getting old. You can't see, you can't hear well, you get confused, and you have trouble walking.* [emphasis added]

In Jessica's account, like that of many seniors, to grow old is synonymous with bodily breakdown. James, the seventy-seven-year-old African American man from Rockport, expressed the same sentiments about health problems being a key aspect of growing older at the senior center where he spent many of his days:

> You have a tendency when you get older to have a problem with your health, walkin'. You have problems, all problems pertaining to your health. You know, it could be walking, sitting, laying. *Those are the things that an old person deals with that's not easy.* [emphasis added]

The observations above illustrate an astute recognition of how the physical predicaments of "getting old," such as increased health needs, the presence of pain, decreasing energy, slowing cognition, and sensory changes described in the previous section structure social life.[25]

In the sixty in-depth interviews I used to supplement my fieldwork, one question I always asked was "How would you describe what it is like to grow old to someone who is younger?" It is telling that although the question deliberately makes no reference to the body or health, every respondent from every neighborhood mentioned physical degeneration and the social consequences as part of their response. The comments of Tim, a sixty-seven-year-old white male living in Baygardens, are representative of a number of central points:

> So I'm really *physically* a wreck. And I'm very, very concerned about being able to *live by myself,* because I've lost a lot of the *flexibility* that I used to have, and that's one of the things that I wanted to mention . . . Seniors are a tough crowd . . . They're old, by definition, they're cranky, they're often in *bad health,* they're frequently in *mourning* for, you know, family or compatriots, and lastly, they're basically sniffing their own *mortality,* which is, you know, it's a tough, tough, tough crowd. [emphasis added]

Tim's answer points to the salience of problems created by the aging body detailed in the sections above, as well as a widespread acknowledgement that these problems were a common source of concern.[26]

In addition to acknowledging the physical changes of aging and how they affected her, the accounts of Janice, a sixty-seven-year-old, upper-middle-class white woman living in a large home in Elm Flats, described the sense of increased risk associated with becoming old. When asked what a young person should expect when growing older, Janice noted,

Well, speaking personally, things that I used to enjoy eating, I can't always eat because your digestion changes. Things do slow down. I've had a problem with my back. I used to be a person that walked a lot, but I've had a particular problem with my back and it's slowed me down. It can be frustrating. *Stuff happens. Heart attacks happen. Strokes happen. And falls happen.* And you have to just be very careful, and you have aches and pains. Your teeth may have to come out, and your eyes get old, it's called cataracts. [emphasis added]

This theme was shared across all four communities. The risk seniors acknowledge is often tied to underlying physical vulnerabilities: the chance of falling, strokes, or catastrophic medical problems. However, many seniors also constantly described fears of being taken advantage of, "losing their [mental] facilities," and/or being victimized by crime as they saw themselves as a more vulnerable and preyed upon population. One senior described the process of aging as "coming to terms with a mindset of frailty," which involved an increased likelihood of catastrophe both in terms of health and crime. Comments such as "I feel safe going out during the day, but I never go out at night" were common.[27]

Seniors across neighborhoods described how the convergent practical and symbolic challenges faced in later life produced a general shift in ways of experiencing and acting in the world. Like Janice, seniors from all four neighborhoods discussed how the general pace of life "slowed down" as they reached old age, often to the chagrin of individuals who built an identity around their ability to "stay active" through work, sports, volunteering, or other forms of social engagement. Many described learning to accept and manage the pain of everyday life as one aspect of a general shift in how they experienced the world. Lila, who is mentioned in the Introduction, conveyed the sentiment of this experiential shift when she noted, *"When you get old things change. How you think and feel."* This echoed James' statement that *"old is a different animal altogether."* Although the seniors above had different degrees of physical and cognitive changes, and were from diverse backgrounds, all were responding to the convergent predicaments of the aging body. As their bodies—the primary physical instruments for acting in the world—changed, their possibilities, and the way they were received by others, changed as well. Consequently, seniors described associated shifts in modes of experiencing and acting in the world—or, as Lila put it, changes in how they "think" and "feel."[28]

Although seniors' narratives of the aging process were fragmented and at times even contradictory, they shared a remarkable degree of coherence around the centrality of the body in everyday life. This coherence arises from the shared "structural dilemmas" rooted in the practical and symbolic challenges of growing old in America and speaks to their salience as a force for structuring life in the end game.

Conclusion:
On the Sociological Importance of Aches and Pains

It is probably not surprising to most readers that growing old is often associated with health problems, aches, pains, changes in cognition, the death of friends and relatives, and declining physical capacities. After all, these phenomena are all well documented in the medical, social-scientific, and popular literatures, and are affirmed by common sense. This fact alone should point to their significance. However, in practice the fact that they are "common sense" can obscure their centrality to, and utility for, understanding social stratification. This is true even among social scientists. After giving a talk on this project a few years ago, I was asked why as an ethnographer I did not choose something more exotic and "less depressing." My response then, and my point now, is that it is precisely the comparative universality, unseductiveness, and very lack of exoticism that makes later life such a powerful and important site for understanding the contours of social stratification and inequality.[29]

This chapter demonstrated that a set of physical and symbolic challenges associated with the aging body traversed the four neighborhoods in this study. These issues often became a structuring force in seniors' lives, a newfound point of common experience, and an axis of distinction. The next chapter shows that although seniors from different backgrounds faced shared challenges, they did not do so on equal footing. Rather than being leveled by biological processes, entitlements, or shared difficulties, later life remains a time of substantial inequality. As readers will see, resource disparities determine not only who survives long enough to reach the end game, but how they can play.

2

THE UNEVEN PLAYING FIELD
Disparate Contexts and Resources in Old Age

There are few sorrows, however poignant,
in which a good income is of no avail.

—Logan Pearsal Smith

While Americans from diverse backgrounds face shared predicaments as they grow old, they do not do so on equal footing. The end game faced by American seniors is defined in part by an un-level playing field, filled with resource disparities operating on both the individual and neighborhood levels. This can be seen in how Pauline, Laura, and Dave respond to the same very concrete problem: running out of Ensure (a liquid dietary supplement providing protein and vitamins).

Pauline, Laura, and Dave Respond to Running Out of Ensure

Pauline, Laura, and Dave each had issues meeting their nutritional needs and consequently rely heavily on Ensure. In this case, although all three sought the same thing—to replenish their supply of the supplement—the differences in how they accomplished this goal illustrate a lot about the unequal contexts and resources that shape their lives. Pauline is a middle-class African American woman living in a house she owns in Elm Flats. When she ran out of Ensure, she walked a few blocks to the local supermarket and bought some. She explained that she could have easily driven her car, but she enjoyed the exercise and the weather was nice. Her kids lived close enough by to help if needed, but she prided herself on her independence and said there was no need to enlist their help. On the other hand, Laura, a middle-class white woman of about the same age, had much more substantial health and mobility issues. She had given up driving years earlier and had recently begun using an electric scooter to get around, although she was not totally comfortable with the device. When she ran out of Ensure, she explained she could not easily get to the store. So she called her son Timothy, who typically visited her several times a week to help with household tasks, spend time with her, and bring her food. On his next visit, Timothy brought his mom more Ensure. Laura explained that she had money and a pension from her deceased spouse, so she could also pay someone to do this task if needed.

While Ensure was a major part of Dave's diet as well, getting the viscous liquid was more of an ordeal for him. Dave is a poor white man who lives alone in a small apartment in Elm Flats. Although he is younger than the other two, he has substantial health problems and few monetary resources: no home, no pension, no income outside Social Security, and no savings. Dave does not have a car and could not drive even if he did. Further, he does not have any close family to help him out. The issue is not that Dave lives in a "food desert," an urban locale without access to affordable food (or, in this case, a nutritional supplement). He lives only two blocks away from a major supermarket. However, given his health problems and trouble walking, the market might as well be across town. It does not help that he lives on the second floor in an apartment complex without an elevator. Dave explained that he could take the senior transportation system to go the few blocks, but, unlike the system in the more affluent Baygardens, it was unreliable at best. A common saying about the service was "they get you there, but . . ." The "but" part is that you have little control over when and if they remember to pick you up. Even if one of his neighbors offered to go for him, Dave did not have the cash. A case of Ensure, which would last him a few weeks, costs around fifty dollars. So what does Dave do when he runs out of the product?[1]

Given his physical problems and lack of material resources, Dave must engage in a convoluted process to replenish his stores. The process begins with a call to his social worker. The social worker insists that he go to the doctor first. This means Dave has to arrange transportation to the clinic weeks in advance with the county ride agency, and hope nothing goes awry. In this particular case, I drove him. While the doctor gave him a prescription for Ensure during their five-minute meeting, he also insisted that Dave come for a follow-up appointment next month and that he see specialists for his other issues. Dave saw this as undesirable, but he explained to me he was going to do it because he "doesn't want any red flags" with the doctor or social worker. He was afraid that missing appointments could result in his losing independence or being placed in a nursing home. In the end, Dave found himself caught in a web of doctor appointments, social worker visits, and other intrusions that took up much of the following weeks. In the end however, he managed to get his Ensure as well as some Vicodin (a prescription narcotic painkiller), which he used for both managing his pain and bartering with neighbors.

Although they may employ different cultural approaches to confront the various challenges of aging (the topic of the next chapter), the differences in how Laura, Pauline, and Dave go about getting Ensure is not reducible to different cultural values. While each has a different outlook on life, in this case all three want the same thing: a supplement used to maintain health. Further, each values their independence and, given the choice, would prefer to just walk to the store and pick some up. However, just as earlier in life, their options are stratified. Dave's range of possible responses is more limited than Laura's, whose prospects are in turn more limited than Pauline's.

The remainder of this chapter charts how disparate material resources and neighborhood contexts limit seniors' options, and how this shapes everyday life across the four neighborhoods in this study. In doing so, it illuminates how the disparate options Paula, Laura, and Dave have in responding to running out of Ensure are not a deviant case, but part of a broader pattern whereby overlapping material inequalities continue to stratify our possibilities later in life.

Contextual Inequalities:
Disparate Neighborhood Resources in Old Age

People confront the challenges of aging against a backdrop of real-world settings such as apartment complexes, neighborhood senior centers, and hospitals. These settings differ substantially between neighborhoods. Further, seniors from different backgrounds reach old age with vastly different levels of material resources both within and across neighborhood contexts. The sections that follow show how differences in both *neighborhood contexts* and *material resources* (e.g., money, health insurance, and property) create a drastically uneven field on which the end game is played and why this persists, despite the provision of potentially leveling entitlements such as Social Security and Medicare.[2]

Social scientists have long shown that where we live matters. The neighborhoods people inhabit affect the resources and opportunities that are available to them throughout their lives. This pattern holds for the increasing physical and social predicaments of aging as well. Compared to middle-class neighborhoods, poor areas in the United States typically have fewer of the health resources needed by seniors. These areas often have fewer hospitals and clinics per capita than more affluent neighborhoods, and those tend to be of lower overall quality. A body of research suggests that areas that are poor and racially segregated sometimes form "food deserts," where high-quality healthy food is more difficult to find and more expensive to purchase. The housing environments and physical infrastructure in poor areas are often poorly maintained, and residents are disproportionally exposed to toxins and other environmental hazards. Consequently, a person's geographical location can profoundly limit access to key resources for managing the physical and social challenges of old age.[3]

The effect of space also has an institutional component that extends beyond differences in individual access to any given resource. The neighborhoods in which people live affect the organizations they interact with regularly, and often how these organizations process them. In addition to divergent patterns of organizational treatment, those in poor areas face compositional "spillover" effects, as the people they encounter also often lack resources and face parallel hardships. Although we know that these structural inequalities shape opportunities over the life course, the knowledge of how these links operate in the everyday lives of seniors is less developed. This section illustrates how aspects of neighborhood context shape seniors' options in the communities included this study.[4]

Getting Around

The degree to which we are geographically confined or mobile profoundly structures behavior. The physical spaces we inhabit form the backdrop of everyday life. In other words, our ability or inability to transverse space limits our social possibilities. While some scholars have argued that the importance of space withered with the rapid technological advances of the past century, the challenges presented by the physical environment were very real for the older Americans in this study. They were not living in a "postspatial" world. Differences in the ability to physically navigate the local terrain both reflected and reinforced broader patterns of inequality. This section examines how this worked out concretely via a concern shared by seniors across the communities in this study: the capacity to get around the neighborhood.[5]

For the seniors in this study, the ability to see a doctor, get healthy food, or socialize with friends across town required finding a way to physically get there. As the previous chapter showed, in our final years we often develop problems moving around environments that we could navigate with ease decades earlier. People generally have less energy available and are at a greater risk of falling. As aging progresses, seniors' physical capacities decline, and their effective spatial range shrinks. Bo, an elderly Chinese man from Elm Flats, voiced this common problem in his local senior center: "Well, you know, like before I could walk six blocks without any problem; now if I can walk a block and a half without getting winded, it's a triumph." This reduction in mobility is spread across different social strata, but seniors' attempts to compensate are structured by inequalities in the spatial allocation of resources such as transportation, social service hubs, and medical facilities. In more extreme cases, seniors became isolated in their homes, their isolation broken only by the occasional visits of social workers, ethnographers, and meal delivery services.[6]

It is important to reiterate that seniors' remaining physical capacities—the basis of their ability to move through space—reflect social inequalities as well. The poor and socially marginal have more medical problems, live shorter lives on average, receive worse medical care, and confront the physiological problems of being "old" at a younger age. The Elm Flats man mentioned above was in his nineties. Seniors living in poverty, such as Dave or the men from Rockport discussed in the last chapter, often face similar issues in their fifties or sixties. These issues have been convincingly documented in the aggregate and are often linked to environmental inequalities. How they create shared difficulties in everyday life was discussed in the previous chapter. Here, I turn to how inequalities in individual and neighborhood resources affected the ability to get around in the four neighborhoods in this study.[7]

UNEQUAL SERVICE PROVISION CASE 1:

Transportation

While past inequality affects the onset of physical mobility challenges, present contextual inequalities exacerbate them. Ostensibly, both middle-class and poor seniors can compensate for their declining physical capacities using other resources to aid mobility. In the case of transportation, if walking to the grocery store becomes harder, they can theoretically drive, take buses, reserve taxis, or have friends bring essentials, such as food or medicine, to their homes. However, middle-class seniors have substantially more resources to offset the logistical problems created by decreasing physical mobility. Consequently, while a combination of physiological mobility problems and uneven access to usable transportation created major issues for seniors in all four neighborhoods, the problems were more acute for those who were ill, had less wealth, and were in poor neighborhoods that had fewer viable options.

It is intuitive but important to note that seniors who could afford cars and still had the physical capacity to drive were better able to get around. That seniors in middle-class and affluent areas were more likely to have cars, and that younger seniors were more likely to be able to drive, are important points of difference both practically and symbolically. The practical significance of transportation in a place like California, where having a car greatly increases your ability to get around a city, is hard to overstate. However, cars also had immense symbolic importance for seniors. As discussed in the previous chapter, owning a car, and having the mental and physical capacities to pilot it, was a substantial status marker and a signifier of independence. Many seniors noted that one of the hardest things to come to terms with in aging was acknowledging that they were no longer able to drive safely. Likewise, seniors who could rely on others in their social networks to drive them places were in a much less uncertain position than those relying on public transit. This was partially an economic issue but also a function of the extent to which people assist others in their networks, as well as their capacity to help (a topic discussed in Chapter 4). While access to automobiles provided an obvious advantage to more affluent seniors, there were also important differences in public transportation options across neighborhoods that profoundly affected the ability of seniors to get around.[8]

It is important to recognize that bus coverage in these dense urban neighborhoods was much better than what would be found in other parts of the state. Most seniors were within a few blocks of a bus line. Seniors who were relatively healthy and mobile were able to get to key locations around town, which would likely not be the case in less-connected rural settings. Still, public transit created substantial barriers, particularly for ill seniors. As anyone who has used public transportation knows, travelling via bus includes walking to bus stops, waiting for the bus, climbing the stairs, riding the bus, often transferring busses, exiting the bus, then walking to the destination. Even with accessibility modifications, public transportation in the neighborhoods in this study required substantially more physical exertion and time than traveling by car. For many seniors, this was difficult or prohibitive; they simply did not have the stability and stamina required. A white woman in Baygardens explained this to me when she said, "Well, I can't stand for a long time, and I need a walker. I'm pretty good while I'm moving, but getting up and down [the bus stairs] can be hard." Over the years I knew her, I observed that this this woman generally avoided traveling by bus and instead used the free shuttle or arranged rides with friends in her building. When regular public transit became too difficult, seniors had to either (1) find alternative services (such as subsidized transportation for the disabled), (2) have food and other necessities brought to their home (and often become more isolated), or (3) face institutionalization in an assisted-living facility.[9]

Even among those seniors who were physically able to ride buses, many seniors felt that the combination of time, physical activity, and incomplete coverage made using public transportation problematic and undesirable. Maurice, a Chinese man from Elm Flats, commented, "Public transportation is very, very bad. I mean if you are old, you can't drive; it makes it hard to get around. You have to depend on your friends and there's very limited public help that you can get." Consequently, being within walking distance of important locations like pharmacies and markets provided a substantial advantage to seniors. Delores, a white woman with substantial resources, commented on this:

> I happen to live close to a grocery store within walking distance, and you know the pharmacy's right there too now, and the banking is now in the grocery stores too, so things have consolidated, where you don't have to go as far. But for anything else there is not enough public transportation. There are buses, but the way they're run and where you have to get them, it's just not helpful.

Seniors like Delores who lived in more affluent areas could take buses if necessary, but often were fortunate in that they were able to get services with less exertion than going to a bus stop by walking. If they needed to go somewhere, they would ask friends or family members for a ride, which was facilitated by the fact that their network typically included other people with substantial resources (including cars). When Delores was unable to drive briefly, her retired neighbors offered to drive her, but she chose to take a taxi rather than impose. The bus was there, but it was seen as a last resort. The key point here is that Delores had access to physical and social resources that expanded her options relative to her less affluent peers.

Seniors suffering from more substantial mobility problems had a much harder time. Transferring buses or even walking to and from a bus stop was a major undertaking. For seniors such as the Chinese man at the beginning of this section, or Dave, who was introduced in the Ensure example, a few blocks became a prohibitive distance. Without access to substantial additional resources (such as a driver or a powered wheelchair), these seniors had a very limited effective range of travel. Some of the people in this study went so far as to count the number of steps they could take before their legs gave out. If they could not get someone to drive them to a doctor's appointment, market, and so on, they would have to rely on supplemental transportation for seniors or the "disabled," as using basic public transportation required exceeding this range.

Even comparatively mobile seniors were concerned with these issues and the implications for their quality of life as they continued to age. For instance, Loraine, an active woman at Cedar Hills, noted,

> The main issue with seniors is transportation. They keep cutting back on public transportation; so many seniors with ambulatory issues are just stuck at home. They eat, sleep, watch TV, and take medicine, but can't go anywhere. They become prisoners in their homes.

Loraine's comments point to a fear that was prevalent across neighborhoods: losing "independence" and the ability to navigate the world. This fear can be conceptualized in terms of a very real threat related to the loss of key "capacities for action," that shape the ability to navigate the world in a physical and social sense; that is, losing the resources that allow people to pursue desired ends. The sentiments Loraine expresses, which were widely shared across neighborhoods, reflect an acknowledgement that (1) the physical problems of old age create issues for navigating their environment; (2) public transportation can be uncertain and problematic even in middle-class neighborhoods; and (3) when these factors converge, seniors' effective spatial range in the world is limited in a way that profoundly shapes their lives.[10]

All four neighborhoods did have supplemental forms of transportation for seniors, although these operated with divergent levels of coverage and consistency. Cedar Hills, Baygardens, and Elm Flats each had senior transportation programs that were funded by grants that city agencies had been awarded. In addition, seniors in these neighborhoods also had access to a county-wide program. In contrast, Rockport residents had access to *only* a county program. The city programs provided shuttles that stopped at senior centers, major senior housing complexes, grocery stores, pharmacies, hospitals, and doctors' offices. When available, these services were heavily used by seniors in all neighborhoods. Residents frequently commented that the shuttle or "free bus" made their lives easier and allowed them to get what they needed without asking for help from friends, family, or neighbors. An elderly African American woman from Cedar Hills who used the shuttle frequently to get around provided a representative view:

Cedar Hills is an unusual place because they have a public transportation network for seniors. This year the senior center has taken over that piece, and they can arrange pretty much anything in this area or in [the hospital] for disabled and older seniors to get picked up and take them where they need to go—appointments, errands, whatever they need to do on a can do basis. It happens daily. Our driver is Danny and the other is Craig; they are very loving and wonderful people. They treat the seniors with love and respect.

Where available, these shuttles provided both an instrumental benefit for accessing resources, as well as a sense of "independence" that is core to many Americans' identities. They also added to sociability in a way seniors felt was beneficial.[11]

In contrast to Cedar Hills, the services in Baygardens and Elm Flats did not run every day, but still provided an easier alternative to bus travel. An elderly white woman from Baygardens described how she took the shuttle to the doctor:

I took that free shuttle. They pick you up right here [in front of building], and drop you off at [the hospital]. They also go to the senior center, [market], and the library. The driver is a real nice young guy, and you know all the people on the shuttle since it is the same each week. It is hard for me to get up and down the steps though. This time the driver helped me, but my legs held up okay. [knock-on-wood gesture] [Researcher: "Don't they have a ramp for your walker?"] Yes, but I feel bad. They work hard enough already, I don't want to make more work or make everyone wait for me. I have to use my smaller walker which I can carry, which is a pain in the neck, but it doesn't make trouble for anybody.

During the last year of my fieldwork, the Baygardens shuttle was reduced to running one day per week. Seniors complained that this forced them to do all of their errands on one day and that it made visiting the doctor an issue when they could not schedule an appointment to coincide with the shuttle timetable. For instance, the senior above tried to take a regular city bus to the doctor after this change. She ended up waiting for forty-five minutes on the way back from the pharmacy, which subsequently drained her energy level, increased her pain, and negatively affected her mood for the rest of the week. The situation in Elm Flats was very similar. There were organized supplemental programs that seniors knew about, liked, and used, but those were in the process of being reduced in scope and or eliminated.

Seniors who lived in Rockport or those off the designated shuttle paths were not as well off. In the absence of developed city programs, they had to rely on the larger county programs, which were notorious for being late or simply not showing up. They also required seniors to file substantial amounts of paperwork and to book appointments weeks in advance. Further, many adult day service programs, nursing homes, and hospitals relied on the county transit program to move institutionalized seniors around in order to reduce their operating costs, taxing an already overburdened service. Because of the size and dispatch structure of the county program, routes were always changing. Consequently, drivers and passengers frequently rotated. Seniors often did not know the other riders or drivers on the shuttles, which reduced the social benefit of shared transportation. While the loss of a shuttle community may have affected seniors' subjective well-being, the fact that the service often simply did not show up led to missed doctors' appointments, delayed trips to the pharmacy or store, and other logistical problems.[12]

In addition to missed appointments, service inconsistencies created a serious drain on the energy levels of ill seniors. For these people, the process of getting ready to leave the house was a major undertaking, something many would spend the whole week preparing for physically and psychologically. Dave commented on these issues when I visited him after a trip: "Getting shaved and cleaned and putting on clothes is a major ordeal. Getting transportation is a major ordeal. Seeing the doctor is a major ordeal and it takes my whole day. It is tempting to just not go and keep my schedule free, but that is the coward's way out." He later added, "If I go to the doctor, I have to get someone to drive me or don't know when I'm getting back. Either way it takes all day and it's a major ordeal."

Dave then explained that although he had previously scheduled a ride to the doctor weeks in advance with a county program, which he then called to confirm days ahead, the service simply did not show up, and he subsequently missed his doctor's appointment. His problems then snowballed, as missing the doctor's appointment resulted in an unwanted social worker visit (an issue expanded upon in the following section on gatekeeping and surveillance).

At best, dealing with the vagaries of these transit programs added stress for seniors like Dave; at worst, seniors found themselves stranded or missing appointments. Unfortunately this issue was not atypical, but part of a larger pattern I observed in both this project and my prior work. Numerous other seniors remarked that they had been stranded by the county program. One senior from Cedar Hills flippantly summed up the situation to a friend at the senior center with a version of a common quip: "They get you there okay, but then they don't bring you back." The senior went on to say how she was a "guest" on the service with a friend, and that, despite repeated calls and an hour-and-a-half wait, the service never picked them up. Although she was mobile enough to take a bus and had money to take a cab, she said that the experience was taxing and that she would not try to use the service again.[13]

Getting Meals

Everyone has to eat. Although they faced broad transportation challenges that affected how they went about acquiring food, the seniors in this study did not live in "food deserts" as conventionally defined. In each of the four areas, including the poor neighborhoods of Elm Flats and Rockport, major supermarket chains were accessible by foot, bus, or shuttle. There were seasonal farmers' markets in each of the areas as well, including regular ones across the street from the senior housing complexes in both Baygardens and Rockport. Further, several senior centers in these areas offered lunchtime meals for around two dollars per day. Many seniors, who otherwise had little to do with the senior centers, would show up for this lunchtime meal. This was particularly true for men living alone and those residing in poor areas. While seniors sometimes complained about the taste, these meals provided large portions and basic nutrition. The senior centers also frequently gave away day-old bread from nearby bakeries and other food donations, although their "first come, first served" policy gave regulars the first pick. In addition, each of the neighborhoods had food banks that provided seniors with free food that was collected via donations.[14]

Each of the communities was also served by county mobile meal service programs, which delivered warm meals to the homes of seniors up to six days per week. These services were particularly important for those who had a hard time leaving their home, for either physical or psychological reasons, but even more active seniors received this service as well, since it was often cheaper and more convenient than buying food. Further, the services tailored the food to the senior's dietary needs (low sodium, low fat, etc.). These meals provided more than the seniors could typically eat in one sitting. Seniors would save the extra food for later, share with friends, or offer it as a reward or gift to helpers. Although seniors sometimes commented that the taste and variety of these meals was not exceptional, most believed that they provided adequate nutrition and left them sated. Seniors who were members of formal religious organizations such as churches and synagogues were also often given food by congregation members. A senior explained to me how she went about getting her food, while I was in her apartment in Baygardens:

> I used to go to [the food bank], but they just gave me too much food. I am only one person and it was too much to push across back here [it was about a block away]. So I got signed up for [county meal service]. I eat a lot of meat now, much more than I would buy. My girlfriend says they only give you what's healthy, and I eat it all except the salad. It uses that iceberg lettuce, and I don't like it. They cut Social Security, so I said I won't pay anymore, but they still bring me the food. [*shrugs*] If it wasn't for the [county meal service], I probably wouldn't be able to get food.

After saying this, the senior opened her refrigerator to show me her leftovers. She added that the preacher from her church also brings her fruit and vegetables every week.[15]

In general, with the possible exception of some extremely isolated seniors and those with advanced mental illnesses or other conditions that prevented them from interacting with other people, the seniors in this study were much more concerned with transportation problems, health issues, treatment by organizations, and issues of surveillance than issues of food insecurity. Although it consumed more of his time and energy than he would have liked, even Dave (the poor senior described in the introduction) was able to get daily meal deliveries and Ensure.[16]

UNEQUAL SERVICE PROVISION CASE 2:
Meal Programs and "Visitors"

Despite the cross-neighborhood presence of essential services such as the meal programs described above, there were noticeable differences in the way services were provided in different locales. This follows a general pattern convincingly charted by historians and sociologists such as James Patterson and Jill Quadagno, in which social services and other programs that ostensibly provide relief from poverty and inequality in the United States have historically been implemented in a way that is piecemeal, localized, and dependent on assumptions about the deservedness of the population. The example of uneven transportation networks was discussed above, but the operations of county meal programs offer another useful example. While all four communities had mobile meals programs, the presence and extent of associated home-visit programs, in which volunteers would check in on and socialize with seniors, varied greatly across communities. These programs were often administered at the county level, which spanned both poor and nonpoor neighborhoods. In general, even in the counties that included poor neighborhoods, the bulk of recipients were from middle-class or affluent neighborhoods. Volunteers also tended to be middle-aged or older people from middle-class or affluent backgrounds who preferred to volunteer near their homes. In practice the coverage provided by the auxiliary programs was concentrated in more affluent locales, where seniors with more resources to start with received more help.[17]

Often, administrators knew very little about poor neighborhoods such as Elm Flats or Rockport, even though they were under their jurisdiction. This was highlighted in my interactions with an administrator who handled volunteers for the larger county containing Rockport. When I tried to volunteer in the city that contained Rockport, the administrator, a middle-aged white woman, shrugged and said, "We have a lot [of need] from [city]. It is difficult to get volunteers because it is a bad area. I had one woman who would go to [city], but she didn't want to be in Rockport. I don't know the area, but she said it is dangerous with lots of gangs." Despite regular follow-up attempts, the administrator was never able to assign me a senior from that neighborhood. Unlike the transportation and food programs, seniors in poorer areas often did not even know these auxiliary social programs existed, perhaps because in practice they did not.

While more basic services such as meal programs eventually made their way into the poor areas, the same was simply not true of auxiliary services. This affected how people from different neighborhoods could approach the challenges of everyday life. Rather than just being a person to chat with occasionally, volunteer visitors often functioned as a key source of social support as well as an instrumental resource for connecting seniors to services or driving them around so they did not have to take the shuttle or bus. Often, volunteers would develop long-term bonds with seniors and provide much more substantial help. For example, one of the volunteers in Baygardens, a white man in his sixties, described his relationship with a senior at a meeting for volunteers held in a local senior center:

> I told Eve that we were going down to LA. She has my phone number because she calls me to ask for things, or to talk. I told her not to call when I was in LA unless it was an emergency. She called within a day, and I asked, "Eve, is this life-or death?" She began crying and said yes. It turns out she could not get an appointment for a flu shot. [*shrugs*] Of course, I made the appointment and took her when we got back. But I could see it being a problem. I also buy her groceries, and take her to the bank.

While calling the volunteer on the trip may seem somewhat extreme, it was not atypical. These visitors were key figures in the seniors' lives. They formed a key resource many drew upon as they constructed strategies for managing the predicaments of growing old.

This is not to say that poor areas did not have volunteers, but the absence of these formal programs blocked seniors' access to a useful resource. The volume of volunteers, particularly in the county-run senior programs, was smaller in the poorer neighborhoods. Further, volunteers often did not have the same level of disposable resources visitors in the middle-class areas possessed, which affected the efficacy of these social ties (a topic I return to in Chapter 4). In poor areas, volunteers were also more likely to be involved with religious or ethnic organizations. Many of these organizations operated as service hubs as well, where more educated members, or ex-residents, of the neighborhood would connect individuals and families to medical or social programs. However, many did not provide services specifically for seniors, and the majority of their clientele were nonsenior families. Additionally, similar programs existed in middle-class areas, with the net effect being fewer services and resources for seniors in the poorer neighborhoods. In sum, older adults in more affluent areas had access to a wider variety of auxiliary services that provided transportation, companionship, and advocacy than did their counterparts in poor areas.[18]

Local Service Hubs

Each of the four neighborhoods had senior centers, hospitals, and housing. Senior centers served as a particularly important gateway for accessing services, recreation, and information for those seniors who attended. Although centers varied in both size and types of services offered, at minimum each center provided low-cost meals, public spaces for socializing, free or low-cost recreational activities, and volunteers or employees who could help refer seniors to additional services. Many of the centers also had free health screenings, auxiliary transportation services, and volunteer consultants who could help with taxes or health insurance issues. Many of the older adults who frequented the centers pointed out that they provided a chance to see their friends, socialize, and exchange news. The centers also held special events for holidays, which were important to the many seniors who had outlived their families. For "regulars," these centers were an immense source of meaning and satisfaction. An African American woman from Cedar Hills noted, "Coming to a place like this and being with my friends here, that is my life. Because most of my family is gone, they passed away, so this is my family right here at the center." Each of the centers also distributed information in the form of free booklets such as senior resource guides, which had an extensive list of phone numbers for senior services provided by state and local authorities as well as nonprofit groups. While I was flipping through one at a senior center in Rockport, a woman commented, "That guide's a bible. It's free, and it tells you where to get anything you need." Other seniors, volunteers, and employees provided informal information and advice. These individuals were often looked up to as neighborhood "caretakers," whom seniors would consult when they were looking for answers or had a dispute. Consequently, senior centers functioned both as service hubs and community institutions that distributed information, provided sociability, and helped maintain the social order of the senior community.

All four neighborhoods were also in close proximity to major health-care services, and within five miles of a major hospital with emergency services. Both poor and nonpoor areas were served by free clinics. Elm Flats and Cedar Hills were close to senior health clinics geared toward individuals on Medicare or Medicaid. Senior centers also often had on-site health professionals who would provide free screening (e.g., blood sugar, blood pressure, podiatry checks) and referrals. Intermittent senior "health fairs" offered free medical supplies, such as blood sugar testing strips, to those who attended.

UNEQUAL SERVICE PROVISION CASE 3:
Senior Housing

Each of the four areas had subsidized housing for seniors. Baygardens and Rockport both had large, centrally located complexes near stores, senior centers, and health care. However, the quality and provision of those resources varied greatly in ways that illuminate unequal service provisions.

This stark contrast was physically evident at the two state-administered senior housing units in Baygardens and Rockport. The Baygardens site had manicured foliage, well-maintained public spaces, and wide corridors with handles. From the outside, it would be difficult to tell the difference between the housing complex and nearby condominiums. Maintenance tasks were handled quickly by the resident administrator, who also facilitated formal events for holidays and provided informal help for seniors such as connecting them with state services, offering general advice, helping with paperwork, and visiting with them. In contrast, the unit at Rockport consisted of large, high-rise, apartment-style buildings that were poorly maintained and dirty on the outside. They had narrower halls and poor maintenance. From the outside, the building looked like the classic "housing project." Rather than being a community "caretaker," the building administrator was rarely on site.

The issue here is not aesthetics. Sociologists have often shown the hazards of judging a book by its cover, or more accurately, judging the social order of a neighborhood by its graffiti and broken windows. Ethnographers have long shown that whether a sidewalk is cracked or a ramp is out of place does not necessarily signal the absence of social order in a neighborhood. Put more bluntly, the "broken windows" model of social disorganization has never held up to ethnographic scrutiny. Scholars in the otherwise internally combative field of urban ethnography have consistently presented compelling evidence showing that poor neighborhoods with markers of physical disarray have discernible social orders, even if the content of these is different from what is found in more affluent settings. These scholars have argued that the notion that broken windows, graffiti, or other such markers somehow reflect an anomic context characterized by social disorder is based on faulty assumptions (i.e., the aesthetics of a physical environment are a proxy for the social environment).[19]

Nonetheless, in this case these physical markers were indicative of different levels of state investment in ostensibly similar facilities. Further, since most of the seniors in this study had problems with mobility, minor differences in the physical environment could create large problems. Uneven walkways or cracks created issues at both sites. This was explained to me when I was accompanying a woman in Baygardens on a walk to the bank. Her walker caught on the pavement, and she said, "See that? It is worse with the other one [walker]. When I take it on the bus it gets stuck in everything." Later she showed me a spot near the housing complex where she fell. She explained, "I did it wrong and I fell." I asked what happened. She said, "People here helped me up. This has been a good year, though. I haven't had a fall." She smiled and told me she managed to avoid a trip to the hospital on that occasion.

Further, after this incident the senior went to Susane, the administrator of her housing complex, who was not only present frequently but also was heavily involved in the social life of the complex. Susane helped her receive a new alert system that she wore around her neck in case she fell again. The senior explained that she asked Susane for help obtaining this, since she was concerned with the many attempts to scam seniors (both imagined and actual) and did not feel comfortable making calls on her own. Susane knew who to talk to and what to say. Like many in the complex, the senior trusted the administrator as a central and respected part of the community. Susane also helped this senior and others deal with myriad other issues such as family troubles, finances, and health problems. While community members in poor areas could go to homegrown caretakers or brokers who were respected in the community, these individuals did not have the formal connections, organizational clout, or cultural tools that made Susane so effective in not only offering advice but also in connecting seniors to external resources.[20]

While both the middle-class and poor neighborhoods in this study exhibited social order, physical differences mattered quite a bit for seniors. The state of a sidewalk, the level of upkeep of stairs, or whether an elevator is in working order substantially affected the ability of mobility-impaired seniors to get around safely. Since a single fall can land a senior in a hospital or nursing facility, this was a major issue across neighborhoods. Seniors in all areas pointed out the difficulties they encountered with cracked sidewalks or buildings requiring the use of stairs. Those who worked with seniors were generally sensitive to this issue as well as the profound ramifications of having an environment that was easy to navigate. However, even the most sensitive senior center administrators have little recourse to ensure that streets get repaved. The director of Baygardens senior center, for instance, often noted that having well-maintained facilities was one of the most pressing issues for seniors. She was especially sensitive to this since her previously healthy uncle (who was in his seventies) had recently fallen, suffered cognitive damage, and was subsequently placed in a nursing facility. Her center, however, managed to secure funding and donations for drastically improving the physical environment—something I did not observe at the other centers, even though the Elm Flats and Rockport centers were degenerating.

Differences in the physical environment, like a chronically broken elevator, compounded mobility troubles. While seniors in all neighborhoods developed strategies for dealing with these issues in both their living spaces and the broader urban landscape (e.g., using a walker in uneven but open environments and using a cane in combination with a wall in narrow environments), the more affluent areas in this study were simply better maintained. Seniors across communities would point out to me spaces where they had fallen, or where other seniors they knew had fallen, and explained that they would try to avoid those spots.

However, since the poorer areas generally had more stairs, fewer ramps, more cracks, and narrower building interiors, these were simply harder to avoid. This increased some seniors' exposure to spots where they could trip, fall, and injure themselves.[21]

Still, those seniors who lived in subsidized housing units or apartment complexes with concentrations of other seniors were often better off than those who lived alone. These environments often had at least basic handles and ramps that made navigation easier and safer. They also provided spaces for sociability with other seniors. Having a common room in which to talk with friends and share information provided seniors in these locations with an additional way to find out about and procure resources (e.g., carpooling or having neighbors pick up free food). Many had systems that made contacting medical providers easier as well. For instance, Jessica, a white woman in her nineties, told me how much she liked her home in Baygardens, in part because of the sociability but also in part because of safety. On the car ride back from a trip, Jessica commented that she liked her place because it was nice and inexpensive, and she got to see her friends. Jessica added, "I [also] like how my place now has a string." I asked, "A string?" She replied, "Yeah. One near the bed and one near the bathroom. In case you need to go to the hospital. I had to go once, but it was my fault. I let it get bad with my tricholitis, and boy did my stomach hurt."

The proximity and concentration of other seniors facing similar problems, as well as the comparative ease of checking in on a neighbor who is just down the hall as opposed to across the street, also meant that seniors could socialize and generally provide or get help more easily.[22]

Entrepreneurial Funding and the Reproduction of Inequality

One likely source of inequalities in the physical environment and services between poor and nonpoor areas is related to the entrepreneurial structure of grant funding. Federal agencies offer broad block grants that can be used for a variety of programs affecting seniors (e.g., housing development or aging services) as well as more narrow categorical grants. Along with money provided by private organizations for work with seniors, city officials and private organizations can ultimately apply for funds from a broad pool of sources if they have the credentials and know where to look.

Cedar Hills and Baygardens were filled with numerous nonprofit organizations, large and small, that continually won grants. Many smaller nonprofits worked with city administrators, although some larger nonprofit organizations functioned like corporations and had employees whose sole job was to write grants. These organizations had people with time and expertise dedicated to obtaining and allocating funding. Further, many had previous experience with grantors that provided them with legitimacy and a track record, which made getting subsequent awards much easier. The more informal organizations found in poor areas, such as local church groups, were not as adept at tapping into these funding sources. Consequently, in practice, the "equal opportunity" of competition funneled money into programs in middle-class areas with established organizations and individuals adept at navigating this funding structure.[23]

In practice, the entrepreneurial system of granting resources funneled limited resources to the most affluent areas—a process that parallels what sociologists Lutfey and Freese label a "compensatory inversion": a situation in which resources for well-being are differentially distributed among those who already have more resources to begin with. While this did not necessarily thwart basic access to food, housing, or medical care, in this study it did substantially affect the amount and quality of auxiliary services available to seniors. Senior housing agencies in the affluent areas had more resources to assist with maintenance and repairs and more of a buffer against cuts. When statewide austerity measures forced the Rockport senior center to drop computer classes and exercise programs or increase their prices, Baygardens was able to maintain their current programs while seeking grant funding to add new computer classes and special events. Seniors in Baygardens and Cedar Hills, the two more affluent areas, were served by an extensive volunteer network that provided not only sociability for seniors but also brought substantial material and logistical resources to the organizations they were involved with. They did this in the context of neighborhoods that were already easier to navigate and populated by seniors who had more social, material, and cultural resources than those in the poor areas.[24]

Disparate Individual Resources in Old Age

The previous section showed that although seniors from across neighborhoods generally have access to basic public services, the services provided are unequal. However, disparities in individual resources acquired earlier in life also carry over into old age. The continuation of wealth disparities adds to the vulnerability of seniors who spent their lives in poverty, relative to their more affluent peers. While nonmonetary resources such as education, physical capacity, and cultural skills undoubtedly matter (a topic discussed in the next chapter), here the focus is on explaining how the advantages of higher socioeconomic status earlier in life translate into durable resources in old age that reproduce inequality, even given the provision of state services and the effect of selective mortality. In other words, it shows why the proposition that the racial and socioeconomic inequalities so prevalent earlier in life are "leveled away" in old age does not correspond to the everyday reality of the aging Americans in this study.[25]

Unequal Assets:
"It's Money"

Just as seniors acknowledged that physical assets such as health and mobility were central to their quality of life, seniors in all communities acknowledged that those with money "had it easier" when dealing with old age. This came up almost without variation in interviews and in elders' spontaneous comparisons with peers in everyday settings. Interestingly, while almost all study participants noted that those with more money "had it easier," the numbers who said race or gender was a key factor were much smaller. Tanya, an African American woman in Cedar Hills, verbalized this common attitude when she noted, "If you have money, you know, you have better benefits. Better food, better transportation and a nicer place. It's money."[26]

The seniors were correct in acknowledging the continued importance of material resources: money from jobs or pensions, supplemental health insurance, or wealth in the form of a home substantially affected how seniors were able to deal with the contingencies of aging. Having more disposable income directly affected seniors' abilities to manage the physical and social challenges of old age. Seniors with arthritis, fibromyalgia, or similar conditions often used massages, herbs, or acupuncture to help them manage chronic pain. Although some health maintenance organizations (HMOs) and supplemental insurance plans covered these alternative forms of treatment, most seniors paid out of pocket. Medicare did not provide coverage for many of these treatments. Consequently, wealthier seniors were both more likely to have these forms of treatment covered by their insurance and to have money to pay for them if they were not. At the senior center in Rockport, two seniors were discussing the absence of a woman named Tina, who used to come regularly. Like many seniors, she had issues with pain. One of the seniors noted, "Tina used to get massages from this girl in [city] while she was going to school for that. It really helped her with her pain. Then the woman graduated, and she wanted too much money, so she stopped going." In these cases, a lack of money became a major issue, as seniors struggled to afford complementary treatment that improved their quality of life. While poor seniors did engage in more informal exchanges of services, lack of money or supplemental insurance limited their options for alternative treatments. On the other hand, seniors in poor areas often had better access to an informal economy that made available narcotic painkillers and other drugs. Many also said that marijuana, which was readily available in Rockport and Elm Flats, helped with their pain.[27]

In his book *Being Black, Living in the Red,* sociologist Dalton Conley shows how home ownership is both a key aspect of wealth and an important axis of racial inequality in America. The most advantaged households, typically made up of whites, own homes, which allows wealth to be transmitted between generations. In addition to helping reproduce the wealth gap, homes also serve as an important source of prestige and "independence" for many Americans. This is true in old age as well. In this study, home ownership provided older individuals with substantial material advantages over their peers who did not own property. Although the upkeep of a house can be expensive, seniors who owned their homes outright did not have to pay rent. For seniors who were able to navigate the paper work, owning a home also opened additional avenues for generating cash, such as reverse mortgages or equity lines. Finally, having a home allowed seniors an additional resource to set up informal exchanges. For instance, several seniors in this study rented out extra rooms or basements in their houses in exchange for some service, such as home maintenance, grocery shopping, or home care. This was part of a vast informal economy among seniors in both poor and nonpoor areas. Younger, more mobile seniors in particular often performed services for older seniors in exchange for a nominal fee, lodging, food, or alcohol. Having a home, a spare room, or disposable income provided seniors with greater resources for exchange. On occasion, however, this could also lead to trouble, such as when "helpers" would move in but could not be easily evicted by the seniors housing them.[28]

In addition to trading living space for services, seniors from more affluent families were often able to hire formal helpers who helped with everyday activities. These helpers were often paid for by insurance, family, or the seniors' own savings. Having a helper improved seniors' abilities to accomplish everyday tasks. These paid helpers, often immigrants and poor people of color, typically cooked, cleaned, drove, and provided companionship to seniors. Health aides also helped with tasks such as bathing, using the restroom, taking medication, and changing medical equipment. While poor seniors were eligible for free or subsidized home-care services if they could demonstrate need, to do so they had to provide documentation and deal with social-worker visits on a regular basis, which again required skills in navigating bureaucracy and the willingness to engage with those agencies. Consequently, in practice, many of those who managed to get subsidized help were people who had spent much of their lives in the middle class but now lived on a fixed income and had substantial health problems.

Not having money also affected seniors' ability to engage in social activities such as trips. This was an issue for seniors who had been middle-class for most of their lives, then found themselves without a substantial income as they got older. Many felt this isolated them from friends and created a subjectively difficult situation, in part because they did not have psychological or practical skills for dealing with material scarcity and its stigma. One senior from a middle-class background explained the issue:

> The money thing is something I think about all the time. I don't go out. I don't. Once in a while I'll buy a coffee. I don't go to a bar to have a glass of wine anymore. I can't do it. I can't go out for a lunch or go

out for a dinner. It's just not within my budget. So when I said a while back there's loneliness, it makes you, um, I can't travel. So I'm stuck at home.

A white man who owned a home in an affluent area explained:

I got to my golden years without enough gold . . . I still don't have enough money. [*laughs*] I'm just living on my Social Security. A very humble existence compared—I had a really good life. My forty years' worth of business, you know, I lived very well. But now I live like a poor person. And I hate it. And I don't see any alternative, unfortunately.

For the people above, and those in their social network, spending money was a key aspect of sociability and their identity more broadly. Old age brought a form of downward mobility in terms of physical resources, social status, and money. Lack of money created a structural barrier for socializing in the manner in which previously middle-class seniors were accustomed and also a sense of stigma at having less than peers. The operation of cultural resources for dealing with both formal organizations and problems of scarcity is discussed in more detail in the next chapter. The broader point here is that even in old age, our lives are structured by persistent material inequalities that stratify which courses of action are possible. This issue is seen clearly in the case of health care.

The Case of Health Care:
Gatekeeping, Surveillance, and Vulnerability

The advantages more affluent seniors held, and the vulnerabilities to which others were subject, can be seen in their experiences with health care. First, having insurance affected where seniors could get care. Although most of the seniors over sixty-five were eligible for Medicare, many of the middle-class seniors held jobs that provided auxiliary insurance coverage into retirement; others could afford supplemental insurance out of pocket. The difference between these seniors and those without supplemental insurance was not so much *whether* they could get health care, but *where*. Those without supplemental insurance could go to free clinics, emergency departments, hospitals, or doctors who accepted Medicare. In contrast, those with supplemental insurance had access to a larger array of providers. Free clinics and emergency rooms were more crowded and had longer waits. Seniors often had to wait in larger rooms with more sick people, where they were at greater risk of catching airborne illnesses. Because of the increased patient load in public clinics and care facilities, doctors and nurses spent less time with seniors than in privately funded facilities.[29]

Further, although they were generally more affluent, those with supplemental insurance often paid less out of pocket for a given trip to the doctor. A senior from Elm Flats who had a union manual-labor job during his working years noted, "My insurance covers everything, the best policy my union provided. Even the eyeglasses, they take about five-hundred-something a year [without insurance]." Poor seniors were still able to see doctors, get medication, and receive prescriptions for basic items necessary for everyday life, such as walkers, canes, and protein drinks, but they had a substantially longer road characterized by financial and logistical barriers. The very poor who were documented as such also did not make copays because of Medicaid coverage. As one senior quipped, "I'm not proud to say it, but they look at me and they know I don't have a copay. I'm the poorest of the poor."[30]

Seniors with less money and insurance had fewer options. They were beholden to greater bureaucratic hoops, gatekeeping by service providers, and surveillance (an issue introduced in the Ensure example). To begin with, they could go only to doctors who were willing to accept state insurance. Further, even when seniors did not want to visit the doctor, they often had to go regularly in order to maintain access to necessary supplies (e.g., Ensure or blood sugar testing strips) that more affluent seniors could simply buy directly. Since poor seniors had a hard time affording these items on their own, they were dependent on prescriptions and referrals from clinicians and social workers. In effect, this made service providers gatekeepers for resources. These "street-level bureaucrats" had authority over whether seniors could get their protein shakes, fix a broken walker, or update their eyeglasses. If providers were unhappy with the senior, they could create problems for them ranging from withholding a social worker visit to a longer wait for services to misplaced paperwork.[31]

The way poor individuals were vulnerable to surveillance and gatekeeping can be seen in the experience of Dave, the poor senior I discussed at the beginning of this chapter. My observations from a trip to an Elm Flats senior clinic provide a typical example. After seeing the doctor, Dave came out of the exam room. He told me that although he got his prescription for the Ensure, he now needed to make an appointment with the hand surgeon, the eye doctor, and his regular follow-up with the general practitioner. We returned to the waiting room. Dave had a hard time standing up for long periods of time and was anxious in social settings, so he sat and waited for the long line to die down. Two elderly white men, who were quite clearly intoxicated, were talking loudly about herbs, marijuana, and the government. Dave looked afraid and upset, noting, "If everyone can hear you, you are imposing on other people's space. It is too loud. They are on drugs and just come here to socialize." Dave eventually staggered over to the line. By time he reached the window, he had already been standing for several minutes and was breathing hard. One of the intoxicated seniors came near, and Dave made a "shoo" motion with his cane. The middle-aged woman at the window gave him a disgusted look. She took his paperwork without speaking and disappeared for at least five minutes, sitting behind the computer.

Every person before Dave had been speedily processed. The attendant eventually came back and gave Dave a paper and said, "There you go." Dave mentioned that he needed to check the date with me, since I had agreed to attend any follow-up appointments with him. I said it was fine. Dave, who was visibly shaking and breathing hard, now said, "I am supposed to have three appointments. That one"—he showed me a piece of paper—"and the one with the eye doctor. They said the hand surgeon would call." The woman nonchalantly said, "I don't know about that." Dave said it was on the chart, and, as he went to pull it out of his bag, she said she would check. She returned to the computer. We waited for ten minutes. Dave was visibly upset. He told me,

> There is no reason for this. We had all of our things together. Those other people were here for a social call. The woman over there scheduled an eye appointment for someone else already. This is very stressful and there is absolutely no need for it. I can't stand up anymore. I only have that hour and a half window [of energy], and I used it just getting to the doctor. I did everything right, this is not fair. I am going to sit down.

Dave went to sit down, and the woman continued at the computer. Other patrons were helped, including an older African American man with his son, and another African American man who was alone.

Dave finally came back up. He said to me, "If they don't come I am going to knock their mail on the floor and start banging." The woman came by, and Dave said, "Excuse me." She said, "I can't hear you." Dave's conditions prevent him from talking loudly, a fact he is embarrassed about. She came over. He said, breathing heavily, "I can't talk loudly. Is there an eye appointment?" The woman said, "Oh, I thought you left." She then handed him a piece of paper and smiled. Dave said he was sorry for knocking over her clipboard, and he mirrored her smirk. I was visible the entire time, but she never said anything to either of us. Dave commented on this when we were outside. "She knew you were my driver." In the car he reiterated how stressed he was, and that this was unnecessary. He had a harder time than normal getting up the stairs to his apartment and asked me to leave because he needed to "recharge his batteries."

In addition to issues with stress and gatekeeping, assessments of doctors and social workers have a profound effect on seniors' lives, often determining whether they were left alone in their homes or whether social services checked in on them regularly. Even those seniors who held a favorable view of doctors (which many minority seniors and those from less affluent backgrounds often did not) noted that this was a major source of anxiety. Although visiting the doctor was necessary to get essential items such as protein shakes and medicine, the resulting surveillance was both undesirable and potentially risky. Dave articulated this clearly on our way to see the orthopedic surgeon two weeks later. He said that the appointment would be more "low-key" than our visit to the free clinic the previous week. I asked why. He responded,

> You know they [orthopedists] aren't going to send you to the hospital or the nursing home so there isn't much to worry about. If I had remembered earlier, I probably would have cancelled, but it is better to just go. If you don't go, then you start getting calls and people coming out to spy on you, plus the cancellation fee. To be honest though, I would pay ten dollars to get out of this. [*laughs*]

Although nothing came of the appointment (the orthopedist was surprised that he was sent there, given that his poor overall health made any surgical treatment risky), Dave was concerned that any failure to attend would get back to his doctor, which could have consequences ranging from paperwork hassles to being placed in a nursing facility. Seniors like Dave who were caught in the medical webs sometimes talked about the importance of "showing the flag" so as to avoid additional contact outside the clinic or hospital. Seniors with greater financial resources, on the other hand, did not talk in these terms, presumably because their additional resources afforded more autonomy.

Relying on clinicians and administrators as gatekeepers created logistical issues for poor seniors. Gatekeepers' assessments, erroneous or not, determined the extent to which various state agencies became involved in seniors' lives. As the example with Dave above suggests, clerks, aides, and clinic operatives have power as well. While being forced to wait is an inconvenience for a healthy person in middle-age, for seniors with limited energy, waiting an extra half hour is not only anxiety-producing but potentially dangerous, because having less available energy increases their chance of a fall. Consequently, even making an unwell individual stand for longer than necessary can be a substantial exercise of power.

Overloaded medical providers sometimes made errors in procedures or paperwork that had major ramifications for elders. Several seniors in this study, mostly from poor areas, discussed how medical errors (e.g., getting the wrong medication) led to them being hospitalized. Even minor errors can affect quality of life and how seniors perceive health organizations. More major medical errors, like botched surgeries, can lead to years of pain and trouble. These experiences affect seniors' orientations and behavior toward peer organizations, a topic discussed in depth in the next chapter.[32]

In a free clinic in Elm Flats, I observed the following interactions, which show how a seemingly minor problem (i.e., an issue with paperwork) created major issues for a senior who needed to get his scooter fixed. Denny, an elderly white man living alone in an apartment near the clinic, did not have much money, so he required bureaucratic endorsements to ensure his scooter was repaired. On this particular occasion, he walked into the area between the waiting room and the exam rooms, where the nurses' station is located and health aides take vitals and do health screening. The man approached the nurses' station. The people behind the station avoided eye contact, a common behavior in nursing homes and clinics servicing seniors. The man slammed down his cane and said loudly, "I'm not going to take this shit anymore. I've been coming here for years. What the fuck do you people do here?" The whole room looked over, and an aide said calmly, "Can I help you?" The man explained that the doctor or someone else had not filed the paper that would allow him to get a new battery for his scooter. He said that the doctor promised it was taken care of, but the company said they never received the paperwork. He added angrily, "I've been stuck at home for three weeks—three weeks because someone didn't fill out the fucking form."

The aide calmly stated that he was using inappropriate language and would have to leave if he did not change his tone. She asked if he had checked in at the front. He lowered his tone and said that this is the second time he had been there without seeing someone, and that he had been without morphine for several weeks and was in pain. He said he was waiting there for over an hour and was not going to wait any longer. He added another expletive, and the aide said that she would pull his chart, but that if he did not adjust his language, he would be asked to leave. The man moved with great difficulty over to a chair. He asked, "Is this one okay?" She said yes, and he sat down. While the aide was actively engaging the senior and ultimately helped him, Denny still felt he had little control over the situation, which added to his frustration and anger.

To remedy his problem, he could not just lay out money for a new battery the way an affluent senior might. Denny's options were structured by a lack of money. He had to go through the clinic and submit to rules, protocols, and gatekeeping if he was going to receive the goods and services he needed. While this is true for most seniors to an extent, particularly those getting narcotic painkillers, poor seniors depended on prescriptions for basic supplements and mobility aids, so the problem was more acute. Consequently, what might have been a minor hassle for someone with more resources (e.g., money to lay out for a medical apparatus, a family member to drive to the clinic, or a health-care center that responded to phone calls) could be a major issue for a poorer senior. Further, when such an error occurred in a more affluent area, the senior would be dealing with a different set of doctors and administrators (who were likely less overwhelmed) and had additional cultural skills for navigating the bureaucracy before it came to such a point. In sum, those with greater material resources had a broader range of options for dealing with everyday challenges and securing outcomes than did those like Denny.

While richer seniors had monetary resources and skills that enabled them to advocate for themselves more effectively, poor seniors often had a distrust of service providers. The case of distrusting doctors, as well as its roots in past experiences with inequality and state organizations, is discussed in the next chapter, but the phenomenon is more general and thus warrants mention here. Many seniors in poor areas often regarded any agent associated with the government or an affiliated organization as a potential threat to their independence. This view is grounded not only in prior experiences but present realities. Social workers and others who visit seniors must legally report any sign of abuse or neglect—which includes the nebulously defined "self-neglect"—to adult protective services or other agencies that can intervene, potentially resulting in a senior being placed in a hospital or nursing home (even if the senior feels this is unnecessary). One senior in Elm Flats articulated the dilemma quite clearly. He was initially introduced to me through a contact at a senior program, but it took months to earn his trust. Eventually he explained his early hesitance:

> When Sandra [senior program administrator] wanted to set me up with a visitor, I was worried. Everyone, I don't know if this is true for you, is a mandatory reporter. They have to report if you are being abused or if "you are abusing yourself." All it takes is one do-gooder misunderstanding something and the social worker is over here, and you lose freedom.

So while many poor seniors relied on government agents and senior organizations to provide essential access to food, shelter, and medical care, they also acknowledged that there was a component of surveillance and vulnerability that made them uneasy. While organizational gatekeepers provided access to key resources seniors needed or wanted, they were simultaneously seen as a potential threat to their independence.[33]

Conclusion:
The Uneven Playing Field

While inequality profoundly influences who lives to grow old, the previous chapter showed that survivors from different backgrounds face "similarly shaped problems" associated with being an American elder.

Even though many of the challenges the elderly face are similar, the individual and neighborhood resources at their disposal for responding are very different. This chapter has shown how material inequalities played out in the lives of seniors across the four neighborhoods of this study. Despite the presence of factors that might mitigate inequalities among those who survive to old age—the presence of government entitlements, biological robustness and selective mortality, and demographic "leveling" in aggregate—in practice the end game is still played on an uneven field. Rather than disappear, many of the same inequalities that structure our experiences earlier in the life course continue to stratify our possibilities in old age.

While "safety net" services helped older adults from each of the neighborhoods in this study gain access to basic resources such as food, transportation, housing, and medicine, seniors in the middle-class locales had access to substantially more services of a higher quality. The entrepreneurial structure of grant funding compounded this problem by funneling competitive resources to the most affluent areas. Likewise, the wealth seniors' possessed in old age, which often reflected inequality earlier in the life course, mattered immensely. Pensions, income, insurance, and home ownership provided some seniors with avenues of care that were simply not available to their less affluent counterparts. Further, their substantial resources allowed them to access resources from government institutions without being totally dependent on them. Poor seniors, on the other hand, were able to get resources but were reliant on state programs. Consequently, social workers, clinicians, and other "street-level bureaucrats" maintained substantial control over their lives. At the same time, ongoing budget cuts and other austerity measures threatened to erode funding at the local, state, and federal levels and consequently diminish services upon which poor seniors were most reliant. The next chapter illustrates that while these material inequalities are key to understanding the end game, how individuals play cannot simply be reduced to material inequality in the present.[34]

3

GAME-DAY STRATEGIES
How Prior Experiences Shape
Cultural Strategies in the Present

Culture is a stake which, like all other social stakes, simultaneously presupposes and demands that one take part in the game and be taken in by it; and interest in culture, without which there is no race, no competition, is produced by the very race and competition which it produces.

—Pierre Bourdieu

As the previous chapters have shown, despite the presence of government entitlements and macrodemographic factors that could level inequality in later life, an unequal distribution of physical and material resources stratifies which options are available to older Americans. This chapter explains that while understanding these structural inequalities in the present is necessary to charting the terrain on which the end game is played, doing so is not sufficient for understanding the diverse ways seniors play it. Understanding why people respond to similar problems in different ways, particularly when the resources available to them provide multiple possibilities, requires looking at the way culture connects prior experiences (and the inequalities that shape them) to how individuals and groups construct meaningful strategies for approaching everyday life. Consider the case of how Jane and Laney, two women with very similar resources, respond to a parallel predicament: early stage breast cancer.

Why Does Jane Skip Chemo, while Laney Doesn't?

Jane is a middle-class white woman living in Baygardens. She has a college education, private insurance to supplement Medicare, her own car, and friends in the area who are willing to help her with tasks. Laney is like Jane in many ways. In fact, on many surveys used to examine how seniors respond to health issues, they would be nearly indistinguishable. Laney also went to college, has supplemental insurance, owns a car, and has a robust social network. The two women are about the same age: Jane is sixty-five and Laney is sixty-four. They each live in a single-family home a few blocks away from each other. Both Jane and Laney face a similar health challenge: early stage breast cancer. Yet despite all their similarities, the two women adopt very different strategies for dealing with this condition.

This is seen most clearly in a simple observation: over the time I knew them, Laney went to get her chemotherapy treatments religiously, while Jane often skipped them. Since both women had very similar material resources in the present, it is impossible to explain the difference in those terms. Thinking counterfactually, Jane could have easily attended her chemotherapy appointments, and Laney could have skipped them. But they pursued fundamentally different approaches to dealing with the same problem. So what explains the difference?

Jane frequently pointed out that she did not want to "live forever," so she wanted to enjoy life while she could. She tried to live in the moment. For her this meant going out to social events and trying to feel well enough to enjoy them. This took priority over treating her cancer or engaging in other life-prolonging activities. For Laney, the idea of skipping chemotherapy to enjoy the present was not only hard to grasp but also irresponsible. Despite their similar capacities and circumstances, Jane and Laney pursued different ends. Jane valued trying to wring as much enjoyment out of life as she could. Laney valued preserving her body and independence as long as possible, even if that meant less excitement. Consequently, the two women employed different cultural strategies when presented with parallel dilemmas.

The divergent ways Jane and Laney responded to breast cancer are representative of broader differences in how the seniors in this study approached the end game. Understanding why these two women pursued very different paths when both responses were available, and the many parallels observed in fieldwork, requires a deeper look at how culture shapes behavior. In the sections that follow, I examine why seniors such as Laney and Jane adopt particular strategies for dealing with the dilemmas they face rather than other viable alternatives. As the data will show, these differences cannot simply be reduced to material resources in the present or random variations in individual psychology. Rather, how seniors respond to the challenges of the end game is conditioned by patterned cultural strategies. These strategies result from lifetimes of shared experiences, structured by prior patterns of inequality, which ultimately shape what seniors understand as *desirable (motivations), reasonable (orientations), possible (cultural resources),* and *practical (strategies)* ways of surviving the challenges of old age in the present.[1]

Doing the "Right" Thing:
Desirable and Responsible Responses to Growing Old

There is vast literature that shows that seniors from different racial, socioeconomic, and gender groups respond to the physiological and social challenges of growing older in very different ways in aggregate. This has been documented with respect to end-of-life planning, the physical issues of aging, patterns of health-care use, and numerous other phenomena. As the previous chapter demonstrated, much of this variation is a function of the continued stratification of material resources and opportunities in later life. However, as the example with Jane and Laney shows, there is also substantial variation even within demographic categories and neighborhoods. Likewise, statistical analyses have shown that even after controlling for variation in health and illness, among seniors living in poverty, whites and women are on substantially more likely to go to a doctor than African Americans and men. Understanding the end game necessitates looking at the sources of variation in how seniors, both across and within neighborhoods, respond to everyday

challenges. Doing so requires charting the way culture—broadly understood as shared understandings, motivations, capacities, and strategies—
shapes behavior and experience in unequal contexts.[2]

Social scientists have long shown that differences in attitudes, dispositions, skills, and understandings lead people to behave in very different ways. A great deal of empirical research continues to show that
"what people want" and what they "value" influences behavior, both
within and across contexts. In recent years, however, scholarly debates
about "how culture affects action" have shied away from the term
"values," particularly when looking at the relationship between culture
and inequality. Contemporary criticisms of value-centered approaches
to culture correctly point out that models that place unified value systems as a driving force have been overextended and need updating in
light of new evidence and advances in scientific understandings of cognition. A parallel body of research convincingly speaks to the way important differences in nonmaterial resources, cultural tools, and "cultural
capital" contribute to the reproduction of American inequality, even
when people value the same thing. Recently, cultural sociologists have
attempted to reconcile and reconnect these seemingly divergent understandings of culture. However, less work has leveraged the advantages of
comparative ethnography to show how various facets of culture shape
everyday social life across the contexts of American inequality. The
design of this study provides a useful opportunity for doing so. Such an
examination is both necessary to understanding how Americans
approach the challenges of the end game and useful for empirically
examining how the relationship of social stratification and culture
operates more generally.[3]

In the pages that follow, I demonstrate how *cultural inputs* such as
motivations and orientations, shaped by social experiences over the life
course, affected how the seniors in this study responded to the dilemmas
they faced in part by "providing the ends people value and pursue." As I
discussed in my work integrating different theoretical models of culture, the effect of inputs is most noticeable when people were able to
pursue various options (as in the case of Jane and Laney) but consistently choose one over the other. In this study, differences in what
seniors valued shaped how they deployed the resources at their disposal.
Consequently there were substantial differences in the strategies people

exercised, even within the same neighborhoods. For instance, some seniors, such as Laney, felt that the best way to deal with aging was to adopt long-term strategies to mitigate loss, conserve health, and maintain independence. That is to say, they valued approaches that reflected a desire to *preserve the body*. Others, such as Jane, felt that the challenges of aging were a reminder that they were nearing their "end," so they might as well have a good time while they could—these seniors' valued approaches allowed them to *maximize enjoyment* before their bodies broke down. Which of these approaches seniors adopted had a profound effect on how they approached old age and how they evaluated the action—and even the morality—of others doing the same.[4]

Preserving the Body:
Playing It Safe to Preserve Independence

For many seniors, preserving the body and a sense of independence for as long as possible is seen as the "right" way to approach growing older. The underlying idea is that the body, and consequently the ability to act in the world, is perpetually at risk as one grows old. The responsible thing to do is to maximize functionality, independence, and life as long as possible. This is the espoused goal of myriad programs for seniors that make proclamations like "Our goal is to help keep you safe in your own home." It is paralleled in academic literatures that talk about "successful aging" and the rewards of a conscientious approach to nearing the end. Quite simply, the notion that preserving the body is a more "responsible" approach to old age is common sense to many of the seniors in this study and perhaps some of the readers of this book. The sociological question, however, is not whether this is the "right" stance to take but rather from where such motivations and "conceptions of the desirable" originate, how they affect behavior, and to what ends. In this book's conclusion, I return to the assumption that any group (e.g., the affluent, the poor, the medical community, social scientists) knows the "right" response to existential questions such as how to deal with life and death in the context of inequality. The point of this section is more directly empirical: to show how cultural understandings of the "right way" to approach the challenges of aging shape social life in the end game.[5]

The focus on preserving the body had far-reaching effects on the behaviors of many individuals in this study. These seniors continually emphasized, through both speech and actions, that the physical vulnerability and challenges of old age necessitated a careful, conservative, and temperate approach to everyday life. One senior described this as "coming to terms with the mind-set of frailty." Another senior broached the topic of risk, worrying, and monitoring when she quipped to a friend at the senior center, "If I didn't have something to worry about, I'd make up something. That's just me. I worry about everything." She went on to connect this to how she dealt with aging by noting that she was constantly researching potential causes and treatments for her health problems, large and small, and that she would spend hours on the Internet researching both Western medicine and alternative treatments for her conditions (as well as preventative measures). In this study, individuals focused on preserving the body were less likely to go out at night, disregard the advice of medical authorities, drink alcohol, or use recreational street drugs. They were also far more likely to carefully track the medication they took, exercise, research treatment options for health conditions, and verbalize their worries. Body-preserving seniors were generally concerned with monitoring their bodies, getting information about health, treating symptoms as soon as they appeared, abstaining from activities that could result in physical catastrophes (such as walking or driving too far), and making sure they had support systems in place for when something bad (such as a fall) did happen.

The motivation to preserve the body was generally not a new manifestation for these people but part of a general strategy of "security maximization" developed over the life course. Although I could not directly observe their lives during their childhood and middle age, the behaviors and strategies during their working years that seniors described lined up closely with how they behaved in old age, as well as which behaviors they considered to be "responsible." Consider Donald, the Chinese senior from Baygardens. Over coffee at the senior center, Donald talked about the importance of saving money. He provided an extended account of how he came to America with nothing, and worked in a factory. He explained he would work as many hours as he could in the factory, then sell shoes he bought with his savings during his day off. By never spending his money except on investments, he said he was able to buy homes and support his family. He attributed this to his "old-fashioned Chinese values. Very conservative. We had no money, but our sons went to [university]. We saved all money even though we were poor."[6]

Just as Donald explained that a responsible middle age involved working hard and saving money to take care of his family, old age necessitated staying on top of health conditions and seeking medical help when something went wrong. When Donald fell after taking an extended walk around town, he immediately went to the doctor to get an X-ray. He subsequently went to his regularly scheduled appointments. He adhered to the dietary guidelines that medical care providers set in response to his diabetes. When there was a health fair at the senior center, he went to check his blood sugar and blood pressure and speak to the volunteers, proudly telling other seniors that his "numbers were good." After the falling incident, he went to great effort not to overextend himself physically after having a fall, such as always using a walker. In short, he sought to protect those physical assets that he had left. For him, it was both common sense and the "right" thing to do.

Inclinations toward preserving the body were also seen clearly in my interview data, which used vignettes to probe what seniors say people *should* do when presented with various concrete predicaments. In my interviews, I read three vignettes describing common physical problems faced in later life. I followed each of these with the question "What should this senior do?" A fourth vignette recounted the behaviors of a hypothetical individual based on my early field observations of Jane's inclinations toward maximizing enjoyment. Seniors who were inclined toward preserving the body and who espoused security maximizing strategies in general had the strongest response to this fourth vignette, which asked the following: "There is a senior I know, who has breast cancer and is getting chemotherapy. Her doctors told her she should not drink alcohol, but all her friends are heavy drinkers. After getting chemotherapy, she would often go out to bars with her friends to drink. What do you think of this?" Here, rather than asking what a senior should do, the question prompts the respondent to evaluate a senior who behaves in a way counter to the ideal of preserving the body. Those who approached old age by trying to preserve the body would often shake their heads and provide comments like those offered by a senior in Rockport: "That's stupid. That's really stupid." Johnny, an African

American man from Elm Flats, offered a similarly indignant and telling response: "I think that's asinine. If you are not gonna pay attention when you have a disease like that, and you feel like you have to take it upon yourself to drink when it's not necessary, then you are asking for trouble. You have no one to blame but yourself."[7]

This sort of behavior was seen not only as "stupid" but also as irresponsible, irrational, and even immoral. Some said it was unfair to their loved ones. Seniors who sought to preserve the body often made similar statements about not wanting to let down friends or medical professionals. For instance, a white senior from Elm Flats noted that although he was sick of doctors, "I feel responsible to them, not to do anything stupid, and let all of these caring professionals down." In contrast, seniors who focused on *maximizing enjoyment* would note that while the behavior in the vignette was clearly bad for longevity, the issue was complicated. Several added that it was not their place to judge. Other said they could not blame the senior for drinking.

Maximizing Enjoyment: "You Only Get One Go-Round"

In contrast to those who sought to preserve the body, a different group of seniors felt that the desirable response to dealing with the problems and uncertainties created by aging was to enjoy life before it was gone. The guiding notion was that to focus on preventing inevitable problems (such as death or institutionalization), rather than taking advantage of opportunities to enjoy oneself, was both undesirable and irresponsible. Here the focus was not so much on seniors letting other people down as it was on letting themselves down. These seniors were quick to make proclamations like the quip provided by one Rockport senior: "You only get one go-round!" Enjoyment-maximizing behavior often translated into a much more laissez-faire attitude toward problems of health and the body. This is exemplified by Sandy, the eighty-nine-year-old introduced in Chapter 2. During one of my visits to Sandy's home, I casually mentioned that my mom was diabetic. Sandy noted that she was as well, adding, "I eat candy sometimes. I know you are not supposed to but at this age who cares?" In a later visit, she articulated the notion behind this sort of behavior:

Next year is my ninetieth birthday. I'm going to have a cake and dinner and they [her family] might as well come. This is going to be the last one I celebrate. I don't really care what happens after that. What is there to live for at this age? All my immediate family is dead. My father died at fifty-six, my mother died two years later. My sister died at fifty-four. Why did I live so long? [*shrugs*] I don't know, but I am going to have a party for my ninetieth. [*smiles*]

Sandy's actions were still oriented toward the future, but the timeline for what constituted the future was compressed. In contrast, Jessica, a ninety-two-year-old discussed in following section on pain and distinction, was hypervigilant in her attempts to prolong her life, health, and independence despite her advanced age.[8]

In this study, individuals who sought to maximize enjoyment were more likely to deviate from medical advice, drink alcohol, smoke cigarettes, use recreational drugs, engage in casual sexual activity, go out after dark, risk falls, and delay getting care until health problems became a major issue. In explaining why he drank vodka and smoked constantly, a man in Elm Flats articulated a common attitude shared by these seniors: "What, am I going to get lung cancer? I've already had it. Liver damage? I already had fifty thousand beers in my lifetime, so what's one more?" Likewise, Jane disregarded the instructions of her oncologist regarding abstaining from beauty products while on chemotherapy (as well as his advice to attend all the appointments). He told her not to use nail polish, but she showed polished nails to me and said, "I think I would rather be sick than have black nails."[9]

My data suggest that, as with inclinations toward preserving the body, the drive toward maximizing enjoyment is not newly developed as people reach old age but rather is acquired over the life course. Although the image of excitement-maximizing seniors bucks common stereotypes about later life, the fact that there is motivational continuity from earlier in life is not surprising, given the vast sociological, psychological, and even economic literatures on the importance of socially mediated motivations, values, and dispositions acquired early in life. Further, although one might expect the potentially jarring experience of growing old to produce a fundamental change in motivation (i.e., a "conversion experience"), I did not observe this. In fact, people's life histories, general motivations, and reported past responses to dilemmas mapped extremely well onto what they sought to maximize in the present. (Differences in the viability of maintaining continuity in identity, however, were discussed in Chapter 1 and will be revisited in the section below on cultural resources.)[10]

Jane, the sixty-five-year-old white woman introduced at the beginning of this chapter and the basis for the breast cancer vignette used in my interviews, provides a good example of an excitement-maximizing senior whose approach to her later years was shaped by prior experiences. When I first met her, Jane explained, "I was diagnosed with rheumatoid arthritis in my early twenties, so I have never really been able to work a regular job, which is hard, because it means I was always dependent on a man even though I had a degree from [university]." She often remarked that she did not like having to depend on people for help but that she was used to it. She also told me she had become accustomed to not having money, so she would try to have fun when and where she could.

Jane described her life in both the past and present as "chaotic." In the period that I knew her, she spent a lot of time with her "group of guys," heavy-drinking younger seniors (mostly in their sixties) whom she dubbed "the lost boys." She met them at local bars and had been in casual sexual relationships with at least three. She said they were all "alcoholics," and she noted, "I don't know if I have a sign over me, or if it is just that I like to go to bars, but I am a magnet for alcoholics." The following example, which is typical of the time I spent with Jane and representative of seniors adopting this approach, shows how excitement maximization can shape responses to the challenges of growing older.

Near Christmas I visited Jane in her Baygardens home. She explained that she had intended to make "the lost boys" a Thanksgiving dinner but ended up not feeling well from the chemotherapy (which she had gone to this time), so she had gotten drunk and called all her friends and family instead. She told me she was having rat problems. This was not much of a surprise, given her living environment. Her house had lots of trash, empty beer cans, and other debris. She explained that she did not want to pay for an exterminator and that she hoped one of the "lost boys" would take care of it.

We subsequently spent the day in several neighborhood bars, which were populated with other seniors. At 4:55 p.m. we drove to a strip mall so she could have overdue blood work done at the small clinic there (which was en route to another bar). The lab closed at 5:00 p.m., which led to an argument between Jane and the technician. The technician relented when Jane explained she was behind on her chemo because they needed blood work and that she could die from cancer. After this encounter, Jane smiled, shrugged, and told me she might as well have the chemo done while we were near the mall and she remembered.

That evening we were at a liquor store, where we were waiting to meet up with her new "guy," a neighborhood man in his sixties with whom she was in a casual relationship. We were waiting for a long time, so I offered Jane a sugar-free candy. She had fibromyalgia, which she said makes the sugar substitutes bad for her, but then shrugged and started eating them. She ate most of the bag. While waiting, Jane mentioned that she had previously been obese and had undergone a gastric bypass (a weight-loss surgery). I asked why she had the procedure. She said, "I wanted to look better for guys. It was about seven years ago." She proceeded to tell me stories about how she regularly gets sick when she eats ice cream, a food generally prohibited after weight-loss surgery of that type. She noted, "I love ice-cream, but you can't process it. Instead of eating the three bites, I eat the whole thing then get sick." After about forty-five minutes, Jane finally got hold of her "guy," who was dealing with police and accident victims after causing a minor car accident and trying to avoid having the incident labeled a DUI. When she heard this, Jane quipped, "See what I said about chaos?" Later, as I went to drop her off with a friend, Jane asked, "Can you go to UPS? I forgot, and they are about to close. If I don't get my fax, I lose my health insurance."

Jane was educated, articulate, and savvy in her interactions with care providers and bureaucrats. She read books voraciously and spent a great deal of time using the Internet for research and leisure. She lived in the center of Baygardens, a middle-class neighborhood with high-quality senior services and medical facilities. She was quite aware of the potential ramifications of her behavior for health and longevity. Yet she chose to skip chemotherapy on many occasions. This was not because she lacked information, access, or even "cultural capital" but rather because she dealt with the dilemma of growing older and getting ill in a way that made sense to her and paralleled her behavior earlier in her life—by trying to maximize enjoyment and live in the moment (which for her case revolved around men, music, food, and alcohol).

Pain and Distinction:
The Case of "Dope Pills" and Pot

In general, seniors enacted behavioral strategies associated with either preserving the body or maximizing enjoyment because they felt that was the "right" way to act. In other words, these responses reflected not just individual psychology but patterned ways of approaching the world based on prior inequality as well as a publically moral component that shaped how behavior was understood (i.e., what is right or wrong). Sociologist Pierre Bourdieu offers insight on this in his commentary on socioeconomic differences in bodily practices and their ramifications when he poignantly notes that "the legitimate use of the body is spontaneously perceived as an index of moral uprightness." This moral dimension of the body and its ramifications are seen clearly in how seniors responded to a common problem: the presence of pain.[11]

As Chapter 1 demonstrated, although the levels and subjective meanings of pain varied greatly for different individuals, managing pain was an issue for seniors from all the gender, racial, and socioeconomic groups represented in this study. Seniors' behavioral responses, even within a demographic category, varied substantially and were not simply reducible to the presence or absence of material resources. Some seniors took narcotic pain pills, some exercised more, others moved less, some wrote poems, others went to doctors constantly, some sought out street drugs, and some, such as Jane, spent more time drinking alcohol in bars. The legitimacy of different strategies for coping with pain was a constant topic of conversation among seniors and a point of distinction that highlights the divide between those who maximized bodily preservation and those who valued enjoyment over longevity. This difference often played out in discussions concerning whether particular seniors in a community used pain medications, which ones they chose to use, and whether this was acceptable for a given level of pain. It is important to note that seniors' general approaches toward moderation and preservation, or trying to feel good to enjoy life in the present, were consistent even when they reported different levels of pain. Those inclined to moderation did not suddenly go to bars when their pain was worse, but gradually increased medications (i.e., the divergent approaches cannot be simply reduced to changing physical status).

The extent to which seniors took pain pills was an explicit axis of distinction among many of the individuals in this study. Seniors who limited their intake of pain pills often cast themselves as having greater will, character, and self-control than those who took "dope" from "Pill Hill." Temperance and self-regulation were valued by these seniors, who were generally inclined toward preserving the body. A representative example occurred when I visited Jessica in her apartment unit in Baygardens. She showed me an 8½″ × 11″ notebook filled with numbers, then explained,

> This is to keep track of my pills. [*points to notebook*] I can take up to ←
> three a day, but I never take that. Sometimes I'll take some other pills.
> They gave me these for sleeping, and these for pain [hydrocodone]. I
> used to joke about them being dope pills, but that's what they are. I
> don't like pills and don't want to be hooked. My daughter says, "So
> what if you get hooked?" But I don't want to.

In the years I knew her, Jessica would often shake her head and talk about seniors who "got hooked." Even though she was unable to manage without the medication, she would still closely monitor her use to remain temperate. In a similar vein, a senior from Elm Flats noted, "Some people just lie down and take narcotics. That is no life." He went on to reinforce this distinction: "If you can work through the pain you have accomplished something and it gives you a sort of clarity . . . It is *better* than laying down waiting to die."

The "moral boundary" around the use of pain medicine echoes the more general distinctions about the desirability of temperate behaviors that conserve the body and prolong "independence." Donald made a point about the importance of temperance more generally when discussing the values he imparted to his children: "All I asked was that my children did not go around with women, or do drugs, or drink, or stay out late, and that I would like them to be in the top ten percent of their class." Although these may seem like rigid expectations, he was not being sarcastic. He explained that two of his three sons met these criteria, and the third "dummy son" had since apologized to him for being a failure.[12]

On the other end of the spectrum, "enjoyment maximizing" elders believed there was no reason to be old *and* in pain, and they distinguished themselves from the body-preserving individuals accordingly. They often saw those who avoided the use of pills and the like as prudish or even irrational. Sobriety and temperance were not seen as ends in and of themselves, and certainly not as markers of higher moral status. Many would take narcotic pain medication regularly (which they could access via doctors or informal markets), even when they were not in severe pain. They were also more likely to use these same substances recreationally and/or use street drugs. At a health event in Baygardens, volunteers were taking the blood pressure and glucose levels of seniors. An African American man walked over from the nearby bus stop and approached me, joking, "I'd have them take it [blood pressure] but they'd say I'm high. I used to be able to say that all the time" He laughed and walked away, and a few minutes later he returned with a plastic baggie containing marijuana remnants. He said, "I just told you about getting high. Look what I found on the street. Let me tell you, though, the Chinese is the ones with the good stuff." There were a lot of Asian American seniors at the event. "They got opium. That's what I use. Good for the pain." He smiled then walked away with the baggie.[13]

Seniors like the man above often deal with their age, pain, and pending mortality through the use of pain pills, recreational drugs, alcohol, or whatever else they can find to take their mind off their predicaments and make life a bit more fun or bearable. Dave, for instance, drank at least a six-pack of beer a day and smoked marijuana regularly. He used the oxycodone he got from his doctor, but he said he was in "constant pain" and that it only made sense to do whatever helped. He added that he did not understand why people were so concerned with pain pills, adding, "I don't understand. They don't get you high. Maybe if you crush them up and inject them or they can help if you are addicted." Like other enjoyment-maximizing seniors, he also looked forward to the "buzz" provided by imbibing various substances. He went on to say that he smoked medical marijuana with his friends, which was always a "nice interlude" in the day. He continued, "I have been smoking marijuana since before you were born. It is interesting, that it actually does help with the pain and appetite. It doesn't stop the pain, but it takes my mind off it, and the waves [of pain] are not so bad, plus I eat more." Dave went on to tell me that the current marijuana was much better than what he had in his "hippie days," and that, as with pain pills, he did not understand why people had such a problem with something that did not affect them personally. He explained that the right thing for people to do was "to mind their own damn business." In another instance I asked a diabetic woman I visited regularly why she did not follow the doctor's advice regarding avoiding sugary foods, and she laughed, responding, "Why not? I don't want to live forever." Temperance and deferred gratification in the service of prolonging life were simply not viewed as desirable, nor were they understood as a more responsible approach to later life.[14]

Acting Reasonably:
Orientations for Responding to the Aging Body

The respective inclination toward preserving the body or maximizing enjoyment affects how older Americans respond to the dilemmas of aging, given the contexts they inhabit. However, these inclinations are not the sole determinant of the strategies elders adopt. For instance, seniors in middle-class areas who are trying to prolong their life at the expense of present enjoyment can pursue numerous strategies, given their structural location and material resources. They can go to an herbalist or doctor for stomach troubles, try to sleep more, go to an emergency room if they are dizzy, check in with a psychiatrist or friends if they feel sad, do yoga, or take Aleve for arthritis. While they face additional hardships and constraints (as described in the previous chapter), seniors in the poor neighborhoods could (and did) pursue quite divergent strategies as well. Even when multiple responses (e.g., for muscle pain, either medicating with marijuana or stretching) were equally viable, which strategy individuals pursued was not random. Rather, the responses seniors saw as more *reasonable* guided their actions. This is because what constitutes a *reasonable* response is conditioned by a second layer of cultural inputs: *orientations*.

Motivations such as the inclination to value bodily preservation over immediate enjoyment drive action by determining what is desirable in general. In contrast, orientations point people toward what is reasonable, given their motivations and specific circumstances. Orientations can be thought of as sets of attitudes relating to a particular subject—in this case, how one responds to aging and its physical dimensions. Rather than shaping "what people want" in a general sense, orientations shape what people see, or what they notice and understand given particular circumstances (e.g., a health problem, trouble paying the bills). Orientations are less ingrained and often more discursive, and thus change more easily over time than do values or motivations. For instance, having a bad experience with a hospital is unlikely to change an individual's underlying motivations or psychological makeup, but it may very well affect how the individual interacts with doctors by shaping both what the individual notices and what he or she views as an appropriate response.[15]

I now examine the two competing sets of orientations that had the most profound effect on how seniors responded to growing old, and in particular how they approached the physical predicaments of the aging body. I refer to these two orientations, seen within each of the neighborhoods in this study, as the *natural body* and the *medical body*.

The Natural Body

Seniors who possessed a *natural body* orientation emphasized that the body is a "natural," self-regulating, and highly individual entity. These people generally saw themselves, rather than doctors, as experts on their unique physical and mental states. The body was understood as possessing everything it needed to repair itself. Chemicals and medical interventions were often framed as counterproductive or even harmful to this natural healing process. Elders with this orientation often distrusted doctors and Western medicine in general, which they frequently described as "money-making schemes," or, as one African American man from Rockport put it, "bullshit systems and programs." Another senior expressed this attitude in a representative way when he commented, "Doctors bug me, because I know that they're just juicing it for money, I know they are." These seniors' responses were guided by the perception that the body "heals itself" and that medical institutions that were involved in interventions were "just a hustle," a scheme to make money.[16]

The natural-body orientation was well articulated by Ray, a sixty-eight-year-old middle-class African American man living in Elm Flats. While at the senior center in Elm flats, Ray explained,

> I don't see doctors and I don't believe in taking medicine basically . . . Friends of mine at work said at a certain age you need to go in and have a doctor shove his finger up your ass so he can check out your prostate, so I went in and did that so I can get back to Jamie [his friend] and say, "Okay Jamie, I did that; I could have done that myself, you know." Anyway, the doctors didn't know what that's all about, I don't know . . . If you get sick you get a lot of rest and then the body heals itself.

Ray went on to say that he had not seen a doctor since the prostate exam twenty-eight years ago. He did, however, take "herbal concoctions," smoke marijuana, and see a chiropractor to feel better, but noted that he no longer did "real drugs" such as LSD or speed, which he felt were harmful. He did point out that when he was middle-aged, he had gone to the doctor after experiencing chronic migraines that he could not manage on his own, and he reported that the medicine that the doctor prescribed helped.

When last observed at the Elm Flats senior center, Ray was preparing for his annual "garlic fast," a month-long period of not eating solid food, except for garlic. Ray explained that this "natural" measure helps the body cleanse itself. Later, when asked what he did if he did not feel well, he commented,

> Rest. I see what sort of herbal concoctions sound best, but mostly just rest. The body heals itself. The body has all types of natural healing agents inside of it if you leave it alone instead of loading it up with chemicals. When you get a cut, I don't care how deep it is, all you have to do is stop the bleeding, and it patches itself up. It's how nature works.

Within the context of this study, the orientation toward the natural body was most often held by seniors who had lived in poverty, had negative experiences with medical organizations, or (quite commonly) both. This orientation was common among the African American men who had lived much of their lives in poor neighborhoods—which is not surprising, given the history of unequal treatment in medical institutions. However, other groups exhibited it as well. For instance, this orientation was also held by smaller numbers of middle-class African Americans, some whites (mostly poor), and some Asian Americans (both poor and nonpoor).[17]

Michele was a seventy-year-old, middle-class, Asian American woman from Baygardens. She was college-educated and had supplemental insurance. Yet how she responded to thyroid problems provides a useful example. Michele frequently reiterated variations on the notion that "the body heals itself." When the doctor recommended surgery for her condition, she refused. Going against the advice of both her doctors and her children, she chose instead to focus on metaphysics and meditation. Like other seniors with a natural-body orientation, Michele continually pointed to the limits of Western knowledge and the insight provided by her own experiences. Similarly, she emphasized that "doctors aren't God" and that the seniors knew their own bodies better than any outsider could.[18]

Seniors inclined toward the natural-body orientation often commented that those who take more conventional biomedical approaches are either responding to custom or falling for a "hustle" that could be counterproductive. James, the seventy-seven-year-old African American from Rockport, invoked these attitudes one day while commenting on how people were dressed around the senior pool hall. He went on to explain why he was not wearing a coat:

> When you wear a lot of clothes, your body has a tendency to not do its job. In other words, the body is designed to make intersections [sic] for the weather. But once you try to make intersections for the weather, it throws the body out of kilter. And you catch a lot of colds. A lot of things happen to you that wouldn't normally happen to you if you didn't have the frame of mind. You don't need a whole lot of clothing. Like today, you got three or four coats on, 'cause in their mind, they think, the season, that's what you are supposed to do. Rather than the way you feel.

Once again, James stressed how the body manages itself and pointed out how interventions directed by both convention and Western medical systems discounted seniors' tacit knowledge of their own bodies.[19]

Often invocations of this orientation were accompanied by discussions of how Western medicine was a "scam" set up to make money.

Further, these seniors connected organizational processing and inequality with a medical approach to everyday life in old age. In doing so they often returned to the way the interests of doctors and privileged institutions diverged from their own. One senior who had lived his life in poverty articulated this while describing his displeasure at having to go to the doctor to get his prescriptions renewed: "[Doctor] makes me come back every ninety days. And I'm not different, you know, I'm no different every ninety days. She's just, I'm sure she's got a tremendous income. I mean, I bet she makes a ton of dough." Even though these seniors' visits were often covered by Medicare and Medicaid (which removed some financial barriers), this orientation made engaging with doctors any more than was absolutely necessary seem unreasonable, even foolish—a problem compounded by the issues of surveillance and vulnerability discussed in the previous chapter.

While holding the natural-body orientation affected action by shaping what was seen as reasonable, it was not a linear determinant of what seniors actually did. When things got bad enough, people still saw medical professionals, but when and how they did this was influenced by their natural-body orientation (i.e., they responded differently than did *medical body* seniors). Even James echoed this point when he reluctantly admitted, "If I don't feel well, then I'll go to a doctor. But I usually don't feel bad enough to have to go to a doctor." Seniors who emphasized the natural body often first tried holistic or folk strategies for staying healthy or dealing with illness, but when something important "broke," they would still end up at the hospital. For instance, Jessica, the ninety-two-year-old white woman from Baygardens, was adamant that she knew her body and that doctors' offices were places people went to "get sick." She stressed that she could handle things on her own and that her grandmother had lived to 105 without ever seeing a doctor or taking flu shots, an observation that reinforced Jessica's beliefs. Jessica would go to her regular doctor only once a year, to placate her daughter. Still, like most other seniors, when something major went wrong, Jessica would rely on doctors and the emergency department. This happened several times during the study, most frequently because of falls.[20]

The following example involving Jessica's trip to the emergency room is typical of how those with the natural-body orientation end up at a doctor or hospital. On this occasion, I went to visit Jessica, who had asked me to take her to the doctor. I asked how she was doing, because going to the doctor, as I had previously observed, was a rare occurrence for her unless something was very wrong. She told me she had a "little problem." Apparently she was having considerable issues with constipation that week and was concerned, because she previously had been hospitalized for intense pain and diagnosed with "the tricholitis." As usual, she tried to take care of it herself, taking lots of Maalox (an over-the-counter antacid), which she believed was a laxative. She got the Maalox from the drugstore across the street. Jessica reiterated that she thought it was best to take care of these things yourself. After having a very solid stool and not sleeping for several days, however, she became very worried and finally went to the hospital, so they could "clean me out and make sure it all came out." She said she took the bus to the emergency room and had to wait a long time. She commented, "I don't like to go to the doctor, so I try not to go unless I can't fix it myself." After visiting the doctor, Jessica explained that she thought the dope pills were the problem. She told me, "I don't take pills unless I have to, but I took one, so maybe that is what happened." Narcotic painkillers can often cause constipation, so Jessica's concern with the "dope pills" may have some validity. Jessica added that she was feeling better, so she would stop taking them. She did not schedule a follow-up with the doctor. She also did not stop taking the pain medication, although she continued to carefully record it in her notebook.[21]

The above examples show how those with natural-body orientations sometimes vary in how proactively or reactively they respond to health problems. Although Ray was distrustful of doctors, he was proactive in using alternative strategies to help himself feel better. Jessica used various strategies, Western and otherwise, to "fix herself." James, on the other hand, was more reactive, usually addressing problems only when he was truly worried about his health. However, all three seniors are typical of those with the natural-body orientation in that (1) they eventually went to a Western medical professional when things got "bad enough," (2) this happened only after trying to treat themselves, and (3) finally turning to conventional medical care involved an emergency room or urgent care visit rather than scheduling an appointment with a primary care provider. The example with Jessica also reveals the way orientations and motivations can be tempered by the demands placed on seniors by their social networks. Although Jessica did not like going to doctors and felt it was largely a waste of time, the insistence of her daughter ensured that she went at least annually (with trips to the emergency room in between). The topic of how networks affect seniors' trajectories, and how this too is premised upon shared cultural understandings, is examined in the next chapter.[22]

The Medical Body

In contrast to seniors who held the natural-body orientation, many seniors espoused the familiar Western model of the *medical body*—that is, a complex biological machine that needs to be observed, maintained, and fixed by experts. In the context of this study, this orientation was most often held by seniors with middle-class backgrounds, particularly whites and Asian Americans. Here, doctors and other medical professionals were understood as experts who possessed specialized knowledge, but seniors were seen as responsible for following their instructions to maintain health. An elderly white woman emphasized this last point to a friend at a senior center when commenting about how another senior was absent with gout. Upon hearing the explanation, the woman shook her head and noted, "People need to exercise, watch their blood pressure. They can't just eat whatever they desire." Talking about diet and exercise can be associated with either natural- or medical-body orientations and often assumes moral dimensions. However, the idea of contrasting desire and regulation, as well as the importance of monitoring medically validated vital signs such as blood pressure, was associated with a medical-body orientation.[23]

Seniors with this orientation often consider aging intrinsically linked to medical processes. Most go to doctors on a regular basis to monitor their conditions, even if they are relatively healthy. A typical response was provided by a Tanya, a sixty-two-year-old middle-class African American woman from Cedar Hills:

> I have to see a nurse practitioner every month for blood work and a checkup. Then I see a doctor about four times a year for a checkup and physical and consultation, and medicine refills, new eyewear, and eye exam, dental work. Whatever I need to do.

Likewise, Bill, a seventy-nine-year-old middle-class Latino man, made a similar statement:

> I have my doctor and we have a regular schedule. We used to see him twice a year. Well, I usually see him in January now. They draw my blood and I come home and have a meeting the following week and he and I check on everything.

The overarching principle was that their doctors and medical professionals should be consulted regularly to catch and address problems early. Consequently, for those who sought to preserve the body, the most *reasonable* thing to do was to go to doctors to minimize or fix the physical problems that were associated with old age. Bill explained this when he noted, "You just make the best of it. Try and keep healthy enough so you don't need that much attention. I'm seventy-nine and I feel great. Although sometimes I ask myself why am I shuffling? I guess the legs just give out."[24]

Many individuals with orientations toward the medical body were also proactive in seeking care when problems would arise. These seniors would go to a doctor, typically a general practitioner or specialist, when they felt they might have a health problem. Many would call the provider early when they felt something was wrong. Sometimes they followed specific guidelines to avoid being labeled a hypochondriac by the providers (or themselves). For instance, Tanya explained,

> My rule is forty-eight hours. I mean, if you have a fever or if you're going to pass out, or if your heart is racing, then naturally you need to call 911 and get to the hospital, but a lot of seniors don't do the right thing. They think that they are keeping their life in their hands when they stay at home and think it's going to be alright, when in fact, you do need to go.

Tanya's quote illustrates several important components of how seniors with medical-body orientations think about and respond to health problems. The first point is that when there is a problem, the doctor is the correct place to go for care. The second is that although what constitutes reasonable behavior is a function of severity, the appropriate response is to get professional care. Finally, Tanya notes that this is "the right thing to do." Orientations are conscious, but that does not mean they are regarded as one equally reasonable response among many. Like motivations, they assume a moral valence.

The belief that one should go to the doctor whenever a health problem arises, and its corresponding behavior, was more common among the women I observed, but it was also shared by men from middle-class backgrounds (a finding mirrored in quantitative research). In describing how he dealt with recent health problems that sent him to an emergency room, Walter, a seventy-four-year-old Asian American retired dentist, commented:

> I had kind of numbness in my arm and everything else, and I thought oh my God I'm having a stroke, went over there and it turned out to be a pinched nerve. [*laughs*] But at least I found out that it was okay. When I went in with bloody stools [several months prior] they kept me over-night because it turned out that I did have the diverticulitis. So they were able to take care of that.

Walter went on to explain that when it turned out to be a pinched nerve, he "felt really stupid, but again as you say, when things don't seem right we are more likely to go to the ER."[25]

Although orientations toward the medical body influenced behavior, as with orientations toward the natural body, they did not determine it. Consequently there was a great deal of variation in behavior. Some seniors religiously checked vital statistics such as pulse, blood pressure, weight, and blood sugar. This was sometimes done pub-lically and turned into a game to see "who had the best numbers." This public ritual was part of a more general process where health and its sig-nifiers represented an axis of status and distinction among seniors with a medical-body orientation. Even among these seniors, however, indi-viduals sometimes behaved in a way counter to espoused ideals. This resonates with much of the work in contemporary cultural sociology, which focuses on how the facets of culture that direct action can be overlapping and even used in contradictory ways, as opposed to the coherent and totalizing systems seen in classical sociology and some veins of interpretivist anthropology. A typical example involves the financier described in Chapter 2. He was a diabetic and proudly touted the fact that he had not had "a real Coke for twenty-five years." Still, he drank alcohol occasionally, even though he knew that it was bad for his diabetes. The typical justification in these scenarios is that maintaining life indefinitely is not worth it if it takes away everything you enjoy. Some code-switching, "excitement-maximizing" seniors would go so far as to say they visited doctors simply because they "loved life" and wanted to stay healthy to enjoy it. In this case, doctors were seen not as "moral authorities" but simply as facilitators who helped people enjoy life by treating their bodies and providing access to pharmaceuticals.[26]

On the Social Origin of Orientations

Orientations are an important pathway that connects culture to action, and, like other aspects of culture, this pathway is not sui generis— orientations reflect past experiences grounded in patterns of social inequality. Sometimes these experiences are tied to the historical memory of group treatment. For instance, African Americans in this study often remembered and referenced the Tuskegee experiments. In many cases, however, orientations were shaped more directly by personal experiences or interactions with medical organizations, health providers, and perhaps even authority figures in general. For instance, many of the seniors who held natural-body orientations described how what they perceived to be medical errors or poor treatment in their own lives shaped their outlook. In a representative example, an African American woman from Elm Flats explained that a botched surgery led to her being incapacitated for a year in her early sixties. She noted that after that experience, she was both more hesitant about doctors and more confident in her ability to manage her own health independently. These orientations also reflect life experiences about "what works," exemplified by Ray's observation that he heals better by himself, Jessica's observation that her grandmother never saw a doctor and never got sick, and Bill's comments that seeing the doctor regularly helped him stay well.[27]

Orientations toward aging are not random aspects of individual personality. They are cultural products connected to experiences earlier in the life course. These experiences are structured by the persistence of inequality. Consequently, past experiences that reflect racial, gender, and socioeconomic divisions often shape seniors' orientations and responses to the new challenges of old age. Yet, as the examples in this chapter show, orientations are not uniformly tied to social position and can cross demographic categories. Consider Ray. Although Ray's responses are representative of the natural-body orientation, he was not poor. He had an associate's degree, owned a home (albeit in a poor neighborhood), and had a car, health insurance, and disposable income. Likewise, Jessica was also a middle-class woman, but her prior experiences with organizations, scarcity, and poor health shaped how she responded to aging. Consequently, it is important to remember that orientations do not reflect socioeconomic or ethnic cultures in a reductionist way. Still, that does not mean there is no connection.

Experiences are stratified by unequal contexts that limit the realm of possibility from birth onward. Culture is connected to shared experiences and publically available ways of responding that reflect this. Individuals from some groups, such as African Americans or those living in poverty, are consequently more likely to have had negative experiences with medical institutions and consequently to adopt skeptical orientations. One important implication is that this can lead to the clustering of orientations along axes such as race, class, and gender—making those with experiences of social disadvantage less likely to seek medical care and providing a cultural mechanism that extends health disparities into later life.[28]

What Is Possible? A Note on the Role of Cultural Resources in Shaping Responses to Aging

Motivations shape which approaches to growing older are desirable, and orientations point toward which responses to particular situations seem most reasonable. However, the resources individuals can leverage in their interactions with other people and organizations determine what is ultimately possible. The previous chapter described how, in contrast to accounts that would cast the end game as a time when inequality is dissolved, structural inequalities and material disparities at the neighborhood and individual level continue to stratify the options and strategies available to older Americans. However, in the past thirty years there has been a growing acknowledgment that culture can also serve as a set of symbolic resources, tools, or capacities that are unequally distributed. As Swidler notes in her classic article on the topic, culture in this sense "has an independent causal role because it shapes the capacities from which such strategies of action are constructed." In other words, rather than only shaping what people want, culture in this sense (like other resources deployed by human actors) determines what they can actually get. Culture, as Bourdieu correctly notes, can be a form of capital. This can been seen clearly in both the skills and capacities seniors deploy as they approach the challenges of their later years.[29]

Cultural Resources in Contexts

The advantages provided by conventional cultural skills and knowledge can be seen in the actions of Hatty, an African American woman from Cedar Hills. Hatty had worked in health care earlier in her life. As she got older, her mobility issues led to increasing difficulties with everyday tasks. Eventually she began to use a wheelchair for most of the day. Hatty realized she was in need of a helper, but she did not have family or close friends that she felt she could call upon to take care of her. Nor did she have the money to simply hire a caregiver on her own, the way some wealthier seniors did. However, given her past experience dealing with older adults and the disabled, she knew that since she used a wheelchair and was getting medical care for various conditions, she could secure the help of a part-time home health aide. She set this up through a social worker. The home health worker visited several times a week. She helped around the house, ran errands, and provided companionship. When talking about where she got her food, for instance, Hatty noted, "There are some local stores like [pharmacy] that I can get in and out of with my chair. Mostly my home worker comes in, that is with the state or county, she does my major shopping for me or with me." While Hatty did not have extensive material resources or close social ties with family, her knowledge and abilities in dealing with formal organizations and paperwork facilitated her ability to secure a helper and consequently her strategies for preserving her body.

The case of Hatty reveals how cultural resources can help older Americans construct strategies for approaching everyday life. However, it is important to note that Hatty was both in a neighborhood with relatively developed senior services (Cedar Hills) and was clearly motivated to preserve the body (an institutionally validated approach to aging). This raises the question, Can these sorts of cultural resources be used to other ends (i.e., maximizing enjoyment) and other contexts (i.e., poverty neighborhoods)? Examining the different trajectories of Lilith and Bernard speaks to this issue.

Lilith and Bernard were both African American seniors living in Rockport. Unlike Hatty, both were inclined to respond to growing older by trying to maximize enjoyment. Similar to many of the individuals in this study, they liked narcotic painkillers (i.e., the "dope pills" described above), both for their analgesic properties and the intoxication they produced. Differences in their cultural skills, however, affected how they could go about securing them. Although they lived in the same geographical area, they had different backgrounds. Like Hatty, Lilith had a background in the health field. Not only did she have a college education (and a confident, middle-class style of self-presentation to match), but also she had worked in hospitals for many years. When she would attend her regularly scheduled doctor appointments, Lilith was easily able to secure and renew her prescription for Vicodin along with her other medications. In contrast, Bernard never went to college and had worked mostly in manual occupations. He did not trust doctors and did not feel comfortable in medical settings. He felt that doctors were mostly hustling, and, although I was never able to attend an appointment with him, Bernard said he felt the doctors did not trust him. Even though he was in worse shape physically than Lilith, he said he was afraid doctors would think he was just trying to hustle for the narcotics (which many seniors acknowledged could sell for upward of several dollars a pill on the street). Although he was prescribed pain medication after visiting the emergency room for an injury, he did not see a regular doctor for a regular prescription, the way Lilith did. Rather, he would acquire various substances with which to medicate (including prescription pain pills, alcohol, and marijuana) on the informal market.

The examples above connect to a key point: while cultural resources are unevenly distributed, what constitutes a useful tool is dependent on the circumstances. The way Hatty and Lilith were able to translate their knowledge, educational background, and skills into securing additional resources is a textbook example of cultural capital. Their styles and credentials mapped well onto those validated by medical organizations. Bernard did not have these resources. However, he did have tools that allowed him to navigate his world. He was adept at securing goods through the informal economy—a different yet important skill set, given his location.[30]

Identity, Resilience, and the Context-Dependence of Cultural Resources

Ethnographers have often charted the way those who have been socially marginalized are not passive victims but resilient social actors who develop strategies for carving out a meaningful world, despite the hardships afforded by their circumstances. These individuals often develop friendships and sources of identity that are not based solely on material wealth, formal education, or occupational ties. This process continued into later life for the individuals in this study. [31]

In contrast, those who were less accustomed to the challenges of scarcity, such as white men from affluent backgrounds, often had a harder time adjusting to the differential treatment and other life changes associated with aging. This was particularly true of people whose identities and networks were closely tied to their occupations but then retired (or were forced to retire). For instance, when asked about friends, Dan from Baygardens noted, "My entire life I've had work friends. So now I have no work, I have no friends. Yeah. Horrible. That's another thing I would tell young people, you know, make some friendships outside of work. Make some real friendships, you know? But I've always just been friends with people at work." In contrast, those who had dealt with poverty tended to have social networks and activities that were not premised upon work connections or spending money. Unlike going out to restaurants, taking paid Jazzercise classes, and going on cruises, hanging around the pool table at the senior center, talking about politics at the cafeteria, seeing friends at church, playing dominoes, or babysitting grandchildren did not require much disposable income. Getting money was sometimes a goal for these seniors, but not having substantial disposable income did not isolate them in the same way. They had developed strategies for coping and sociability that were more easily transferable to later life in the absence of great material resources.

The man described above was comparatively healthy. He had a house that was paid for as well as a car. Yet he talked about aging only in terms of loss. He continually remarked that he had a hard time dealing with his diminished status as an "old guy" who no longer worked. He did not have many resources for constructing an identity outside of his occupation and wealth. He was unhappy and became increasingly withdrawn over the years I knew him. In contrast, Tamilyn, a poor African American senior I visited regularly in a nursing home, was always smiling. Tamilyn had lived much of her life in poverty, but she was placed in a Baygardens nursing home following a stroke that left her unable to care for herself. Although she was bed-bound, she continually emphasized how "blessed" she was to have friends, family, and a roof over her head. She told me that she had had bad times before and had been poor for much of her life, but she had also experienced joy that could not be tied to money or jobs. She told me she always enjoyed her life, adding, "We may not have always had a lot of money, but love is the most important thing." Although objectively her situation could be seen as more dire (she had less money, more health problems, and was institutionalized), in many ways she was better equipped culturally and psychologically to deal with the challenges of aging than those less accustomed to hardship.

What Is Practical? Strategies for Managing the Aging Body

Sociologists often use the term "cultural strategies" to refer to general ways of approaching persistent problems shared by groups of people over periods of time. In this study, different strategies of approaching later life, premised upon motivations, orientations, and resources, determined how individuals responded to concrete problems they faced. I observed four basic cultural strategies that seniors adopted as "practical responses" to the physical predicaments of growing old, each of which was predicated on particular motivations, orientations, and resources (cultural and otherwise). Although many of the actual behaviors are discussed above in more detail, this section summarizes the characteristics of the broader strategies, which I label "Better safe than sorry," "Be healthy, but get help if sick," "Fix for fun," and "Damn the torpedoes (until you are in the ER)." The sections below describe the characteristics of these strategies in a bit more depth.[32]

Better Safe Than Sorry

"Better safe than sorry" was a proactive strategy driven by the motivation to preserve the body and prolong independence. Seniors who adopted this strategy dealt actively with health problems that arose as well as problems that could potentially arise. How they went about this was affected by orientations toward the medical body or natural body. For those who had an orientation toward the medical body, the ideal behavioral strategy was simple: go to the doctor and do what the doctor says. The responses of Tanya and Donald described above are indicative of how this was performed in both health and illness. Tanya and Donald monitored their health closely, went to doctors when ill, and had regular checkups when well. Although they did not always follow medical advice exactly, they were more likely to follow this advice than was any other group. For those who held a natural-body orientation, the correct way to actively engage with the body was to help the body heal itself. Jessica provides a good example. She paid attention to her body, assessed what it needed, and attempted to provide it. She was proactive in that she tried to assess and act before, and if necessary after, something became a problem. She went to medical professionals, but only after her initial strategies for helping the body heal itself failed, or when feeling external pressures from her networks unrelated to what she thought she needed (i.e., her daughter's insistence that she get an annual checkup).

Fix for Fun

Those who adopted the "fix for fun" strategy were enjoyment maximizers who took a proactive strategy toward confronting the aging body. Rather than trying to minimize the problems of the body or enhance longevity, they tried to maximize the enjoyment they were able to get out of later life. How they did this depended on whether they oriented toward the natural body or medical body. Those with a medical-body orientation engaged with doctors readily but did so strategically and instrumentally, in order to facilitate enjoyment. Jane's behavior is consistent with this strategy. Jane went to doctors, got transfusions, and had surgeries, but these were done to facilitate an enhanced ability to enjoy life rather than prolong it. She had weight-loss surgery to be more desirable to men (by her account), rarely missed blood transfusions (which gave her more energy), and interacted with doctors (to get medicines that helped her feel good). In addition to an acknowledgment that doctors can be beneficial in reaching particular ends, such a strategy presupposes material resources and cultural skills that are not equally distributed across groups (e.g., Jane or Lilith's institutional savvy). Seniors with orientations toward the natural body acted in a similar way, but they differed in how they interacted with medical institutions. These individuals did what they could to help themselves feel good as well, but they believed doctors and Western medicine were typically antithetical to this goal. This is seen in Ray's behavior. He actively seeks to feel better through the use of marijuana, herbal supplements, garlic fasts, and other "alternatives" in stead of engaging with doctors. These people also frequently made use of "complementary and alternative medicine" practitioners, such as herbalists or acupuncturists.

Be Healthy, Get Help if Sick

Those who adopted the "be healthy, get help if sick" strategy aimed to preserve the body, but they did so in a more reactive way than those who employed the "better safe than sorry" strategy. Once again, how they approached this varied by their orientation toward the medical body or the natural body. Those who saw the body as a medical object would try to follow the doctor's advice in order to stay healthy, but they would still reluctantly go to the doctor for occasional checkups or when something "broke down" (e.g., they faced a problem that had physical dimensions). This strategy was seen in Bill, who went to the doctor once a year in addition to when he had a major health problem. Still, Bill viewed the body in medical terms and consequently tried to achieve security and independence by "staying healthy" in accordance with doctors' advice. For those who adopted the natural-body orientation, this involved "listening" to the body. This is seen in James's discussion of paying attention to the body's demands, as opposed to doctors or social conventions, while still going to see someone when there was a serious problem.

Those who employed a "damn the torpedoes" strategy aimed only to maximize enjoyment and generally dealt with health more reactively. The overarching principle was that one should do whatever feels good, since death or institutionalization are never far away (e.g., "We are all one fall away from the home"). This is seen in Sandy's discussion of why she eats candy and in Dave's justification of drinking, smoking, and marijuana use. People with this orientation emphasized that they should live one day at a time, and that, regardless of whether the body was "medical" or "natural," enjoying oneself is the prime directive. Consequently, whether they held a medical-body or natural-body orientation was largely irrelevant to their strategies. The larger determinant was the material context discussed in the previous chapter and the cultural resources they had available, as these structured how they could maximize their enjoyment.

Table 3.1 summarizes the role of different elements of culture in shaping seniors responses to the physical predicaments of aging.

Conclusion:
Connecting Past, Present, and Future

Pierre Bourdieu poignantly remarked, "There is no way out of the game of culture." As Bourdieu theorized, and others have shown empirically in studies of youth and midlife, culture is an inextricable part of inequality and its reproduction over the life course. This chapter has shown that culture's influence does not dissipate in old age but rather continues to profoundly shape how older Americans approach the end game and the inequalities it contains. In the context of this study, culture provides a key empirical link between prior inequality and present behavior. What people want, how they see the world, and what they consider the best course of action affect how they respond to the predicaments they face in everyday life. Culture shaped how seniors made sense of the past, how they related to the future, and how they acted in the present by shaping how they saw, and lived, their lives. While charting this is key to understanding why seniors with seemingly similar

Table 3.1   Cultural elements and their role in later life

Cultural element	Affects action by shaping . . .	Examples of manifestations in old age	Seen in . . .
Motivations	*What is desirable*	"Preserving the body" "Maximizing enjoyment"	Why Jane skips chemo while Laney attends Different moral implications of pain management and "dope pills"
Orientations	*What is reasonable*	"The natural body" "The medical body"	Why Ray goes on garlic fasts as a precaution, while Bill goes to the doctor as a precaution
Resources	*What is possible*	Skills and capacities for navigating organizations (formal and informal) Resilience and tools for identity construction	Why Hatty and Lilith get what they want from the doctor, while Bernard does not Why Dan and Tamilyn have different capacities for coping with loss
Strategies	*What is practical*	"Better safe than sorry" "Fix for fun" "Be healthy, get help if sick" "Damn the torpedoes" (Until you end up in the ER)	Tanya Jane James Dave

resources act in different ways, it is important to understanding inequality more generally. [33]

   This chapter traced how seniors' responses to physical challenges were ultimately premised upon and linked to cultural motivations, orientations, resources, and strategies, which influenced what was experienced and understood as *desirable, reasonable, possible,* and *practical* ways to approach aging and to respond to concrete predicaments. How people responded to a challenge, such as a diagnosis of breast cancer, was contingent upon whether they were motivated to *preserve the body* or *maximize enjoyment*. Whether a senior would visit a doctor or acupuncturist was shaped by whether they had a *medical-body* or *natural-body orientation*. Likewise, whether individuals were able to get what they wanted out of a doctor (or to secure medication on an informal market) reflected whether they had the right cultural tools for navigating the context.

The specific content of these cultural elements was not sui generis, or reducible to individual differences in psychology, but rather acquired over the life course and grounded in past experiences that reflect systemic inequalities around socioeconomic status, race, and gender. The strategies seniors ultimately employed in the present often mirrored responses that had worked for them in the past. Put simply, while it is not necessarily sufficient as a reductive explanation, understanding why people respond differently to similar problems necessitates taking the role of culture seriously. As the next chapters shows, culture also shaped the efficacy of elders' strategies by altering the meaning and operation of social networks.

4

TEAM DYNAMICS
The Meanings of Social Ties

Invisible threads are the strongest ties.

—Friedrich Nietzsche

Past chapters have illustrated how friends, family, and neighbors play key roles in helping seniors deal with the material, physical, and psychological challenges of growing old. This chapter examines the *meanings* and *efficacy* of these social ties more directly. It shows that even seemingly similar social ties operate differently, depending on their social context, in practice making network inequalities in later life even greater than they seem. Consider the following example of how two groups of seniors responded differently to the same commonplace event (tripping) in an ostensibly similar setting (a senior center).[1]

Ruth, Eli, Clinton, and Charlene were similar in a lot of ways. Each spent a large portion of the week at their local centers in the presence of a regular group of friends and acquaintances. They all had degenerative physical conditions, such as arthritis, that limited their mobility and created problems navigating the physical environment. Like many of the people in this study, each used aids, such as a cane or walker, to move about. In the examples below, all four seniors experienced a comparable event related to the declining mobility most seniors eventually face. However, the way each responded to their foundering mobility varied substantially in ways that reflect the contingent operation of social ties.[2]

Ruth was an elderly white woman heavily involved with the Jewish community in Cedar Hills. On this occasion she entered a room where a group of other seniors she knew from temple were discussing a *New York Times* article. As Ruth struggled through the door with her walker, the discussion stopped. One of the nearby male seniors got up and held the door open. Another man cleared a spot at the table, and a third pulled up a chair for her. The woman said thank you, and the others smiled and nodded. The discussion resumed. During the lunch that followed in the larger recreation room, there was a similar instance of a senior struggling with mobility. An older man named Eli came in the room with a walker. Another man cleared a path for him and helped him into a chair. Eli said thank you. The helper smiled and nodded.[3]

I observed parallel events at the senior center in Rockport. At a nearby table there were three African American men who were discussing their desire to "get with some ladies." All three had canes. The youngest one, Clinton, who was very overweight, tried to stand up. He grimaced with pain and fell back in his chair. He did this several more times, rocking his body back and forth before he finally made it to his feet. Nobody at the table acknowledged the failures. When he finally made it upright, Clinton smiled and looked at his neighbors, at which point he said, "One, two, three; take a licking and keep on ticking. That's how we do it, that's how we've got to do it. Ain't that right, Johnny?" Johnny, who had not moved during this event, smiled broadly and said, "Yes sir." Clinton smiled back. Clinton walked with great difficulty to the bathroom, stumbling along the way with his cane but not falling. After about ten minutes, he returned and sat down again. While he was in the bathroom, an elderly African American woman named Charlene slowly got out of her chair and began moving toward the lunch table with her walker. She was having a hard time making headway and kept bumping into tables and chairs. There were men and women around but no one moved the chairs. No one said anything. She continued to a nearby table where she sat down with several other African American women who greeted her as they waited for lunch.

In the case above, similar events (mobility problems), in a seemingly similar setting (a senior center), in the presence of friends and acquaintances, played out differently. Some common survey measures might categorize the four seniors in the events above as equally "socially connected." Each saw and talked to friends and family within the span of the last week and attended lunches at the local senior center. What such a measure would not predict is how the underlying meanings of these connections led to their being activated differently in the context of the senior center. More nuanced measures might show that the four differed with regard to their membership in formal organizations (i.e., Ruth, Eli, and Charlene were involved in religious groups, whereas Clinton was not), but the variation might simply be reduced to ethnoracial membership. One might even mistakenly conclude that middle-class Jews will help a foundering senior, while poor African Americans will not. That conclusion would not only be incorrect but would also miss the larger point about how contextual factors shape the operation of networks. In my records, every time a senior experienced a serious fall (i.e., one resulting in an injury requiring medical attention) in the presence of others, someone helped. However, examples like the cases above highlight how the meaning of "being together" can shape different responses to everyday events in a way that has larger implications for how social life is constructed. These differences are grounded in shared understandings, resource disparities, and organizational contexts that shape the meaning, efficacy, and activation of social ties across the life course—often in counterintuitive ways.[4]

The data presented throughout this chapter show that past scholars are indeed correct in their acknowledgement that social connections matter a great deal as we age. However, exactly how friends, neighbors, and acquaintances support seniors depends on contexts shaped by inequalities past and present. When, why, and how people engage with one another cannot be adequately explained without acknowledging how shared cultural understandings and resource differences in these contexts shape the meaning of social ties. For instance, whether supporting others is seen as an obligation (*generalized reciprocity*) or direct exchange (*earned reciprocity*) influences how people relate to each other. Likewise, the efficacy of a connection to a friend or family member for securing specific ends (such as a ride to the doctor or money for a helper) varies in accordance with individual and neighborhood level resources available to that person. Further, while seniors from all four neighborhoods had to deal with the challenges of shrinking networks in old age due to the deaths of friend and family, there were profound differences in what this meant for their everyday lives. In practice, the instrumental effects of ties lost to "network shrinkage" varied in accordance with the unequal physical, material, and cultural resources at their disposal. In the end, some seniors were much more vulnerable than others. They had fewer resources to compensate for lost ties, and the meaning of the ties they still had sometimes limited their utility for solving the challenges of everyday life. The end result is that the team dynamics essential to understanding the end game are an even greater source of inequality than they might first seem.

The Meaning of "Who You Know"

Social science research has often demonstrated that there is more truth to the proverb "It's not what you know, but who you know that counts" than most Americans readily admit. Sociologists have long shown that both strong and weak connections to other people can profoundly affect our lives. These "social ties" to family, friends, neighbors, and acquaintances can help people get jobs, find a mate, maintain health, disseminate ideas to communities, and perhaps even increase happiness. However, how to accurately measure and categorize these ties has been a point of ongoing contention. Much of the research on the effects of social connectedness tends to operationalize interpersonal relationships as either a dichotomous measure (people are connected or isolated) or a continuous measure (some people are more connected than others). The term "social capital" is frequently attached to highlight the way these social ties function as a resource, which, like other forms of wealth, can affect outcomes such as health and well-being. Social capital is sometimes presented as unequivocally positive for the possessor—that is to say, all else being equal, it is better to have "capital" than not. In much of the urbanism literature, the relative levels of "social capital" possessed by individuals are directly or indirectly connected to differing degrees of social organization in the communities they occupy. Scholars operating in this tradition argue that those who occupy organized (generally nonpoor, white) areas have more robust connections to others, are more integrated into social and economic systems, are more accountable to norms of social control, and are more likely to be efficacious both individually and communally in securing outcomes. We are warned about the deleterious effects of declining community and social capital in America and the specter of the social disorganization that lurks on the other side of the tracks.[5]

Work among the elderly has echoed these sentiments—continually pointing to the importance of social connectedness for understanding behavior and outcomes. Connectedness is frequently contrasted with disengagement and isolation; order is contrasted with disorganization. In *Heat Wave*, Eric Klinenberg explains the life and death outcomes of the 1995 Chicago heat wave in these terms. Specifically, he argues the lack of connectedness, community organization, and social integration were key attributes contributing to the large number of African American seniors who died in their homes. The social networks that tied Latino elders to their community, on the other hand, reduced their risks of dying alone. Hochschild provides a more optimistic but analytically similar case in *The Unexpected Community*. In her study, seniors who were more socially connected were more effective and found more meaning in their lives than those with fewer ties. In each of these cases, social connectedness is clearly positive. Those who have it benefit. Those who do not, suffer. Although these works provide useful insights, many accounts of social capital are thin and undiscriminating in their attempts to chart the complex and often counterintuitive ways social connectedness affects behavior and outcomes.[6]

There is a growing body of scholarship that emphasizes the historically contingent structure and meaning of networks and isolation, the cultural underpinning of networks, and the potential downsides of being connected. What these accounts recognize, either implicitly or explicitly, is that the net effect of social ties is contingent on the contexts that influence people's everyday lives and the efficacy of their networks. For a senior, seeing family members can provide reassurance or aggravation. Being visited by a friend with a car can provide the chance to get healthy food or go out drinking. Consequently, social connectedness cannot be presumed to mean the same thing for everyone. The sections that follow explain that understanding why there are differences and how they matter requires a renewed attentiveness to the role of not only structural inequality but also cultural meanings that vary across contexts.[7]

The previous chapter showed how cultural motivations and orientations determine what is seen as a desirable and reasonable response to concrete problems like developing an illness. The sections below focus on how publically acknowledged cultural *schemas* limit what is a justifiable interpersonal response in a given context by shaping interactional *norms* that guide how people relate to friends, family members, and acquaintances: that is, the team dynamics that shape how they can respond to the end game. They point to the importance of integrating insights from social psychologists', sociologists', and anthropologists' long-standing concern with forms of reciprocity, identities, and the meaning of exchange. In this study the role and form of reciprocity and the correspondingly valued forms of identity found in different contexts were key to understanding how social networks enabled and constrained the strategies seniors used to respond to the challenges they faced. For instance, whether helping was understood as an obligation or an exchange affected when, how, and to what extent seniors could rely on friends and family as they navigated predicaments such as declining mobility or health issues.[8]

Culture, Context, and Justifiable Action

The examples of how people responded to a stumble in the senior center highlight two divergent sets of cultural understandings about how people should relate to others in their networks. In concrete organizational contexts such as senior centers, these translate into what social scientists have often called *norms*—that is, recognized parameters for socially acceptable or justifiable ways of acting. Norms reflect broader *normative schemas:* broad, organizationally backed cultural models of the way the world operates and how people *should* interact with one another. Like other cultural understandings, the power to limit how people explain their actions, and the threat of organizational or group sanctions for violating norms (ranging from shunning to incarceration), can limit how people behave even if they are not believed or internalized. In other words, people can choose to ignore norms or invoke alternative schemas or justifications, but they typically do so at some cost.[9]

The case of tripping in the senior center highlights the differences between two different normative schemas that shape seniors' social networks: *generalized reciprocity* and *earned reciprocity*. Which of these schemas is operative in a given context translates into different acceptable behavioral responses to a situation like a friend struggling with mobility issues or a family member with declining mobility. These schemas molded the operation of both strong and weak ties among the older Americans in this study, and in doing so, shaped how seniors' networks functioned.

Generalized Reciprocity: "When You Need Something, They Should Be There"

The underlying premise of generalized reciprocity, seen in the Cedar Hills examples, was clearly stated in an interview with Beth, a middle-class Jewish woman. When discussing whether family and friends have a responsibility to seniors, she said simply, "Yes." When I asked her what that responsibility was, she replied, "When you need something, they should be there." Similarly, when discussing the role of family, Tommy, a middle-class Chinese man from Elm Flats, commented:

So I really think family is there for each other, for one another. It's, you know, you look after them, they look after you if they need help— take care of them. I need help, come help me. Yeah, I mean they don't know what you need. So if I have, if I have something, I probably tell them. I'm sure they will come and help me.

At a class on current events at a Jewish senior center in Cedar Hills, seniors were discussing which charities to donate to in order to respond to the then-recent Haiti earthquake (a major natural disaster and humanitarian crisis occurring at the time). Their responses revealed a more general understanding about providing assistance. One woman noted, "It is our responsibility to help because we can help." The facilitator, a middle-aged white man from the local adult school, played devil's advocate and asked if it was America's problem. He asked, "What about the UN and the other countries?" The woman replied, "When people are in need like Haiti, in poverty with a disaster, the whole world should help them." The facilitator countered, "What about the poor in other places?" Another man said, "We should all help those in need, wherever they are, whatever country they are from." The class nodded in agreement.

What these examples reveal is that in contexts defined by generalized reciprocity, helping others is publically acknowledged and reinforced. It is a norm because it outlines what they *should* do. These understandings provide a template for justifiable action. While the resulting norms may or may not align with individual motivations and orientations, their codification affects group behavior, regardless of personal beliefs, by providing default expectations of behavior in one's network. Generalized reciprocity is premised on the idea that helping is a general social good, and that if people help each other, all will benefit. While there can be the possibility of individual gain, people should not help with the expectation of either direct or immediate rewards. Helping is expected. Of course, these norms are contextual. In this study ethnic organizations often reinforced generalized reciprocity. Tight-knit religious communities, regardless of race, class, or denomination, also fostered these types of helping norms. While specific helping roles were often mediated by gender at various points in the life course (i.e., the notion women should help with the elderly, men should help by bringing in income), the underlying principle was that everyone should help those in need—male or female.

Seniors whose actions were shaped by generalized reciprocity often implicitly or explicitly connected their understandings of helping to a sense of group history and filial or communal orientation. This was a common topic discussed among seniors at these organizations and encouraged through regular events that publically emphasized this. After spending a day in an Elm Flats Chinese senior organization, Shane explained how modern family obligations are linked to cultural adaptations based on historical circumstances of life in China:[10]

> You know, the Chinese philosophy is you raise a kid like insurance, you know for old age. Well because in China it's different, there is no social security, you know when you get old, you know your kid don't take care of you, nobody take care of you. So I really think family is there for each other, for one another it's, you know, you look after them, they look after you if they need help—take care of them. I need help, come help me.

Similarly, although she did not explicitly relate this to the context of the Philippines, Sage, a woman in Baygardens who was heavily involved in her church and ethnic community, explained that her expectations were built around a sense of ethnic identity and transposed from that context. "I was the oldest so I take care of my sisters. Now I live with my daughter; she is unmarried. I have five children, but Filipino people live with the unmarried daughter. Unless they need you to take care of grandchildren." Religious communities often encouraged generalized reciprocity even in white and African American communities, although the roles and obligations were generally not as rigidly defined as those described by Shane or Sage. Beth, for instance, explained what she expected of her family: "If I wasn't feeling good they would take me to the doctor. If I wasn't feeling good they would get somebody to clean my house for me. They would go to the market for me. Thank God I don't need anything. But that should be their responsibility." Although her words reveal that there is variation in the extent to which obligations are framed in terms of ethnic history, religious imperative, or rigidly defined social roles, in each case the obligation to help was influenced by the understanding of the meaning of group membership in general and the role of family in particular. In all cases, helping was expected.[11]

In contexts underpinned by generalized reciprocity, "strong ties" such as blood relations carry strong expectations—particularly for family members. An African American man from a religious family, who was heavily involved in his church community in Elm Flats, explained:

> When you got family they sort of tend to, if they care anything about you, they want to do the best for you that they can, so that means looking after certain things for you, looking at you to see if you are healthy, should you go to the doctor, should you do this or should you do that. In your best interest. So that's what we do.

Family members are expected to take care of seniors, so intergenerational ties are often key to how seniors approach everyday life. Although seniors who can drive themselves or get around by walking usually prefer to do so, when they cannot, family members are expected to step in. They frequently help seniors to doctors' appointments, prepare food for them, and, if necessary, bring the senior into their home to live with them. In some cases, there is a designated individual tasked with caring for an aging parent (e.g., the youngest unmarried daughter), but in most cases the responsibility falls on whoever is geographically closest to the senior and willing to fulfill the obligation. In each case, the expectation is that when a senior cannot take care of him- or herself, the family will step in. As Tommy noted, "They will take care of me. [I] don't worry about it, 'cause my kids are good kids, both kids."

How families go about helping, however, varies with material and neighborhood resources. Those with substantial wealth can often simply hire helpers to ease the burden. For instance, one ninety-one-year-old senior from Cedar Hills was provided a helper by her family, which allowed her to get around town and feel more independent while creating less work for her children. At lunch at the senior center, she noted, "My bones hurt, and my head is fuzzy. I am lucky I have Anna. She is a beautiful woman." Other families with fewer resources often brought seniors into their homes and then tasked them with caring for grandchildren or great-grandchildren, which allowed them to provide resources for the seniors while also allowing the senior to serve a need in the household.

Although one might imagine that close ties supplant the government safety net, this was not the case, particularly when family members become caretakers until death. The use of state support was widespread, but seniors' relative dependence reflected resource inequalities. Out of necessity, poor and working-class families often relied more heavily on state support. In many cases these families could not afford to have a family member stay home to provide care for a senior. As mentioned above, if the senior was capable of providing child care, this could work for a time. In other cases (i.e., where there were no children or seniors could not care for them), family members were still seen as responsible for the seniors but would aim to fulfill this obligation through securing state services (Medicare, transportation, meal services, etc.). Even many middle-class families could not afford to provide constant care or to hire health aides to take their place. Consequently, these families used state resources as well but would personally handle the logistical arrangements for the seniors. In each case, families supplemented the state-provided services with their own resources (time, money, and housing). Of course, as discussed in Chapter 2, those seniors who lived in neighborhoods with strong resources (typically the more affluent) had more and better service options.[12]

While some seniors stayed with their families until the end of their lives, many were eventually institutionalized in facilities such as nursing homes before their death, even though this was not their preference and did not resonate with the espoused ideology of how strong ties work. However, the practical demands of dealing with physical or mental breakdown became an overwhelming force in determining end-of-life care. Even when families and seniors wanted the senior to be cared for in the home, there was a point at which this was not feasible on a practical level. Typically, the senior would come to require more resources than the household could, or was willing to, provide. Often the path was not linear. Seniors would have a problem that involved a substantial physiological component (e.g., a fall that limited mobility or a major respiratory infection). The senior might wind up in the hospital, stay in a nursing facility for rehabilitation, then return home, only to repeat the pattern several times. Eventually, this pattern would stop when seniors (1) asked to go to an institution on their own, (2) required more care than the household could provide, or (3) died. The small number of seniors asking to go to institutions typically had the resources to go to high-end assisted living or continuing-care facilities. Most frequently, the seniors would require more care than the household could provide. In the case of severe cognitive issues with limited rehabilitation options (e.g., Alzheimer's-induced dementia), the path was more linear. Seniors would stay home until the logistical demands on family became too great. In practice, the strain on households increased dramatically as seniors developed conditions with substantial ramifications for the amount of care they required, such as severe cognitive issues or incontinence. These conditions markedly increased the emotional, physical, and logistical toll of caring for the senior.[13]

However, there were differences even in institutionalization. Compared to groups operating under the schema of earned reciprocity, family members functioning under generalized reciprocity were more likely to regularly visit seniors in the facility. Some would go weekly or even daily. Likewise, for seniors who were part of close religious communities, priests, rabbis, and congregation members would occasionally visit as well. Many of these seniors maintained a sense of continuity and connection that was not seen elsewhere. For instance, Tamilyn was an eighty-six-year-old woman bed-bound in a Baygardens nursing home. While many of the seniors I visited in this institution felt lonely and isolated, Tamilyn was constantly upbeat. Although she could not move around and was often in pain, she would always note that she was "blessed." She told me, "Everyone comes to visit and I am treated like a queen." In addition to visits from her children and grandchildren, members of the church, where she was a Sunday school teacher for decades, would bring her gifts and visit with her. Her walls were lined with pictures and cards. In contrast, Jason, another bed-bound senior mentioned in Chapter 1, did not see his family and rarely saw visitors. He was not religious and did not believe in any higher power or universal order. In contrast to Tamilyn, he described his life as miserable and described the facility as "just a bunch of people sitting in wheelchairs dying. It's no way to live."

Connections to friends, neighbors, and acquaintances (i.e., "weak ties) were also key to how seniors approached the end game. In contexts of generalized reciprocity, friends would give one another rides, bring food to the sick, check in on seniors if they did not show up to the senior center for a few days, or visit those who had been institutionalized. They neither charged for these services nor expected any sort of direct or immediate return. As a Chinese senior noted, "The main thing is to be there to lend support." However, the bounds were more limited than with family. It was rare for friends or other members of a senior's network to submit themselves to any sustained financial losses or other extended difficulties that were borne by family members. While help was much more limited, it was still given rather than exchanged. The comments of a religious, middle-class Latino man explaining his relationship with his neighbors were typical: "One of our neighbors got put in the home, and that's where she's at right now. We would make it a point to go and help her. We look after each other." They help each other, not because of an expectation of immediate instrumental gain, but because it is "what people do." In other words, it is expected and justifiable in the contexts in which they live. Whether someone has done something good for you in the past, or even whether you like them, is seen as largely irrelevant—helping is an obligation that group members are simply expected to fulfill. This can be seen in another interaction between two Jewish seniors involved in an ethnic organization at Cedar Hills. During a communal lunch, Delilah was complaining about "people who sit there and don't talk." Moshe took offense at these comments, which he thought were directed at him, and said in an agitated tone, "You leave them alone. If anybody needs help, I am here. If you fall down on the street, I will be the first one to help you up. Do you need help with anything?" The woman said no, sat quietly for a few moments, then left.

Although expectations of help vary according to the relationship between people (e.g., friends, family, neighbors), being too focused on personal gain at the expense of others is frowned upon in contexts shaped by generalized reciprocity. However, fulfilling obligations may provide individual psychological rewards (e.g., feeling good for "doing the right thing") as well as status within the group. Helping others, and having a family that does the same, is often a point of honor or pride. A Filipino woman in Baygardens explained this to me as she showed me pictures of family members who cared for her and said that she was "very proud, because they help [others in] the community and don't cause trouble." Discussions of whose family helped and lived up to these obligations was a constant theme in organizations such as senior centers or Bible-study groups. One woman pointed out to me that the discussions about whose family helped and whose kids were doing the best were ongoing sources of competition among "the old ladies." While the family's fulfillment of obligations did not necessarily result in concrete material benefits, seniors benefited from both increased status and the expectation that support would be there if needed.

Earned Reciprocity:
"What You Give Is What You Get"

While generalized reciprocity is guided by broad obligations, the overarching principle behind earned reciprocity is one of a more moderated and specific exchange between individuals. Help is like any other transaction between people in the marketplace: people provide assistance with the expectation of a timely return. *The idea is, if someone helps me, I owe them for the service.* This schema corresponds to a more limited, individualistic, and contractual set of relationships in which helping is less unequivocally positive and expected. Help implies a debt on the part of the person being helped. This is often seen as undesirable, as it can (1) signal what can be perceived as the senior's weakness or a loss of independence, and (2) create the expectation of a repayment that is difficult to provide. Sometimes this can contribute to preemptive disengagement from a social circle. An African American woman in Elm Flats described her disappointing experience with neighborhood friends in the context of earned reciprocity:

> Well, a good friend is a give and take thing. What you give is what you get in friendship. Some people, as the friends get older and things happen in their lives, they just don't give anymore, and they are always afraid that you are going to ask them for something that they can't provide.[14]

Help in this context is not something that is given to the group with the expectation that everyone helps those in need—it is a direct relationship between individuals. Consequently, even well-intentioned help can result in indebtedness that stresses relationships. The recipient is forced to acknowledge both an undesirable lack of independence and his or her imposition on others. In other words, intended or not, as Marcel Mauss famously noted, gifts are not simply free—they involve power and expectations of return. Helping in contexts shaped by earned reciprocity involves specific obligations on an individual level rather than just general social expectations.[15]

As with generalized reciprocity, earned reciprocity was not reducible to neighborhood or socioeconomic status but a function of broader organizational contexts. Many settings that lacked a religious or ethnic component encouraging a sense of generalized reciprocity, such as the senior center in Rockport, operated under the parameters of earned reciprocity, which closely approximates American ideals of individualism and independence. Those individuals operating in settings lacking organized communalist undercurrents (in the context of this study, often nonethnic whites or African Americans not involved in religious organizations) were also most influenced by American notions of independence, individualism, and competence that made receiving help a point of stigma.[16]

In contexts of earned reciprocity, not only were individuals more reticent about helping others, but also the sense of obligation to other members of a network was more limited. Family members were still often asked to help, but this was premised upon past behaviors: for example, having been a good parent, brother, or sister. Many commented that they expected help from their kids, but only because they raised them right and took care of them. When asked if family had a responsibility to seniors, an African American man in Elm Flats noted, "Well, if you are lucky enough to have a family that cares, yes. Many of us don't have the luxury of family that cares about us. Some of them are hit or miss." One African American woman noted that she would not expect anything if she had been in jail or a drug addict, but since she put clothes on their backs and food on the table, she expected her sons to help. In contrast to the seniors who invoked familial obligations as a general set of normative expectations they imagine will be met, these seniors were both less certain about their futures and more sensitive to the issue of receiving help. A white senior in Baygardens articulated this ambivalence:

> What am I going to do if I get to the point where I can't take care of myself? I have no idea. I have no clue. Is there anybody to take care of me? No. Would I want anybody? No. I don't want to be a burden. No. I don't want that.

In general, while many relatives still provided social support, they were less likely to drive seniors around, provide extensive material help, or visit once the seniors were institutionalized. The level of support provided to a specific senior under earned reciprocity depended less on a generalized obligation of helping family, and more on the contractual understanding that past care creates a debt that can be paid in old age. One of the major consequences was that in the case of serious health problems, seniors could not necessarily rely on extended family care. This was not necessarily ideal for the senior, but neither was it a breach of norms. The trajectory from home to hospital to nursing facility was consequently much more linear.

The contractual nature of earned reciprocity affected how people responded to friends, neighbors, and acquaintances, as well. Like those operating under generalized reciprocity, seniors would still check in on friends and share information. Many of the people in this study noted that they were thankful to see their friends every day in a building's common room or happy to have someone check in on them in person or over the phone—however, seniors felt people connected to them in this way were not obligated to help them in the more substantial ways expected under generalized reciprocity. One white senior noted,

> It's good to have people to even talk to over the phone, because it's like a, it's like, if someone doesn't hear from you for a while, they call you. If you don't hear from someone for a while, you call them. You have to have a network. Do I have any what I call close friends? No. Not really.

Among groups where earned reciprocity was operative, seniors still helped each other, but this help functioned much more like an economic exchange.

Interestingly, economically oriented assistance enabled the development of substantial informal senior economies, particularly in the state senior complexes in Rockport and Baygardens. For instance, one enterprising senior in Baygardens would drive her friends to bingo but would charge them each five dollars for the trip. Seniors acknowledged that this was a help and that it was easier than taking the bus, but there was no continued debt, because they paid for the service. While both parties seemed to benefit, this would be seen as mercenary behavior and frowned upon in settings underpinned by generalized reciprocity. Likewise, younger seniors often helped friends and neighbors, but received food, alcohol, drugs, or money for doing so. The resources that were exchanged depended on the socioeconomic status of the neighborhood. Seniors in poor areas were more likely to provide marijuana, prescription drugs, or alcohol for help with a task such as shopping, whereas middle-class seniors might provide lunch or cash. For instance, Dave, the poor white senior described in Chapter 2, would often trade his Vicodin for rides or shopping help. When Caroline, a middle-class African American woman, had surgery and needed a ride, she bought her friend (a neighborhood senior) lunch. Despite the differences in the goods and services exchanged, the principle that a service was offered and that the person being helped reciprocated in kind was the same.[17]

"When You Get Old You Lose All Your Girlfriends": The Predicament of Network Shrinkage and Differential Vulnerability in Later Life

Dealing with network changes related to the deaths of friends, loved ones, and acquaintances created predicaments for seniors across neighborhoods and network types. However, the ability to adapt was conditioned by circumstances that molded the meaning and efficacy of their remaining ties—including advantages acquired over the life course as well as forms of reciprocity. Consequently, while the seniors in this study faced shared challenges related to network changes in later life, the effects were more pronounced and damaging among those who were made more vulnerable by the relative absence of mitigating physical, material, and cultural resources. This section examines the shared challenge of contracting networks as well as differences in the ability of seniors to compensate.[18]

As seniors and the people they know grow older, they typically have to contend with the deaths of others with greater frequency. However, recent social science research suggests that death in this sense does not act as the great leveler. Network inequalities continue into, and are compounded, in later life, as seniors' networks shrink due to institutionalization and death. Seniors with advantages such as greater levels of education are better able to maintain and form ties than their peers, all else being equal. Those in their networks share these advantages and are more likely to be healthier and live longer. Still, like other aspects of old age, dealing with the loss of people was a shared predicament that crossed the four neighborhoods in this study. Seniors within the four neighborhoods I studied were all faced with the ramifications of lost friends, family, acquaintances, neighbors, and pets, regardless of whether they operated in contexts shaped by generalized or earned reciprocity. Seniors continually pointed out that this was a major aspect of the experience of aging. The loss of people through death produced concrete problems in both the instrumental and psychological arenas that are important to both understanding the experiences of old age and tracing the way inequalities differentially shape seniors' responses.[19]

One issue for seniors was acknowledging and developing strategies for facing the prospect of their own death. As seniors watched friends and family die, they often came to recognize that their own bodies were not as strong as they once were. They were presented with the inevitability of death. Gao, a ninety-five-year-old Chinese man from Elm Flats, reflected on this problem and responded, "Nobody lives forever. Death's inevitable, right? Sooner or later, so I don't worry about dying, I'm just liv[ing] one day at a time and do it best I can. I do something to help people, if I need help I ask for them to help me. So that's my philosophy." While Gao's response to the problem was conditioned by a set of cultural factors (i.e., norms of generalized reciprocity and an inclination toward bodily preservation), the acknowledgement that growing old meant approaching the end of life and a related set of predicaments was widely shared by the seniors in this study. In addition, the loss of others also had a potentially less existential but still sociologically substantial effect on everyday life. Dying friends meant having fewer people with whom to recreate and "conversate." Locations seniors once enjoyed came to remind them of the friends they had lost. The deaths of others involved the loss of emotional and social pillars in the form of family or close friends. Even the loss of pets often carried a great deal of emotional resonance. The practice of keeping pictures or albums of dead pets was surprisingly common among the seniors in my study. Many seemingly unemotional individuals would break down talking about cats or dogs that had passed away, indicating a substantial sense of loss.[20]

The effects of network shrinkage were seen even among locations with high concentrations of seniors, where there were more opportunities for rebuilding lost ties. One woman in a single unit in Baygardens senior housing remarked that her social life was less active at present than a few years earlier. When I asked why, she responded flatly, "I used to have more friends in the building but four died." She explained that while she still talked to neighbors, she had not made any real friends to replace them. On a trip to a senior center, a man asked another senior with whom I was spending the day, "How is the gang over there [at the apartments]?" She responded similarly, noting, "Most died. That's what happens when you get old, you lose all your girlfriends." While perhaps less acute, even those whose networks involved large numbers of nonseniors had to confront the deaths of friends, family members, or pets. A middle-class white woman in her early seventies summed up a common predicament: "I've had a lot of death in the last few years, so I've lost a lot of people I was very close to." Statements like "All of my immediate family is dead" were not uncommon among seniors. This was particularly true for those in their eighties and beyond.[21]

The deaths of others were also often associated with a variety of instrumental losses that affected how elders went about their daily activities. One senior articulated this when she explained that she used to get rides with her friends to the grocery store and church, but now that they are dead she has to take the bus, even though she is less mobile from advancing arthritis. She responded by going out less. The disruption of routines was exacerbated by the sadness of losing someone for whom the senior cared. Often the result was depression or social withdrawal that could compound seniors' other difficulties or lead to the new problems associated with isolation. As with other challenges in old age, the manner in which seniors could respond to losses was shaped by differences in the other resources seniors had available.[22]

Often, for those with fewer resources, the instrumental effects of losing a key person in their network revealed and exacerbated their greater generable vulnerability. Losing a friend or family member one cares for can be even harder when there are few left—and more so when you depend on them. This can be seen in the experiences of Bernard, the African American baseball fan from Rockport introduced at the beginning of this book. When his mother died, Bernard was put in a difficult spot. He was sad, as many are when a family member passes. Yet her passing also created instrumental challenges that were made more acute by his lack of physical and material resources. Bernard and his mother had worked together to handle the challenges they faced. He took care of errands outside of the home for her, and she fed him her leftovers from the meal program and sometimes gave him money from her Social Security to supplement his disability check. When she died, he lost a key source of social support, income, and food for which he did not have an immediate replacement. He did not have any other "strong ties," and his "weak ties" to other seniors at the senior center were shaped by norms of earned reciprocity and "independence" that limited their utility for solving most problems. Further, like many who have spent their lives in poverty, Bernard was not in the best health before his mother's passing—that is, his physical resources were also more limited than most seniors of the same age who had experienced fewer disadvantages over the course of their lives.

In the period after his mother's passing, in addition to becoming depressed while grieving, Bernard began to have greater problems getting around. Bernard was a natural-body-oriented senior who avoided doctors and regular checkups when he could, so he did not go to see the doctor about the depression or physical issues. He ultimately responded by spending less time with others at the senior center and spending more time watching TV at home alone. Unlike his counterparts in middle-class neighborhoods such as Baygardens, and even some more affluent seniors in Rockport, Bernard did not have many resources to cope with the converging challenges. His options were limited by social disadvantages accumulated over his lifetime as well as the context in which he lived in the present (i.e., a poor neighborhood with sparse services). He did not benefit from the help provided by a church or ethnic organization that encouraged generalized reciprocity, because he was not part of one. The loss of his sole "strong tie" was acute not just psychologically, but physically and materially, as he had fewer other resources to mitigate the loss.

In this study the effect of social ties on outcomes such as health or well-being for a given senior also depended on the resources of those to whom they were tied. Consider the case of hiring helpers. For those without family, or those who had family who were not involved with the senior's daily life (due to distance, etc.), helpers made a substantial difference in their ability to get transportation, clean their homes, and get food they liked. As discussed in previous chapters, access to helpers was uneven and reflected inequalities past and present. Elders who lived in well-served middle-class neighborhoods such as Baygardens had greater access to these individuals because of the programs and service hubs located in the neighborhood. Further, seniors from middle-class or affluent backgrounds typically had greater individual resources (e.g., savings, pensions, long-term care insurance) that could provide such a helper. Likewise, when they did have "strong ties," the individuals to whom they were tied could more effectively furnish material resources for the senior. Consider Laura, first introduced in the Ensure example in Chapter 2. Laura often relied on her son for helping with all manner of everyday activities. She did not need a helper, because he served this role. Yet, even if something happened to him, she had money to hire someone else to help. Further, even if he had moved away, his six-figure income would have made it possible to hire a helper from afar. For seniors with affluent family in the area, even when family members did not want to help directly, the way Laura's son did, they sometimes hired a helper. These seniors benefited not only from strong ties but also from the obligation they carried and the resources of those to whom they were connected.[23]

The resources for coping with loss were not just material. Family structure and forms of reciprocity provided some seniors with advantages not available to those with thinner networks or networks with weaker expectations. For instance, seniors with larger families operating under generalized reciprocity often relied on the greater number of "strong ties" in their network instead of on hired aides. This strategy could be economically viable even in less affluent areas, especially if the senior could contribute in a way that made this workable—for example, caring for young children during the day or helping to run a home business. Further, as discussed above in the section on generalized reciprocity, in some cases there was even a formal expectation that a designated family member (e.g., an unmarried daughter in a large family) would take care of elders. While this differential burden could be a substantial axis of gender inequality for the caregiver, it provided a powerful resource from which some seniors benefited.

Efficacious strategies that helped seniors address the challenges of late life were seen in both poor and nonpoor neighborhoods. Yet strategies and outcomes reflected broader inequalities in physical, material, and cultural resources. Consequently, the disadvantages for seniors such as Bernard often converged in a way that enhanced vulnerability. Bernard had to face declining physical capacities. He did so with a thin network and a small family. He subsequently lost his sole "strong tie." He had fewer material resources to compensate (both on the individual and neighborhood level), and he lived in a context where it was harder to rebuild ties. In contrast, Laura had a dense network and a large family that considered helping an obligation. She still needed help because of her physical issues. Yet she had more options that made her less vulnerable. If she were to lose a tie, she had individual resources to help compensate. She also lived in an area with more services. Likewise, the people in her network had greater resources they could bring to bear in helping her. In the end, her more robust and efficacious network paralleled the other advantages that shaped how she could approach the end game.

Cultural Inputs, Contexts, and the Ambiguity of Social Ties

In examining the variability of networks in later life, it is essential not to lose sight of an important fact: as past scholarship has repeatedly shown, those seniors who were more connected to friends, family, and neighbors were generally better off. Likewise, in this study social ties remained a key resource that separated connected seniors from their more isolated peers. Seniors with more robust social networks generally had more options for getting around the city, taking care of problems in their homes, and socializing. Yet, as the sections above indicate, connections were more unequal than they might seem at first glance. Some ties were more effective in providing seniors with options and securing outcomes. Forms of reciprocity and material resources at both the individual and neighborhood level influenced the efficacy of ties. Those with fewer ties were more vulnerable to network shrinkage. Further, it is important to acknowledge that while social ties could help seniors pursue particular goals, the benefit of being connected was often more ambiguous than some sweeping accounts emphasizing "social capital" (and in particular its connection to factors such as health outcomes) might suggest. This section looks at how and why this is the case.[24]

As Chapter 3 explained, even within the same neighborhood, people often pursued very different ends, such as trying to *preserve the body* or *maximize enjoyment* before death. How seniors used their networks depended in large part on these cultural inputs. Consequently, a dense network of local friends could help a senior secure a ride to the doctor, but it could also facilitate a trip to the bar instead. In addition, different forms of reciprocity affected not only the utility of ties for pursuing given ends but also shaped what was a justifiable, and even obligatory, form of action vis-à-vis others in a network. For instance, for some seniors, obligation and love for family under generalized reciprocity meant that they felt an imperative to maintain health. For others, the desire to maximize enjoyment and stay connected with fast-living friends was a similarly powerful force. This leads to a question of causal ordering. Do unequal contexts and situations primarily shape networks, as scholars such as Mario Small suggest, or do people with like values and motivations group together, as Vaisey, Lizardo, Sánchez-Jankowski, and others argue? The short of it is that within this study, both processes could be seen, but they varied in timing and effect.[25]

Seniors with like motivations formed *groups* or cliques when given the chance, but individuals with divergent motivations were also *grouped* together in families and neighborhoods. Consequently, organizational contexts and resource disparities continued to influence the operation and efficacy of ties for people in shared circumstances. Yet, while situational expectations limited justifiable action, they still did not determine the ends people pursued. That is to say, motivations varied substantially within contexts. As Chapter 3 showed, any given senior saw particular ends (e.g., having fun at the bar or going to the doctor) as more desirable, reasonable, and particular responses to their circumstances. In other words, divergent motivations and orientations continued to shaped the ends they pursued—and these were not simply situational.

Additionally, friendship networks emerged among people who shared similar worldviews, motivations, and dispositions. This connected those who were motivated toward similar ways of acting (i.e., maximizing enjoyment or preserving the body). Consequently, behaviors that might have been hard to justify outside the clique of likeminded individuals became more defensible. Once the distinction between going out dancing or seeing the doctor loses some of its moral grip (or seeing the doctor is seen as the foolish response), the former is a lot easier to justify. So, while the depth and efficacy of seniors' networks was influenced by inequalities, people formed networks through volitional behaviors that reflected their motivations and orientations and deployed these networks to pursue divergent ends that were not simply reducible to race, class, gender, or neighborhood differences in the present.

This complex interplay of factors is seen in the case of Jane, the white chemotherapy-skipping Baygardens senior discussed in Chapter 3. As noted earlier, Jane had a lot of friends and neighbors, but this did not lead her to preservation-driven behavior. Jane often spent her days socializing rather than visiting the doctor. She often explained that she wanted to have fun while she could. In her words, all her good friends were "alcoholics" who would hang out at bars, so if she wanted to be with them that's where she would go. She wanted more help around the house but did not want to hire a helper and was hesitant to ask her friends for help without offering some form of payment (in accordance with norms of earned reciprocity). As a result, things around her house often remained broken. Although she was not isolated, it was hard to mobilize her weak social ties effectively, an issue compounded by her desire to project independence. While I was driving her around (which she saw as an exchange for helping me with my book), she commented:

> I have trouble even getting basic things done. Running errands. The meds make me worry about driving. Even the ones that are not super-duper meds, that the doctor said I could drive on, make me nervous. I am so worried about hitting something and can't concentrate. Then I went to the pharmacy, "Pill Hill." People don't help you. I needed to get a nonalcoholic mouthwash. The guy at the store sent me to aisle seventeen A. I couldn't find it, and he said go back to seventeen B. "Are you sure you looked?" I finally found it, but there were like fifty different mouthwashes, and the print was so small I could not read any of it. Finally another customer helped me. Unfortunately I don't have money to pay someone to help, and my husband, if I move back with him, is not healthy either.

Even though she had a dense network containing friends and a husband, she had a hard time bringing herself to call on them for help.

Jane's network did not efficiently solve practical problems related to basic needs (securing food, maintaining the living environment, etc.) in the same the way it did for seniors such as Jessica, a white woman in her nineties who lived in the same neighborhood. Jessica was involved with a church, and her church friends would often bring her food. She was also a regular at the local senior center. If she missed a day, people would inquire about her status and call her. Although she valued her independence and said she did not "need" help by her estimation, members of her family, including siblings, nieces, and nephews, would come over and fix things in her house and take her shopping (even if she did not ask them). In her circumstances, unlike Jane's, norms around generalized reciprocity meant this was expected. Her interactions with her family were a source of satisfaction, and her sense of obligation encouraged her to maintain health through exercise, diet, and even an occasional doctor visit, even though she felt going to the doctor was "not really necessary."

In contrast, Jane's marriage and family were sources of continual stress. She was in a feud with her brothers over her mother's home. Jane took care of her mother for two years, until her mother's dementia necessitated placement in a nursing home. Once her mother was no longer living in the house, her brother decided to sell the home, because the property was in his name. Although Jane did not want to move, her brother said she was no longer caring for the mother, so she was forced to move out. As she was explaining this situation to me in her living room, she got a call from her husband, from whom she was separated, saying that he was coming into Baygardens the next week. She asked me to drive her to the local bar, where she chatted with her friends and introduced me around. Sitting at the bar (where one of her friends was teasing me for drinking coffee instead of a real drink at three in the afternoon), Jane told me,

> My first husband died, but we had sixteen great years together. He was a professor . . . I don't like the current one, and we have been living in different cities for two years now, but he is a man, he has a pension and health insurance, so we are going to try to make it work, especially with my brother pressuring me to leave here.

Her network, particularly her marriage, provided her access to important resources, but it was also a source of immense stress. Further, she preferred to deploy the resources she had toward maximizing enjoyment. She felt no strong obligation to family that tempered her enjoyment-maximizing behavior or gave her pause. Jane was connected and enjoyed "hanging out" with her friends. However, contrary to accounts that suggest this universally leads to improvements in health and longevity, spending time with them encouraged behaviors associated with negative health outcomes (e.g., excess drinking, eating pub food) and increased her exposure to situations involving physical risk (e.g., driving in cars with people who were drunk or high). So while having a family and friends affected how both Jane and Jessica responded to problems in old age, the effects were contingent on the broader organizational and cultural contexts that shaped various facets of their lives, as well as how each was motivated to activate the ties available to them.[26]

Conclusion:
Social Ties as a Fundamental but Contingent Resource

In understanding action and outcomes in the end game, it is essential to look at variation in not just the structure but also the meaning and efficacy of social ties. The data in this chapter have shown that while seniors across neighborhoods and racial and socioeconomic groups contend with shared challenges, including network shrinkage, how they can respond depends on their access to other resources as well the resources available to other people in their networks. Further, even similar social ties can mean different things in different organizational contexts. In practice, when, how, and to what extent seniors were able to seek or provide help were influenced by understandings of earned or generalized reciprocity that shaped expectations in the contexts the seniors inhabited. In other words, while networks form structures of social relations, the effects of those relations are mediated by cultural understandings as well as differences in the material resources they provide.

This explains why the responses to stumbling incidents in the senior centers were different. In the case of the Cedar Hills center, social norms dictated that people should help one another whenever they are able. This was an extension of a set of cultural understandings that framed helping as positive, obligatory, and moral. It was part of a general expectation that people help others and in turn will be helped when they need it by another member of the group. By helping the stumbling senior, other seniors fulfilled designated social roles associated with these understandings, and did so with little cost to the person being helped. In contrast, in the Rockport center, providing help would have been an acknowledgment of the foundering senior's loss of independence and an imposition on him or her. Helping someone in such a context creates a debt that requires repayment, and, following Mauss and Bourdieu, can even be an act of aggression by signaling someone is incapable of managing on their own. Not providing aid is then ironically the expected, most reasonable, and compassionate way to help.

In sum, the intricacies of how social ties shape the end game cannot be understood without examining both how cultural understandings and continued resource disparities shape the meaning, efficacy, and deployment of social ties in the context of American inequality. Further, the team dynamics of the end game cannot be understood without considering the effects of network shrinkage and the differential vulnerabilities they produce (i.e., some teams are better able to weather the loss of a key player). In later life, as in much of the life course, "who you know" matters a great deal for getting what you need or want; however, so does the "meaning" of who you know and the resources available to those in your network. These team dynamics reflect and reinforce broader patterns of inequality that continue to shape our final years. The next chapter returns to the goal outlined in the introduction to this book—connecting the facets of the end game that structure the lives of older Americans and examining what this tells us about inequality and stratification more broadly.[27]

CONCLUSION

How Inequality Shapes Our Final Years

How beautifully the leaves grow old.
How full of light and colour are their last days.

—John Burroughs

In the introduction to this book, I introduced the reader to my friend Bernard. Bernard taught me that appreciating baseball requires understanding how its various pieces—rules, players, strategies, team dynamics—come together to form something greater than the sum of their parts. This book has shown that the same perspective is necessary for understanding how inequalities, past and present, shape the final years for Bernard and other older Americans. Just as it is impossible to understand the game of baseball by looking only at pitching, focusing only on a singular mechanism of social stratification—such as health disparities, uneven material resources, culture, or social networks—is inadequate for understand the structure of the end game. Explaining why James and Lila describe aging in similar terms, how Dave gets his Ensure, why Jane skips chemo, why Ray avoids doctors like the plague, or why in some cases people ignore stumbling seniors as an act of compassion requires moving beyond reductionism. It requires shifting the focus from *which* facet of stratification shapes social life, to *when* and *how* various facets shape our opportunities, behaviors, and experiences over the course of our lives. Doing so is not only essential for charting the shifting contours of American society but also for understanding how inequality shapes our lives from the cradle to the grave.

This chapter reconnects the "on the ground" observations presented in Chapters 1–4 to the larger analytical task of this book, explaining how key mechanisms of stratification shape later life in America and what their operations can teach us about inequality more generally. To do so, the pages that follow return to the analogy of the game. Understanding how the end game unfolds, as well as its logic, experiences, and contradictions, requires looking at five interconnected facets that structure the contest: (1) who gets to play in the final innings (health disparities and selection into old age), (2) the game's shared challenges (the predicaments of later life), (3) the unevenness of the playing field (unequal contexts and material resources in the present), (4) the different strategies and styles of play people employ (cultural responses to inequality), and (5) the role of team dynamics (network inequalities). After drawing out these connections, I turn briefly to some "postgame" lessons for policy and practice before briefly concluding with an experience that reinforces why these issues remain urgent.[1]

Who Gets to Play?
Prior Inequality and the Chance to Grow Old

The first important factor in understanding the end game is that not everyone survives long enough to step onto the field. Aging is a stratified process.

Who lives to grow old in America, and who dies before having the chance, is determined in large part by social inequalities that reflect the persistent racial, socioeconomic and gender-based divisions that are central to social stratification in America. Just as these "durable inequalities" influence where we can go to school and the jobs we get, parallel inequalities differentially limit our ability to maintain health and take care of ourselves when ill. The socially disadvantaged are subject to greater psychosocial stress loads, higher levels of violence, unequal treatment by medical institutions, and often the need to live or work in toxic environments—each of which can directly or indirectly shorten lives. Consequently, some of the most powerful connections between inequality and old age play out before old age is ever reached. Further, the stresses and challenges provided by their social location leads the bodies of the socially disadvantaged to "wear out" and "break down" faster. The first implication is profound: who shall live and who shall die, the most fundamental and visceral form of inequality, depends in part on social position at birth. Simply put, not everyone makes it to the later innings. The slightly more subtle implication is that, among those who do step onto the field, some are more beaten-up and worn down from prior innings than others.[2]

While understanding who lives to grow old is key to understanding both social stratification and American inequality, charting how long people from different groups survive, and the timing of physiological breakdowns, is ultimately a topic best investigated using demographic and epidemiological approaches. These population level trends are key to the larger story about the inequalities of the end game, but they cannot be adequately charted using ethnographic methods. However, there is still much to be learned by examining the experiences of those whose resilience allows them to survive long enough to play. Consequently, this book and the remainder of this chapter focus on a complementary question for which comparative ethnography provides unparalleled insight: How do those who survive play out the last days of a waning season?

The Basis of the Game's Final Innings: Physiological Challenges, Categorical Inequalities, and the Aging Body as a Structural Dilemma

Growing old in the context of American inequality creates shared practical and symbolic challenges for all who survive long enough. These challenges cannot be understood without examining the physical dimensions of aging and the centrality of the body in social stratification.

As Chapter 1 demonstrated, people from different backgrounds, with different life experiences, face a set of shared physical and symbolic predicaments associated with the aging body. Rich or poor, male or female, those who grow old confront a new phase of life that includes social challenges intertwined with physiological elements such as decreased energy, declining mobility, sensory changes, altered appearance, expanding health issues, the deaths of friends and family members, and the erosion of prized characteristics grounded in the operation, appearance, and reception of their bodies. In part because of its physical aspects and their associated challenges and stigmas, old age becomes a category of inequality that shapes the lives of older Americans and sets them apart from their younger counterparts (and often one another). Despite their past differences, the problems of aging lead seniors from diverse backgrounds to shared experiences and the corresponding realization that being an "old person," or at least being seen as one, is an important force that shapes many facets of their lives. For many, this involves coming to terms with new sources of physical and social uncertainty.[3]

The convergent experiences and realizations of American seniors reflect an underlying sociological reality: old age serves as a both categorical and gradient form of inequality that sets the "old" apart from the young and creates shared issues and new distinctions that are key to understanding social stratification. These issues are largely connected to older adults' changing physiological resources, what these signify to themselves and others, and the resulting responses of individuals and organizations. This is true on the macro level (age stratification across society) and the micro level (the challenges people face in everyday life). This book has focused on the latter, but they are related. In the American case, some physically rooted predicaments carry existential weight (e.g., the dilemma of when to give up driving or move in to a nursing facility) in part because they have implications for where people fit into the bigger picture and whether others understand them—and if they understand themselves—as "independent." Other predicaments are seen in more immediate and pragmatic terms (e.g., how to deal with arthritic knee pain or trouble opening jars). In each circumstance, however, the degeneration of the body, changing physical resources, and what these mean for everyday life in an age-stratified society create what sociologist Ann Swidler calls structural dilemmas: "tasks or practical difficulties of action, to which the wider culture generates many different, sometimes competing, and always only partially satisfactory solutions."

As Chapter 1 showed, old age is a structural dilemma that affects people from all racial and socioeconomic groups.[4]

The larger implication for understanding inequality is that the body and the social resources it provides are central to understanding social stratification. This is because the body constitutes both our basic *instrument* and a key (and unequally distributed) *resource* for acting in the world. On the first point, philosophers have long recognized that as humans, we are tied to our bodies. The body is our most fundamental instrument for experiencing and acting in the world. As people grow older, that instrument changes, as do our physical capabilities and embodied experiences. James put it most poetically when he said, "Old is a different animal altogether." But the body is also a resource in the more traditional sociological sense, and old age often involves its erosion. Strength, agility, intellect, appearance, and endurance are all resources we use in interacting in the world. Each is grounded in the human body, even though their labeling, and the associated processes of moral signification, requires a social response. Having the right "physical capital" or bodily tools can be essential in securing desired ends, such as money, sex, status, or even a bag of groceries.

Just like more conventional forms of wealth, our "physical capital" limits what we can do socially and how our actions are received. This was seen in the way a lack of energy limits what Dave can do in his life, where Donald can walk, and whether Sandy can leave her home. This is what Jason realized in the extreme when he commented to me in the Baygardens nursing facility, "I just sit around all week dying, and watching others waiting to die. I'm a fucking cripple, and I can't go out." Without the physical resources, the self-proclaimed "action man" lacked the capacity to act. A retired teacher at a senior center in Baygardens perhaps put this most clearly when she noted, "You don't realize how precious your body is until you get old." The body not only acts as a powerful axis of distinction, but it also can come to fundamentally structure the possibilities available to us.[5]

The Uneven Playing Field:
Social Contexts and Disparate Resources for Action

Understanding the end game requires recognizing that while growing old involves shared predicaments for everyone, both the contexts in which this unfolds and the ways individuals can respond are shaped by material and economic inequalities that continue into later life. Consequently, despite the provision of entitlements, some individuals and groups face the challenges of growing older with access to *substantially greater resources and opportunities.*

While "old age" creates shared challenges that cut across color, sex, and occupation, people do not face these difficulties on a level playing field. Despite the aggregate effects of selective mortality, the presence of shared challenges, and government entitlements, inequalities do not dissolve in old age. Disparities in material resources and wealth, at both the individual and neighborhood levels, continue to profoundly shape options, opportunities, and outcomes in later life.

As Chapter 2 demonstrated, unequal *neighborhood resources* continue to matter in the end game. In this study, seniors from all neighborhoods relied extensively on "safety net" services provided by both government and volunteer organizations. These services provide basic access to food, housing, and medicine, all of which are central to the survival strategies of many seniors. However, the gaps in the "safety net" are wider in some spots than others. In practice, those in more affluent areas have access to a greater variety of services, and these tend to be of a higher quality. As one senior in Elm Flats noted, the safety net in his particular neighborhood was particularly "thin" and at times coercive.

In this study, living in the more affluent areas of Baygardens and Cedar Hills conferred numerous advantages. Well-organized formal agencies and senior groups actively worked to secure funding and services that were of benefit to the larger senior community and the places they congregated (e.g., parks, senior centers, and housing units). For instance, the well-funded Baygardens state housing facility was cleaner, better maintained, and safer than its counterpart in Rockport. Seniors living in the more affluent neighborhood were likewise better supported by all manner of auxiliary services, from meal programs to volunteer visitors to adult education. Seemingly small issues, such as whether a broken light fixture was replaced or whether a rug that people trip on was adjusted, had major ramifications for older individuals, as an incident such as a fall can become a catastrophic and life-changing event. In more resource-rich communities, these small issues were substantially more likely to be addressed, even if seniors did not make exceptional efforts. Even those who did not go about proactively seeking out resources generally benefitted from the "spillover effects" of living in a more resource-rich environment. This is consistent with a claim sociologists have made for the past century: neighborhoods and communities have an effect on social life that cannot be directly reduced to the characteristics of their residents. Context and space do matter.[6]

Yet differences in *individual resources* remain essential as well. Just as those in affluent neighborhoods have more options even when they have similar individual resources, those with greater individual resources have an advantage even within the same neighborhood. Wealth continues to shape our options in later life, even with the potentially mitigating effect of Medicare and other entitlements. Seniors from middle-class or affluent backgrounds often own homes, receive pensions, have family members who can hire health aides, and maintain supplemental insurance that gives them greater flexibility for dealing with the everyday challenges of aging. Seniors from poor and working-class backgrounds, on the other hand, have fewer resources of this type and have little choice but to engage with public services, even when they would prefer otherwise. Consequently, getting the month's protein shakes or replacing a scooter's batteries require interacting with state agencies and oftentimes giving up the freedoms afforded the more affluent. This provides social workers, clinicians, and other "street-level bureaucrats" with substantial control over the everyday lives of less affluent seniors. While many poor seniors in this study were able to meet their everyday needs with government support, indicating that policy interventions can help, they had to do so under a more uncertain context of bureaucracy and surveillance that they found undesirable and even coercive. Even when they felt they were treated poorly, they had no real way to opt out if they were to survive.

Some continue to argue that the combination of selective mortality (inequalities in who lives to grow old), the robustness of survivors, and the promise of state entitlements turns the later years into a time when disadvantages accumulated earlier in the life course dissipate. Despite the shared challenges faced by seniors, and the important aid provided through public services and volunteers, the evidence on the ground suggests that we are not there yet. Traditional resource inequalities, with their socioeconomic, racial, and spatial components, continue to shape the lives of aging Americans. These are compounded by

Table C.1 Summary of disparate resources for action in the end game

	More contextual	More individual
Physical	Environment	Bodily capacities
Material	Services and programs available in neighborhoods	Wealth and insurance
Cultural	Forms of reciprocity Network dynamics	Cultural skills and capacities

health inequalities that reflect unequal circumstances over the life course. At the same time, ongoing funding cuts and austerity measures continue to threaten the already precarious position of these most vulnerable seniors. The reality is that material inequalities shape our everyday lives until the end, and quite often the disadvantages we face accumulate rather than dissipate.[7]

Table C.1 summarizes the various resource types that shape how those who survive to old age can respond to shared predicaments.[8]

Styles of Play:
Cultural Responses to Inequality Past and Present

Understanding the end game requires recognizing and examining how culture provides a key bridge that connects prior experiences, and the inequalities that structure them, to strategies and outcomes in the present.

Popular and scholarly accounts that attempt to reduce differences in behavior to material resources, access, and information alone cannot explain how people behave when those factors are held constant. Further, they miss the way skills and styles of interacting shaped by life experiences provide some seniors with concrete advantages in navigating institutions or responding to the hardships of later life. These accounts obscure how key mechanisms of inequality, such as the importance of "cultural capital" in dealing with institutions, stratify outcomes.

This book has shown that the different game-day strategies that seniors pursue reflect divergent cultural *motivations, orientations,* and *resources* developed over their lifetimes. Chapter 3 showed that how seniors approach their present circumstances largely depends upon whether they are motivated to *bodily preservation* or *maximizing enjoyment*. Yet, even when they value the same ends, there are often multiple strategies available to seniors, given the resources at their disposal. Orientations toward aging, health, illness, and medical institutions affect what people see as the most *reasonable* way to pursue these ends, given what is structurally possible. For instance, although many seniors share the same basic inclination to preserve the body, whether they orient toward understandings of a *medical body* (i.e., the body is seen as a complex machine needing expert maintenance) or a *natural body* (i.e., the body is a naturally self-regulating unit) affects what they do when faced with a concrete predicament—for instance, whether they go to a doctor or an acupuncturist when pain threatens their mobility. While these responses can vary within neighborhoods or demographic groups, it is essential to note that motivations and orientations are not just random variations in individual psychology. They are influenced by prior social experiences with school, work, and an unequal social world more generally, and they often assume deep moral valence. Motivations are imputed and evaluated by peers and organizations who see different behaviors not as just one way to respond but as the "right way" to act.

Nonetheless, the ability to secure an outcome (e.g., seeing an acupuncturist or rheumatologist) is constrained by present resources—both symbolic and material. Just as it is harder to see a specialist if there are none in your neighborhood, it is harder to navigate medical institutions if you do not speak the same language as the doctor. *Cultural resources,* such as language skills, knowledge of institutions, and general styles of interacting with authority figures ultimately play a substantial role in mediating outcomes. The ability of seniors to invoke socially validated medical knowledge to get what they want from a doctor or the ability to navigate the medical bureaucracy (or the informal economy) affected which strategies were possible and practical. In this study, seniors enacted four general strategies in responding to the challenges of the aging body: "better safe than sorry"; "be healthy, but get help if sick"; "fix for fun"; and "damn the torpedoes (until you are in the ER)." These strategies reflect clusters of motivations, orientations, and cultural resources that assumed coherence in different neighborhood and organizational contexts.[9]

The larger implication for understanding social stratification is rather straightforward: culture cannot be ignored. Culture is necessary for understanding why Jane skips chemo, why Donald sees the doctor regularly, why Ray believes in his "herbal concoctions," and why Bernard has a harder time getting what he wants from doctors than Hatty does. Culture shapes what is believed to be worth pursuing, what is seen as a reasonable way to go about that pursuit, and, in its capacity as a resource, whether the desired ends are ever reached. As this book has shown, this does not mean culture is sui generis—rather, it is forged in prior experiences that are organized by inequality. Yet the resulting product is carried into the present. While it is not *sufficient*, culture is *necessary* to explain variation in how people respond to the challenges they face. Quite simply, culture matters for understanding stratification and inequality because it profoundly affects actions and outcomes over the life course.[10]

Team Dynamics:
Networks and Inequality in Later Life

Explaining the end game requires not only recognizing that networks matter but also understanding how differences in the meaning of ties and the resources they provide in unequal contexts stratify the options available to seniors.

The relationships we have with friends, family, and acquaintances profoundly influence how we can respond to the challenges we face over the course of our lives. Consequently, differences in our networks can be a form of inequality that stratifies our options and outcomes. This remains true in later life. Seniors with robust social networks generally had advantages unavailable to their more isolated peers. Yet inequalities in this study were not limited to the division between the "connected" and the "isolated." Networks were embedded in broader contexts that provided unequal access to material and symbolic resources. Consequently, even networks that looked similar on the surface functioned very differently. Having friends in the apartment complex could translate into getting a ride to the doctor, a trip to the bar, or neither. Nearby offspring could provide support with instrumental tasks, stress, the threat of institutionalization in a nursing home, or all of the above. Further, even when like ties (e.g., a strong relationship between a senior and adult offspring) were being used for the same end (e.g., helping a senior get medical treatment), disparities in financial and cultural resources affected their efficacy.

How connections functioned in the four neighborhoods of this study also depended on differences in the underlying meaning of ties. Chapter 4 showed that underlying notions of *generalized reciprocity* (helping is an obligation) or *earned reciprocity* (helping is an exchange) affected the mobilization and efficacy of ties. As with other aspects of culture, these meanings were not sui generis—they reflected material differences in past and present. Further, while seniors across the board had to contend with new gaps in their networks due to the deaths of lost friends and family members, the effect was not even. "Network shrinkage" did not mitigate inequality by leveling differences or hurting everyone similarly. Rather, it highlighted differences in seniors' vulnerabilities and exacerbated them. Seniors from more affluent backgrounds often had more physical, material, and cultural resources for reconfiguring their everyday strategies when they lost a friend or loved one. The ties they maintained were more likely to connect them to material resources that made them more efficacious in many settings. Examining different levels of vulnerability in the response to network shrinkage highlights how social ties are often a resource, but their value is dependent on the broader cultural and material contexts in which they are situated.[11]

The larger implications for connecting inequality and stratification are (1) how social networks function depends on cultural meanings that are organized by unequal contexts of past and present; (2) these differences can become an important aspect of stratification by shaping when and how specific social ties can be used; and (3) even when seemingly similar ties are used for similar ends, they vary in efficacy in ways that map onto inequalities in material and symbolic resources. Of course, it is true that examining how social connectedness varies from isolation is essential for understanding phenomena like the end game. However, it is also important to look at the more nuanced meaning of social ties, the concrete contexts that organize them, and the underlying cultural meanings seen in those contexts. The effect of social ties is thus dependent not just on "who you know" but also the "meaning of who you know," as well as the resources those connections provide. This book shows that social ties are indeed a key resource in old age (as earlier in life), but, rather than being a universal form of capital, they are complex, contingent, and perhaps even more unequal than they appear on the surface.

Postgame Lessons:
Connecting the Pieces and Changing the Game

In the sections above, I outlined how various mechanisms of social stratification and inequality fit together to create the end game that shapes our final years. Each piece furnishes lessons that inform social-scientific understandings in their own right, but the larger game cannot be understood without looking at how their convergence structures everyday life for aging Americans. These connections and a few key contributions derived from each aspect of the game are summarized in Table C.2 below. I now turn to some postgame lessons: the broader implications for social policy and practice.

It is my hope that those equipped to address the issues faced by the growing population of American seniors might use the empirical evidence presented throughout this book to devise ways to advance the quality of later life while improving equity. In practice, resolving social problems—often even finding the will to recognize that they exist— is hard. Nonetheless, there are a few implications that immediately stand out as important considerations for improving the equity of the end game:

1. One basic implication of this work is that we need to continue improving the quality of the data that we have at our disposal. Good data, at both the macro and micro levels, is necessary to craft effective evidence-based policy responses. I am hopeful that the findings in this book can be employed both in the improvement of survey measures and as an example of how comparative ethnographic research can reveal how social mechanisms operate on the ground.

2. Given that the survival and timing of old age is a major axis of inequality, it is necessary to continue to look at and address inequality from a life-course perspective.

3. Addressing the substantial challenges older adults face also requires a serious discussion that moves beyond narrow disciplinary debates about whether aging is *really* biological or social. As this book has shown, the reality is that both are involved. The question should

Table C.2 The unequal end game

Aspect of the game	Mechanism of stratification	Manifestation	Broader implication for stratification
Who gets to play	Health disparities	Survival and timing of "old age"	Health disparities are central to understanding inequality over the life course.
Shared challenges	Physical changes and their social reception	Practical and symbolic challenges associated with the aging body	The body is a key *instrument* and *resource* in stratified social systems. "Old age" can be a durable and important facet of inequality.
The uneven playing field	Structural inequalities	Resource inequalities in how challenges manifest and how people can respond	Rather than being "leveled away," material disparities on both the neighborhood and individual level continue to stratify later life. Organizational processes related to gatekeeping, surveillance, and compensatory inversions remain key forms of inequality, even with current entitlements.
Styles of play	Culture	Prior experiences shape motivations, orientations, resources, and strategies for responding to challenges in the present.	Culture is a key mechanism of social stratification that connects prior experiences to present action. Culture is not sui generis. It is grounded in past and present inequalities. Culture shapes what we see as desirable (motivations), reasonable (orientations), and possible (resources) responses to the specific challenges we face.
Team dynamics	Network inequalities	Social ties affect how we approach and interpret present challenges.	Social ties are not universal but dependent on cultural and contextual factors that shape their meaning and efficacy. It is not just "who you know" but also what these connections mean and which resources they provide.

not be "which" factor matters, but when, how, and which interventions are effective.

4. It is important to recognize just how vital government services and volunteer programs are to the survival of American seniors from across the social spectrum. Issues that may seem minor to those in capital buildings, such as the disruptions to Meals on Wheels services during recent budget debates, have a profound impact on the lives of seniors who depend on these programs in multiple ways.

5. It is also necessary to recognize how the competitive funding structure and lack of coordination seen in senior services creates predicaments that can exacerbate inequality. In practice, current funding mechanisms can lead to resources being funneled away from those communities that need them most direly. The way to improve this is not only through more cooperation but also through broader coordination and planning.[12]

6. While adequate funding and coordination is key, as Chapter 2 showed, even low-cost interventions (such as the volunteer visiting program in Baygardens) can be meaningful and locally effective, given a concerted community effort to help.

7. If getting Americans to be less hesitant to see doctors or interact with state agencies in later life is a goal, it is important to recognize that barriers are not just physical. Many of the seniors in this study who chose not to use the clinics in their areas or tried to avoid social workers did not do so because they lacked physical access or information. Rather, they had had bad experiences, and knew others who had had bad experiences, with these agencies. Improving these experiences from early life on, rather than assuming that behavior can be reduced to access and information, is a necessary step.

8. On a related note, it is important to realize and respect that not everyone wants the same thing. Instead of imposing our view about the "right way" to go about a problem (e.g., aggressive medical treatment or working with state agencies), it is essential to acknowledge that intelligent, rational, informed people can come to different conclusions about how to approach their lives—and to respect that.

9. That said, resources and access still matter immensely. If people choose to pursue divergent paths, that *can* reflect differences in preferences or cultural orientations. However, when certain paths are

systematically cut off, that is a disparity. In addition to targeted interventions into specific phases of the life course, general investments in reducing inequality more generally, such as improving public transportation options or having high-quality medical services available to all, will help give seniors (and others) a choice.[13]

10. While one of the sociological points in this book was examining why networks vary in important ways, it is essential to not lose sight of a key issue that affects seniors: despite the variations I have documented—the stories I have told of burdensome kin and wayward friends—those who are connected generally fare better. Addressing the isolation of some seniors, facilitating opportunities for community, and encouraging intergenerational ties can be extremely useful in expanding meaningful options in later life.

Making Good on a Promise

In 2013 I was invited to give a talk to a prestigious sociology department about my work on inequalities in later life. Shortly after boarding the plane, I received a call from a nurse working at a hospital in Baygardens. She told me that Jason, whom I had been visiting regularly since the beginning of this project, was "ready to go." Jason had become my friend. I was sad his life was coming to an end, but I was not surprised. I had visited him recently in the hospital after he had contracted pneumonia. He was not doing well. I was increasingly finding that many of my older friends, who were such a big part of my life for so long, were dying. I proceeded to ask the nurse if she spoke to the family. I don't know why I assumed she had not called them first, but I did. Maybe it was intuition. The nurse sympathetically explained that she would be calling the family, but that he wanted me to be notified first, because, he said, nobody else cared. Upon hearing this last part, I teared up and thanked the nurse.

During the course of the project, Jason, along with other seniors from all four neighborhoods in this study, explained to me that it was important to them that people outside their enclaves understood their lives and the challenges they faced. Many, like Jason, felt abandoned by family, friends, and society. They implored me to tell others what I learned during my time with them. I promised I would. This book is an initial attempt to make good on that promise. Throughout, I have described how inequalities, both past and present, shape the lives of older Americans such as Jason, Bernard, and Jane. This work has demonstrated that inequality does not end with the promise of Social Security and Medicare, and that old age is an important categorical inequality that exists alongside (and in interaction with) others, such as race, socioeconomic status, and gender. I have explained that while growing old in America creates shared challenges for all, individuals face them with vastly unequal resources. The result is an end game that we all must play, even though we do not do so on even ground. The rules, players, and strategies that form the "logic of the game" have a lot to tell us not only about stratification in later life but also about how inequality and stratification work more generally.

On the plane, I had a drink in honor of Jason and then worked on my PowerPoint slides for the rest of the flight. I gave the talk and it went well. I had the opportunity to present it several times over the next few months. During one of the question-and-answer periods, a sociology professor at a major research university asked me, "Why should we care about old people?" While similar projects on inequality in childhood rarely elicit this response, I held back my indignation. Rather than talking about how social scientists should care about people at all phases of life, I reframed the question in a way that touched on what I hoped was the point of the query: clarifying how the case of old age contributes to understanding stratification and inequality more broadly. I said the "right things," given the settings. I reiterated that later life was a key site for examining how the mechanisms of inequality work, pointed out that shifting demographics meant that there were more seniors than ever before, and added that there were few comparative ethnographic examinations of this type aimed at fleshing out mechanisms. The response I received was a dismissive "This is just depressing." And that is part of the problem. Old age is important analytically because it can teach us a lot about society, but it is also important on a human level. It is something we should care about, even when it is hard to watch. Rather than ignoring the challenges and inequalities that shape the end game, we should work to improve them. Only then will it be less depressing. Only then will we have made good.

METHODOLOGICAL
APPENDIX

Field Methods

As is common for many sociological ethnographies, this book relies heavily on the use of participant observation: prolonged immersion in nonlaboratory social settings, with the intent of understanding how and why people behave in real-world settings and how they make sense of their lives as they do. In particular, this study focuses on explaining how patterns of American inequality shape the everyday lives of seniors living in four urban neighborhoods and what this can tell us about key mechanisms of social stratification more generally. Explaining how these processes work in everyday life requires observing a wide range of behaviors in situ. Doing so complements existing population-level insights by showing how microlevel processes operate and are connected to the broader operation of social systems.[1]

Multisite ethnography was thus particularly well suited for this project, as it allowed for the observation of individuals from diverse backgrounds as they went about their lives in preexisting social and organizational contexts. By combining observations with in-depth interviews as well as informal conversations, I was able to catalog how people understood the predicaments they faced in later life, examine how they made choices and justified their actions, and observe how this worked out within and across different neighborhood contexts. The broader goal of this analytical-sociological approach to comparative ethnography, however, is using systematically collected comparative observations, and the observed patterns of similarity and difference they reveal, to understand how key mechanisms of social stratification shape everyday life within and across contexts more broadly.

SITE SELECTION

I initially operationalized neighborhoods as sociogeographical units located within a larger metropolitan setting. While this is not a study of neighborhoods, I expected that allowing the observation of neighborhood variation would be key to charting the operation of inequality in the end of later life. Hence, focusing only on individuals in a single neighborhood would have been inadequate, given my analytical goals. Although neighborhoods were initially screened for demographic suitability using tract-level census data to ensure they met the inclusion criteria described in the introduction (i.e., poverty status and racial homo/heterogeneity), neighborhood boundaries were not imputed strictly based on census tracts but, as in Small's study, were grounded in "socially recognized and ecologically reinforced" local boundaries. Neighborhoods were classified as "poor" if the percentage of households with incomes below the federal poverty line adjusted for family size (e.g., the standard poverty index) was 30 percent or higher. Within each socioeconomic grouping (poor/nonpoor), I selected one neighborhood that was more racially mixed and another that was more homogenous—although there was some racial, ethnic, and socioeconomic variation, even in the more homogenous settings. All neighborhoods were in, or connected to, major metropolitan areas in the Greater Bay Area of Northern California. The neighborhoods are described in the introductory chapter, but I summarize their key characteristics from a sampling or case-selection perspective in Table A1.[2]

A BRIEF NOTE ON THE ADVANTAGES AND LIMITATIONS
OF THE CALIFORNIA BAY AREA CONTEXT

While this study uses comparisons of individuals within and across four urban neighborhoods that vary with respect to racial and socioeconomic composition, it is important to note a potential limitation: all research was conducted in California. In theory, it could have been quite useful to conduct additional fieldwork in other states to see how regional

Table A.1   Neighborhood demographic characteristics

	Poor	Middle-class
More racially mixed	Rockport (AA, LA, WH, API)*	Cedar Hills (WH, API, AA, LA)
More racially homogeneous	Elm Flats (AA, WH)	Baygardens (WH, API)

*Abreviations are as follows: AA (African American), LA (Latino/Hispanic), WH (Non-Hispanic White/Caucasion), API (Asian/Pacific Islander).

effects, more extreme weather patterns, systems of local governance, different urban environs, and so on affected social life. The decision to stay in California was partially pragmatic. I began the project as a doctoral candidate in sociology at the University of California at Berkeley and thus found myself living in the Bay Area. While the structure of my program provided substantial time for conducting fieldwork, the cost of regular travel to different regions of the country would have been prohibitive, given my modest income. Further, the addition of more sites would have entailed substantial compromise: either a much longer stay in the field or spending less time with individuals at each location. These issues would be compounded by time lost to travel. Although I initially considered adding sites in Southern California, as I conducted field work and preliminary interviews, I came to the conclusion that the Greater Bay Area (including San Francisco, the East Bay, the North Bay, and the South Bay) not only provided tremendously rich variation, but also it was a particularly useful test case for charting differences and commonalities in later life.

Conducting fieldwork in the Bay Area had numerous advantages. First, California is among the most ethnically and racially diverse states in the nation, and the Bay Area is one of the most diverse parts of the state. According to a recent report by several prominent demographers and sociologists, the San Francisco–Fremont–Oakland metropolitan area is the second most ethnically diverse locale in the country (second only to Vallejo-Fairfield on the northeast side of the Bay). Further, the Greater Bay Area has both some of the richest neighborhoods in the country, as well as areas characterized by persistent poverty. By focusing my observations in the Bay area, it was possible to select sites with substantial socioeconomic and racial variation (both at the neighborhood and individual levels) and to be able to visit those locations regularly (even visiting several over the course of the same day, when the flow of events in seniors' lives made this necessary). Although the proportion of the California population over sixty-five is lower than the national average, it has the largest raw number of persons sixty-five and older in the nation (roughly 4.4 million). Consequently, there are numerous neighborhoods where the population was substantially older than the national average (although I did not sample on this, Baygardens turned out to be one). Additionally, it was not uncommon for neighborhoods with very different characteristics to be part of the same large counties. This allowed me to trace how the provision of local, county, and state services varied even when served by ostensibly the same agencies.[3]

There are a few unique aspects of Northern California that warrant mention. Like much of the country, it remains a car culture, although the Bay Area has better public transportation than most other parts of the state. The area is more politically liberal than other parts of the country. The climate is temperate. While inequalities in the physical environment affected both the risk of injury and the opportunity to socialize with other seniors in this study (the topic of Chapter 2), they rarely provided the sort of dramatic life-and-death differences found in past research conducted in less temperate regions. Summers in Northern California can be warm and winters chilly (and sometimes vice versa), but they rarely reach the sort of deadly climate extremes experienced in Chicago or Michigan. Further, as mentioned in Chapter 2, farmers' markets are ubiquitous. By removing some of the more extreme challenges faced by seniors in other parts of the country (deadly weather, a lack of public transportation, lack of access to fresh produce, etc.), these factors provided a conservative test of the notion that inequality continues into later life. Yet, as the chapters throughout this book show, the effect remained profound, even given the relatively favorable geographical circumstances for aging.[4]

OBSERVATIONAL STRATEGIES

Within each neighborhood my observational strategy was two-tiered, and it included both general observations of communal settings and organizations and closer observations of individuals as they went about their daily lives. For my general observations, I spent time in organizations and public spaces frequented by the elderly. Initially I observed senior centers and housing units that had primarily senior residents. I also regularly visited nursing facilities in Rockport and Baygardens. By the end of the project, I expanded my pool of general observations to include various settings I discovered were frequented by neighborhood seniors: apartment building common rooms, doctors' offices, emergency rooms, pharmacies, senior centers, bars, corner stores, shopping centers, pool halls, hair salons, coffee shops, and discount stores.

Over the course of my fieldwork, I observed hundreds of elders and developed close relationships with a number of them. After meeting specific individuals, I would ask permission to spend time with them as they went about their daily lives. When speaking to them for the first time, I informed people that I was a sociologist working on a book about aging in different communities. Since I was an obvious outsider (always by virtue of my age, and occasionally by virtue of my race and gender), many seniors would ask me why I was at that location—which allowed me to explain my project. I also typically wore a hat or shirt with my university's insignia, which served as both a conversation starter and a declaration of my affiliation. Although I was not employed by any senior agency, I was granted permission by authorities to observe organizational activities at various senior centers, housing units, and nursing facilities. This was in addition to gaining the consent of the specific seniors with whom I interacted. My transparency about the project, my willingness to listen to peoples' stories, and the sheer amount of time spent in the various locales provided me with a great deal of freedom and local legitimacy to strategically position myself in order to see social processes at work. I did, however, occasionally help out as a volunteer at various organizations serving seniors. Although this limited my ability to move around particular sites during these times, it was advantageous in signaling my respectability and institutional legitimacy to the seniors, who were often concerned about being taken advantage of by individuals who prey on the elderly.

While I was in the field, I generally spent between twenty and forty hours per week with the elders in my study as they went about their daily routines. I listened to them as they discussed the issues involved with aging (such as the loss of mobility, pain, attempting to follow a complicated pharmaceutical regimen, or being treated differently by younger people) through complaints, jokes, and the formulation of ear-nest strategies for managing their problems. I talked with them about their many concerns. I followed them as they went to the doctor and saw how they interacted with different people in medical settings. I listened to their accounts of what went on when I was not there. I observed the environments in which they lived, the food they ate, whether and how they took their medicines (and why), and seemingly mundane processes such as how often they bathed. I observed the way they interacted (or avoided interacting) with other people. I watched what they did when they became ill. I saw to whom they turned, what remedies they took, and at what point they sought out medical professionals or healers (Western or otherwise). I watched what they did when they were feeling well and examined what "feeling well" meant to different groups. I watched them interact with friends and family. I listened to them talk about their hopes and concerns and their sources of joy and sadness. I spent time with elders after they were placed in "total institutions" such as skilled-nursing wings of hospitals or assisted-living facilities. I observed how sick elders managed their dying bodies, how they approached the deaths of friends and loved ones, and the social and psy-chological strains this entailed. In what was perhaps the most difficult part of the research process, I witnessed people with whom I developed friendships die.

I generally staggered the day and time of my observations in an attempt to minimize the chance of missing some key time- or day-dependent variation in behavior, although I also made an attempt to attend events seniors identified as meaningful. I took notes by hand in a 3″ × 5″ paper notebook while in the field. I sometimes did this out of sight of the seniors. This is not to say the ethnographic component of this study was covert—rather, some of the seniors simply seemed more at ease when I did not write the notes directly in front of them (even though they knew I was taking notes for a study). I assured subjects of confiden-tiality, and over the years I became a trusted friend for many. Still, many seniors in this study were accustomed to interacting with social workers, doctors, and other institutional representatives who held some degree of direct power over their lives. These people would often take overt notes that could affect the services at seniors' disposal or alter their living situation in a profound matter. My not taking notes in the manner they did helped remind seniors that I was not one of these people—that I wanted to understand rather than "evaluate" their lives. I generally typed full field notes immediately upon returning from my research sites each day. On the few occasions when this was not possible, I typed notes as soon as I was able. Although I follow the common practice of using pseudonyms to protect the confidentiality of the individuals in the study, it is important to note that the observations provided refer to real people and real events rather than "composites."[5]

Interview Methods

The second method I employed was semistructured in-depth interviews. With the help of two research assistants, I collected sixty interviews ranging from twenty minutes to over two hours in length. Most interviews took around one hour. These research assistants, whom I trained and mentored over a period of two years, assisted in the collection, transcription, and coding of these interviews. Having additional interviewers allowed me to collect more data than would have been possible on my own, at the potential cost of introducing response variation due to researcher characteristics. However, since this strategy allowed me to collect more perspectives than would have been possible otherwise, and the interviews were always triangulated with observation, in my estimation the potential breadth added by the introduction of these auxiliary interviews was worth the risk. For this reason, having multiple interviewers is increasingly commonplace in large qualitative studies. Sociologist Annette Lareau deploys a similar strategy in a well-known study involving interviews and observation.[6]

The interviews contained ten broadly defined topical domains: (1) background/life-history, (2) thoughts on aging, (3) navigating everyday life, (4) social connectedness, (5) everyday behaviors, (6) care-seeking behaviors, (7) general attitudes, (8) health conditions, (9) vignettes about appropriate behavior (i.e., what should a senior do if he or she has had a lump on his or her back for one month), and (10) demographics. Although there were some standardized questions, such as the demographics and vignettes, seniors were also given the opportunity to discuss topics they felt were not addressed. The interviews provided additional data about how the elders in this study think about and represent the world. Further, the interview data complemented the observational data in identifying behavioral norms, shared meanings, and collective representations that proved essential to understanding responses to health and illness.

By comparing interviews with my participant observation data among seniors, I examined what people say others "should do" when presented with a physical dilemma; what they consider "reasonable" for themselves and others, given their social location; and what they ultimately do. Examining both the points of congruence and discord between interview and observational data provided leverage for understanding how various aspects of culture, grounded in inequalities both past and present, affected seniors' responses to challenges in social context. Additionally, these interviews allowed me to collect more systematic life history data. Thirty-two of the sixty interviewees were female (53 percent). The median age of interviewees was 69.4 years. Twenty-six were white (43 percent), twenty-one were African American (35 percent), ten were Asian Pacific Islanders (17 percent), two were unspecified (3 percent), and one was Latino (<2 percent). The interview schedule used as a rough guide for these interviews is found at the end of this appendix.

Table A.2 summarizes what each type of data contributes to my broader analysis.

Data Analysis

I entered all field notes and transcripts into ATLAS.ti, a current generation computer assisted qualitative data analysis software (CAQDAS) package that facilitated the systematic organization, coding, and analysis of the data. I conducted an iterative analysis that used both deductively and inductively generated concepts, codes, and themes to evaluate and expand existing models of the relationship between inequality and later life. I was fortunate enough to have the aid of a research assistant who helped with the initial coding of behavioral occurrences. I subsequently went back and did a deeper thematic coding of the data on top of this initial indexing. I used patterns of code associations generated in ATLAS.ti to orient me to occurrences that were central to understanding my research questions: that is, how seniors dealt with growing old, how this varied within and between social groups, how individuals

Table A.2   Forms of evidence provided by each method

Method	Participant observation	Interviews
Evidence provided	*What subjects do in everyday life:* • Social and physical issues faced • How those issues manifest and are negotiated in concrete contexts • How seniors make sense of issues together • How seniors explain behavior in context • Informal conversations	*How seniors make sense of past and present:* • Which issues seniors identify as salient • How seniors describe/frame issues • How seniors describe appropriate responses to issues • How seniors justify behavior • Life history data

and organizations responded to them, and how seniors made sense of the process. I also used codes to mark critical events and deviant cases. All my data were categorized by site, time, and data-type to facilitate comparisons. Interviews were grouped by neighborhood and individual demographics (race, age, sex, and a rough estimation of socioeconomic status earlier in life). It is important to emphasize, however, that these categorizations and codes did not reduce the underlying data to numeric values. They were simply used as an orienting tool that helped identify patterns and contexts, which were then analyzed in more depth as the behavioral sequences and narratives seen throughout this book.[7]

I also regularly wrote analytical memos. These memos helped me make sense of what I was seeing, pointed me toward new questions to ask (in the field and formal interviews), and helped me collect better data. Likewise, each interview had a memo summarizing key characteristics of the respondent, themes that came up, issues with question phrasing, and what the interview added to the project. I also wrote field event summaries about both specific occurrences I witnessed (e.g., Dave's interactions at the clinic) as well as classes of occurrences I witnessed (e.g., variation in responses to stumbling in the senior center). These writings, as well as larger thematic memos (on social networks, culture, material inequality, etc.), were each connected to the underlying text using hyperlinks. Reading memos, going back to the underlying data, and doing text and code searches to establish common patterns and variation were each essential to making sense of the voluminous data collected during this study and constructing the book manuscript. Below I include a sample of a memo describing what seniors' attempts to obtain Ensure (a protein supplement) suggest about the ways material inequalities can shape seniors' responses, even in the context of a "safety net."

MEMO ON ENSURE AND MATERIAL RESOURCES

The way inequalities in neighborhood, individual, and nonmaterial resources shape seniors' range of available actions is seen in how different individuals respond to similar challenges. In this example, Pauline, Laura, and Dave each ran out of Ensure (a protein supplement) and needed to replenish it. Pauline drove to the store and bought it herself; Laura's son bought some for her (although she had resources to hire a helper to do the same); and Dave was forced to engage in a convoluted process that involved calling a social worker who came to check up on his home, going to a doctor (which lead to more unwanted medical appointments), then convincing someone to take him to the pharmacy, where he had to negotiate with a teller who at first did not want to recognize his prescription. All three individuals wanted the same thing: to get a health-maintaining supplement with the minimum amount of hassle. Their different manners of getting Ensure were not an artifact of "value differences."

Pauline, Laura, and Dave possessed drastically different resources for action. While Pauline lived in a neighborhood with fewer contextual resources and services (Elm Flats), she possessed powerful individual resources for action that allowed her to compensate. First, she was physically well off. This provided her with a much greater range of activities (walking, driving, carrying boxes of supplements) than what would be available to Dave or Laura. Second, she had material wealth in money and a car, which opened up direct paths to the Ensure, given her physical capacities. Third, although she was fiercely independent, she had close social ties with her family, which she could call on if need be. Laura's options were substantially more limited by the fact that she was physically unable to get to a store. Her neighborhood had more resources that could help (social workers, visiting programs, etc.), but her strong social tie with her son made this unnecessary. Further, her wealth in the form of savings and a home would have allowed her to hire a helper even if her son did not see this as his duty. Dave had few options. He was not physically well. He lived in a neighborhood with spotty services. He did not have any savings or a car. Although Dave had a brother, he lived a distance away, the two did not have a close relationship, and there was little help expected. Consequently, he had to engage with a web of doctors, social workers, and pharmacists, as well as the unwanted surveillance and time demands this entailed.

The example of how these three individuals sought the same basic end, a nutritional supplement, points to both how unequal material resources structure their options and how their lines of action involve key nonmaterial resources that extend beyond inequalities in wealth and organizational funding. Differences in embodied capacities for acting in the world, cultural skills for interacting with others (as well as dispositions toward independence) and the presence and meaning of social ties were key.

A Brief Note on Ethnography, Policy, and Public Engagement

It is important to note that a comparative ethnographic approach that places empiricism as its central tenant is not a rejection of principles of socially engaged scholarship. On the contrary, it is guided by the belief that accurate, data-driven explanations are necessary to address persistent social issues such as poverty, health disparities, or discrimination. Sociologists like myself have historically been, and continue to be, concerned with not only their contribution to knowledge in an abstract sense but also with how this knowledge might help address (or exacerbate) the shared challenges we face. Emile Durkheim, one of the discipline's founding figures, provided a useful clarification of the moral imperative of sociology:

> Yet because what we propose to study is above all reality, it does not follow that we should give up the idea of improving it. We would esteem our research not worth the labor of a single hour if its interests were merely speculative. If we distinguish carefully between theoretical and practical problems it is not in order to neglect the latter category. On the contrary, it is in order to put ourselves in a position where we can better resolve them.

In a similar vein, this work proceeds under the assumption that accurately charting social problems is a necessary precursor to addressing them. Of course, it would be naive to think that sociological investigations of inequality necessarily produce a better world by being published. Nonetheless, rigorous work striving toward objectivity is essential to formulating effective evidence-based interventions. It is my sincerest hope that the data and analyses presented in this book can be used in that regard.[8]

Sample Interview Schedule

[*Elicit consent in accordance with approved script from institutional review board.*]

PREFACE

Most of the questions I will ask you are pretty broad and open-ended. There are no right or wrong answers, and everything you say is confidential. I am just really interested in your thoughts. I am going to start with some basic questions:

I. INTRODUCTORY INFO/RAPPORT
- How old are you?
- Where were you born?
- Where do you live now?
    How long have you lived there?
- When you were middle-aged, what did you do for a living?
- Are you retired now?
    IF YES: Do you ever still work? What do you do?
    IF NO: What do you do now to pay the bills?
- *Follow-up: Some seniors look at retirement as a chance to move to a new place, maybe with nice weather or fun things to do; other seniors want to stay around the people they've known for years and in their own neighborhoods. How do you feel about that?*
    Why?
    What have you done?
    Why?
- Can you walk me through what a typical day looks like for you?
    For example, what sorts of things do you do from the time you wake up until the time you go to bed?
    Let's start in the morning when you wake up . . .

II. TRANSITION/THOUGHTS ON AGING

- How would you describe what it is like to grow older to someone who is young?

    For example, what should I expect as I get older?
- What gets harder as you grow older?
- Is there anything that gets easier?

    What is it?
- Are there things young people do not understand about seniors? What about getting older?

III. NAVIGATING AS A SENIOR

- If you need something from the store, how do you get it?
- If you need medicine for the pharmacy, how do you get it?
- If you need to go to the doctor, how do you get there?

    Are there other ways for a senior like yourself to get around?
- Is it easy for a senior to get where he or she needs to go in your community?

    Ask about interviewee specifically
- Is your neighborhood safe?

    Why or why not?
- Do you like your community?

    Why or why not?
- Do you ever have a hard time paying the bills?

    Please explain.
- Do you ever have any other trouble with finances or money?

    Please explain.
- Has this ever affected the food you bought?

    Please explain.
- Have these ever affected getting medical care?

    Please explain.

IV. SOCIAL CONNECTEDNESS

Family

- Are you married?

    Follow-up—*Were you married previously? How long?*
- How often do you see other members of your family?

    What do you do when you see one another?

    Kids vs. siblings, etc.

> *When was the last time you remember seeing a member of your family?*
> *What did you do?*

- How often do you talk on the telephone?
  > *What do you talk about?*
- Do members of your family ever help you?
  > *How do they help?*
- Do family members have responsibilities toward seniors?
  > *What are they?*

Friends

- How often do you get together with your friends?
  > *What do you do when you see another?*
  > *How did you meet?*
  > *When was the last time you remember seeing a friend?*
  > *What did you do?*
- Do you have a close group of friends?
  > *How did you meet?*
  > *Tell me about them.*
- How often do you talk to friends on the telephone?
  > *What do you talk about?*
- Do your friends ever help you?
  > *How do they help?*
- Do friends have responsibilities toward seniors?
  > *What are they?*

Neighbors

- Do you see your neighbors often?
  > *What do you do when you see one another?*
- Do your neighbors ever help you?
  > *How do they help?*
- Do neighbors have responsibilities toward seniors?
  > *What are they?*

Other

- Do you get help from any senior organizations?
- Do you belong to a religious organization like a church mosque or synagogue? Do they help?
- Is there anybody else that helps you?
  > *If no, what about the government?*
- Does the government have responsibilities toward seniors?

What are they?

What about society in general?

- Some seniors get a lot of help from their grown children; others feel that they should not bother them. How do you feel about that?

   Why?

   What have you done?

   Why?

- Do you feel seniors are treated well in your community?

   Why or why not?

- What about in America overall?

- Are some groups of seniors treated better than others?

   Can you give me an example?

- How should seniors be treated?

V. EVERYDAY BEHAVIORS

- Can you describe what you eat on a typical day?

   Breakfast, lunch, dinner

- Do you ever drink alcohol?

   How often?

   Why?

- Have you been prescribed medications?

   For what?

   How often are you supposed to take them?

   How often do you take them?

   IF DISCREPANCY: Why?

- Do you ever take over-the-counter medications [e.g., medications that don't need a doctor's prescription]?

   For what?

   How often do you take them?

- Do you ever take prescription medications that were not prescribed for you?

   How often?

   Why?

- Do you ever use vitamins, supplements, alternative, or herbal medicines?

   How often?

   Why?

- Do you ever take other drugs?
  - *How often?*
  - *Why?*
- Would you say you are physically active?
  - *What do you do?*
- How many hours of sleep do you usually get per night?
- Do you ever have trouble falling or staying asleep?
  - *Why?*
  - *What do you do when this happens?*

VI. CARE-SEEKING BEHAVIORS

- When you don't feel well, what do you do?
- When do you decide it is time to see someone else for a health problem?
  - *Who do you usually see?*
- When was the last time you saw someone for a health problem?
  - *Describe.*
  - *How did you know it was time to go in?*
- Have you ever *not* gone for care and regretted it?
  - *Describe.*
- Do you have a usual doctor?
  - *How often do you see them?*
  - *Do you have a good relationship?*
- What do you think about doctors in general?
- Do you see any specialists?
  - *How often do you see them?*
- Do you ever see anybody else for health problems?
  - *For example, massage, acupuncture, curandera, neighbor, nurse.*
- Have you ever gone to the emergency room?
  - *When was the last time you went?*
  - *Why?*
  - *Did you end up in the hospital?*
- Have you ever been in the hospital?
  - *Why?*
  - *When was the last time?*
  - *What do you think about hospitals in general?*

- Thinking back, what is the best experience you have ever had with a health care provider (doctor clinic, nurse, herbalist, etc.)?
    Describe?
- Thinking back, what is the worst experience you ever had with a health care provider?
    Describe.

VII. MORE GENERAL ATTITUDES ON HEALTH, ILLNESS, AND AGING
- What is a good reason for a senior to go to the doctor?
- What is a bad reason?
- Do you know seniors who go to the doctor too often?
    Why do you think they do that?
- Do you know seniors who do not go often enough?
    Why don't they go?
- Have you ever visited a nursing or rest home?
    What do you think of them?
    Have you ever been a patient in one?
    What was that like?
- Is there an appropriate time for a senior to move to a nursing or rest home?
    When/Why?
- Do you have a general philosophy or way of thinking about how to deal with health and illness?
    Please explain . . .

VIII. HEALTH CONDITIONS
- How would you describe your overall health?
- Do you have any specific problems or conditions?
    How do these affect your everyday life?
    How do you deal with the conditions?
- Are you ever in pain?
    How often?
    How does the pain affect you?
- Do you ever have problems getting around?
    Why?
    How does this affect you?
- Do you drive a car?

IF YES: Do you ever worry about driving?
IF NO: Did you have one before?
Why did you give it up?
Do you miss it?
- Do you have a hard time doing certain things that are physical?
  What are they?
- Have you ever fallen?
  Describe.
- Are you sad often?
  How often?
  Why?
- Do you worry a lot?
  What do you worry about?

IX. VIGNETTES ABOUT "RESPONSIBLE" BEHAVIORS

- I'm going to give you some examples of things that sometimes happen to seniors, and ask what you think they should do.
  In the last two weeks, a senior you know has been bothered by scaly, itchy skin between his or her toes. The spots are spreading. What should this person do?
  A senior you know fell while trying to step into the bathtub last week, and this person is having a harder time moving around than he or she used to. What should this senior do?
  A senior you know has a lump on his or her back that has been there for a month. What should this person do?
  There is a senior I know who has breast cancer and is getting chemotherapy. Her doctors told her she should not drink alcohol, but all her friends are heavy drinkers. Even after getting chemotherapy, she would go out to bars with her friends to drink. What do you think of this?

X. CLOSING DEMOGRAPHICS

- What was the highest degree in school you received?
- How would you describe your religion, if any?
- How would you describe your race or ethnicity?
- Is English your first language?
  If no, what is?

- Thanks again for a great interview. That was really helpful, and I appreciate your time.

     Is there anything else you would like to add, or anything you feel you did not get a chance to say?
- Thanks so much. Two last questions:

     First, would you be willing to have me follow up?

     Second, would you be willing to refer me to other seniors?

NOTES

Introduction

1. All the people described in the pages of this book were observed during the multiyear ethnographic research on which this book is based. The names of neighborhoods and individuals have been replaced with pseudonyms to protect the identities of the people and organizations involved.

    Throughout the book, I use the terms "elderly," "aged," "older persons," and "seniors" interchangeably to refer to individuals sixty-one years of age or older, to reduce redundancy. The section describing the operationalization of "old age" in this introduction ("Is Age Just a Number?") discusses the issue of the chronological, social, and biological facets of age in more depth. Sections in Chapters 1 and 5 continue this discussion.

2. In contemporary sociology, the term "social stratification" generally refers to the valuation, allocation, and movement of resources within and across social systems. See David B. Grusky, ed., *Social Stratification: Class, Race, and Gender in Sociological Perspective,* 2nd ed. (Boulder, CO: Westview, 2001), 3–51. For important discussions of stratification and aging, see Toni M. Calasanti and Kathleen F. Slevin, *Gender, Social Inequalities, and Aging* (New York: AltaMira, 2001); Robert H. Binstock and Linda K. George, eds., *Handbook of Aging and the Social Sciences,* 7th ed. (London: Academic Press, 2010); and James S. House et al., "The Social Stratification of Aging and Health," *Journal of Health and Social Behavior* 35 (1994): 213–234.

3. My intent in advancing this analogy is not to trivialize the challenges faced by seniors, or to try to add levity or lyricism to a topic that deserves the utmost earnestness. Since human beings understand the world through the use of analogies, it is my hope that using this widely understood frame can help communicate complex sociological processes. In other words, without being *reductionist,* the metaphor of the game provides an organizing heuristic for analytical *reduction* and *representation.*

4. I use the term "mechanisms" to refer to the intermediary pathways that connect explanatory variables to observable outcomes. As Hedström and Swedberg note, "This style [of theorizing] can roughly be characterized by a focus on middle-range puzzles or paradoxes for which precise, action-based, abstract, and fine-grained explanations are sought" (Hedström and Swedberg 1998: 25). See Peter Hedström and Richard Swedberg, "Social Mechanisms: An Introductory Essay," in *Social Mechanisms: An Analytical Approach to Social Theory*, eds. Peter Hedström and Richard Swedberg (Cambridge: Cambridge University Press, 1998): 1–31. See also Peter Hedström, *Dissecting the Social: On the Principles of Analytical Sociology* (Cambridge: Cambridge University Press, 2005); Martín Sánchez-Jankowski and Corey M. Abramson, "Direct Observation and Causal Inference: The Function and Practice of Participant Observation in the Positivist-Behavioral Tradition," working paper, *American Journal of Sociology Conference on Causal Thinking and Ethnographic Research,* https://sites .google.com/site/ajs2012conference/2011-ieee-ss. and Peter Hedström and Petri Ylikoski, "Causal Mechanisms in the Social Sciences," *Annual Review of Sociology* 36 (2010): 49–67.

5. Consider, for instance, the fact that most African American men born in 1900 would die before they reached age thirty-three, more than a decade before their white counterparts. In 2010 newborn African American males fared better. They could expect to live to around seventy. (Still, this is over five years less than a white male and almost ten years less than a white woman, a topic discussed shortly. See Schreta 2005, C-13). One of the reasons for the expansion of life expectancy is that compared to children born a century or more ago, new Americans can expect their lives to be comparatively free of fatal accidents in the factory and on the farm; debilitating diseases; disruptions from war and famine; and early, violent deaths. For a discussion of historical changes in American aging, see Claude S. Fischer, *Made in America: A Social History of American Culture and Character* (Chicago: University of Chicago Press, 2010); and Steven Mintz, *Huck's Raft: A History of American Childhood* (Cambridge, MA: Belknap, 2004). See also "A Profile of Older Americans," US Administration on Aging (Washington, DC, 2009), http://www.aoa.acl .gov/Aging_Statistics/Profile/2009/index.aspx; and Kaare Christensen et al., "Ageing Populations: The Challenges Ahead," *Lancet* 374 (2009): 1196–1208. See also *Life Expectancy in the United States,* ed. Laura B. Shrestha, Library of Congress (Washington, DC, 2005), http://www.cnie.org/nlecrsreports/05mar /RL32792.pdf (it was republished as a paperback in 2013, http://www .barnesandnoble.com/w/life-expectancy-in-the-united-states-laura-b-shrest ha/1114943707?ean=9781288672585); and Calasanti and Slevin, *Gender, Social Inequalities,* 2001. Likewise, fewer than seven out of every one thousand children die in infancy: see Donna L. Hoyert and Jiaquan Xu, "Deaths: Preliminary Data for 2011," *National Vital Statistics Reports* 61, no. 6 (2012): 1–52; yet race, class, gender, and age divisions remain. For more recent statistics, see Deaths: Final Data for 2012, *National Vital Statistics Reports* 63, no. 9, forthcoming (http://www.cdc.gov/nchs/data/nvsr/nvsr63/nvsr63_09.pdf).

6. Arlie Hochschild notes that these "recent trends in the United States have expanded the need for care while contracting the supply of it, creating a 'care deficit' in both private and public life." See Arlie Russell Hochschild, *The Commercialization of Intimate Life: Notes from Home and Work* (Berkeley: University of California Press, 2003): 214. See also Emily K. Abel and Margaret K. Nelson, *Circles of Care: Work and Identity in Women's Lives* (New York: State University of New York Press, 1990). Meika Loe makes a similar case in her book on Americans over eighty-five: *Aging Our Way: Lessons for Living from 85 and Beyond* (New York: Oxford University Press, 2011).

7. See Pierre Bourdieu, *In Other Words*, 1990; as well as Omar Lizardo, "The Cognitive Origins of Bourdieu's Habitus," *Journal for the Theory of Social Behaviour* 34, no. 4 (2004): 375–401.

8. Further, unlike children, older Americans have already been exposed to a lifetime of social inequalities, which allows social scientists to trace connections between prior inequality and present responses. For the continuing popular support of entitlements, see Jill Quadagno and JoEllen Pederson, "Has Support for Social Security Declined? Attitudes toward the Public Pension Scheme in the USA, 2000 and 2010," *International Journal of Social Welfare* 21 (2012): S88–S100. For a general review of the sources and effects of social inequality, see Kathryn M. Neckerman, ed., *Social Inequality* (New York: Russell Sage Foundation, 2004). For a review of the relationship between education, mobility, and social attainment, see Richard Breen and Jan O. Jonsson, "Inequality of Opportunity in Comparative Perspective: Recent Research on Educational Attainment and Social Mobility," *Annual Review of Sociology* 221 (2005): 223–243.

9. I have found the same pattern in my quantitative work. See, for example, Corey M. Abramson and Martín Sánchez-Jankowski, "Racial Differences in Physician Usage among the Elderly Poor in the United States," *Research in Social Stratification and Mobility* 30, no. 2 (2012): 203–217; and Corey M. Abramson and Martín Sánchez-Jankowski, "Inequality, Race, and Emergency Room Use among Older Americans Living in Poverty" (working paper, Faculty of Sociology, University of Arizona, Tucson).

10. The way overlapping inequalities shape everyday life and identity is a topic that has also been examined by intersectional theorists and feminists. See for example, Kimberle Crenshaw, "Demarginalizing the Intersection of Race and Sex: A Black Feminist Critique of Antidiscrimination Doctrine, Feminist Theory, and Antiracist Politics," *University of Chicago Legal Forum* 140 (1989): 139–167; Kimberle Crenshaw, "Mapping the Margins: Intersectionality, Identity Politics, and Violence against Women of Color," *Stanford Law Review* 43, no. 6 (1991): 1241–1299; and Patricia Hill Collins, *Black Feminist Thought*, 2nd ed. (New York: Routledge, 2000). See also Katherine Mason, "Social Stratification and the Body: Gender, Race, and Class," *Sociology Compass* 7/8 (2013): 686–698; as well as Rachel Kahn Best, et al., "Multiple Disadvantages: An Empirical Test of Intersectionality

Theory in EEO Litigation," *Law and Society Review* 45, no. 4 (2011): 991–1025.

11. See S. Jay Olshansky et al., "Differences in Life Expectancy Due to Race and Educational Differences Are Widening, and Many May Not Catch Up," *Health Affairs* 31, no. 8 (2012): 1803–1813.

12. See Mel Bartley, *Health Inequality: An Introduction to Concepts, Theories and Methods* (Cambridge, MA, Polity, 2004); Matthew E. Dupre, "Educational Differences in Age-Related Patterns of Disease: Reconsidering the Cumulative Disadvantage and Age-as-Leveler Hypotheses," *Journal of Health and Social Behavior* 48 (2007): 1–15; House et al., "Aging and Health," 1994; and Scott M. Lynch, "Explaining Life Course and Cohort Variation in the Relationship between Education and Health: The Role of Income," *Journal of Health and Social Behavior* 47 (2006): 324–338. There is also a growing body of evidence, employing methods ranging from statistical analyses to the measurement of telomere length in cells, that shows the bodies of the disadvantaged age faster in the biological sense. For more on differences in the timing of aging and its causes, see Teresa E. Seeman et al., "Social Relationships, Gender, and Allostatic Load across Two Age Cohorts," *Psychosomatic Medicine* 64, no. 3 (2002): 395–406; Pamela Herd, Brian Goesling, and James S. House, "Socioeconomic Position and Health: The Differential Effects of Education Versus Income on the Onset Versus Progression of Health Problems," *Journal of Health and Social Behavior* 48 (2007): 223–238; Debra Umberson, Robert Crosnoe, and Corinne Reczek, "Social Relationships and Health Behavior across Life Course," *Annual Review of Sociology* 36 (2010): 139–157; and David F. Warner and Mark D. Hayward, "Early-Life Origins of the Race Gap in Men's Mortality," *Journal of Health and Social Behavior* 47, no. 3 (2006): 209–226. For information on telomere length and its relation to aging, see Athanase Benetos et al., "Telomere Length as an Indicator of Biological Aging: The Gender Effect and Relation with Pulse Pressure and Pulse Wave Velocity," *Hypertension* 37 (2001): 381–385; and Geraldine Aubert and Peter M. Landsdorp, "Telomeres and Aging," *Physiological Review* 88, no. 2 (2008): 557–579.

For a review and elaboration of the literature showing how socioeconomic inequalities are a "fundamental cause" of health disparities, see Jeremy Freese and Karen Lutfey, "Fundamental Causality: Challenges of an Animating Concept for Medical Sociology," in *Handbook of the Sociology of Health, Illness, and Healing,* eds. Bernice A. Pescosolido et al. (New York: Springer, 2011), 67–82. For an earlier articulation of this perspective, see Bruce G. Link and Jo C. Phelan, "Social Conditions as Fundamental Causes of Disease," *Journal of Health and Social Behavior* 35 (1995): 80–94. See also Christopher J. L. Murray et al., "Eight Americas: Investigating Mortality Disparities across Races, Counties, and Race-Counties in the United States," *PLoS Medicine* 3, no. 9 (2006): 1513–1524.

13. See James S. House, Paula M. Lantz, and Pamela Herd, "Continuity and Change in the Social Stratification of Aging and Health over the Life

Course: Evidence from a Nationally Representative Longitudinal Study from 1986 to 2001/2002 (Americans' Changing Lives Study)," *Journals of Gerontology, Series B: Psychological Sciences and Social Sciences* 60, Special Issue 2 (2005): 15–26; see also Diane S. Lauderdale, "Education and Survival: Birth Cohort, Period, and Age Effects," *Demography* 38, no. 4 (2001): 551–561; Pamela Herd, "Do Functional Health Inequalities Decrease in Old Age?: Educational Status and Functional Decline among the 1931–1941 Birth Cohort," *Research on Aging* 28, no. 3 (2006): 375–392; and Jinyoung Kim and Richard Miech, "The Black-White Difference in Age Trajectories of Functional Health over the Life Course," *Social Science and Medicine* 68, no. 4 (2009): 717–725. For a recent work examining the crossover effect, see Jessica M. Sautter et al., "Socioeconomic Status and the Black–White Mortality Crossover," *American Journal of Public Health* 102, no. 8 (2012): 1566–1571. See also David E. Hayes-Bautista et al., "The 'Browning' of the Graying of America: Diversity in the Elderly Population and Policy Implications," *Generations* 26, no. 3 (2002): 15–24.

14. See Timothy Owens and Richard Settersten Jr., "New Frontiers in Socialization: An Introduction," in *Advances in Life Course Research: New Frontiers in Socialization,* eds. Richard Settersten Jr. and Timothy Owens, vol. 7 (Oxford: Elsevier, 2002), 3–11. See also Andrea E. Willson and Kim M. Shuey, "Cumulative Advantage Processes as Mechanisms of Inequality in Life Course Health," *American Journal of Sociology* 112, no. 6 (2007): 1886–1924; Lynch, "Explaining Life Course," 2006, 324–338; and Kim M. Shuey and Andrea E. Willson, "Cumulative Disadvantage and Black-White Disparities in Life-Course Health Trajectories," *Research on Aging* 30, no. 2 (2008): 200–225. For a recent example, see Ryan K. Masters, "Uncrossing the US Black-White Mortality Crossover: The Role of Cohort Forces in Life Course Mortality Risk," *Demography* 49, no. 3 (2012): 773–796. For a history of the life-course perspective on inequality, see Glen H. Elder, Monica Kirkpatrick Johnson, and Robert Crosnoe, "The Emergence and Development of Life Course Theory," in *Handbook of the Life Course,* eds. Jeylan T. Mortimer and Michael J. Shanahan (New York: Springer, 2003): 3–19. For more on the "rising importance" effect, see Brian Goesling, "The Rising Significance of Education for Health?" *Social Forces* 85, no. 4 (2007): 1622–1644; Jinyoung Kim, "Intercohort Trends in the Relationship between Education and Health," *Journal of Aging and Health* 20, no. 6 (2008): 671–693; John Mirowsky and Catherine E. Ross, "Education and Self-Rated Health: Cumulative Advantage and Its Rising Importance," *Research on Aging* 30, no. 1 (2008): 93–122. See also Dupre, "Educational Differences," 2007; and Scott M. Lynch, "Cohort and Life-Course Patterns in the Relationship between Education and Health: A Hierarchical Approach," *Demography* 40 (2003): 309–331.

15. For two ethnographic exceptions that examine these issues, see Elena Portacolone, "The Notion of Precariousness among Older Adults Living Alone in the US," *Journal of Aging Studies* 27, no. 2 (2013): 166–174; and Katherine S. Newman's contemporary account of urban inequality in late

life: *A Different Shade of Gray: Midlife and Beyond in the Inner City* (New York: New Press, 2004). See also Arlie Russell Hochschild, *The Unexpected Community* (Englewood Cliffs, NJ: Prentice Hall, 1973); and Judith Noemi Freidenberg, *Growing Old in El Barrio* (New York: New York University Press, 2000).

16. Conventional wisdom in the biomedical community explains biological aging, or senescence, in terms of the biological organism as "the eventual failure of maintenance" in the cells, tissues, and organs that allow an organism to stay alive. Put more simply, aging is the process whereby living beings "wear out" and "break down" over time. However, as social scientists have argued since the time of Durkheim, when the organisms being studied are human bodies operating within societies, the cause, effect, and experiences of "wearing out" and "breaking down" become sociological topics as well. For the biology of aging, see Robin Holliday, "Aging Is No Longer an Unsolved Problem in Biology," *Annals of the New York Academy of Sciences* 1067 (2006): 1–9. See also Suresh I. S. Rattan, "Theories of Biological Aging: Genes, Proteins, and Free Radicals," *Free Radical Research* 40, no. 12 (2006): 1230–1238. As Holliday notes, on a biological level senescence is a complex and multi-causal process. As in any element of science, there is no absolute consensus about how all aspects of aging work. However, the statement above is a point of much more agreement than contention.

Even within the scientific disciplines that powerfully shape our understanding of the world, opposing perspectives compete with one another. For more on this point, see John A. Vincent, "Ageing Contested: Anti-Ageing Science and the Cultural Construction of Old Age," *Sociology* 40, no. 4 (2006): 681–698. For the classical sociological discussion of scientific paradigms, see Thomas S. Kuhn, *The Structure of Scientific Revolutions,* 3rd ed. (Chicago: University of Chicago Press, 1996).

On the sociological side, in her recent book examining how Americans over eighty-five construct meaningful lives, Meika Loe well makes an important observation when she notes, "Aging is a universal human experience, a bodily process, a social process, and a process that is different for everyone" (Loe, *Aging Our Way,* 2011, 414). For an overview of theories on aging, see W. Andrew Achenbaum, "A Metahistorical Perspective on Theories of Aging," in *Handbook of Theories of Aging,* ed. Vern L. Bengtson et al., 2nd ed. (New York: Springer, 2009), 25–38. Achenbaum notes that reductionism and dichotomization are not limited to theories of aging, but theories of aging are indeed characterized by these features. For a critical review of this debate, see Vincent, "Ageing Contested," 2006. See also *The Futures of Old Age,* eds. John A. Vincent, Chris Phillipson, and Murna Downs (London: Sage Publications, 2006); Sharon R. Kaufman, *The Ageless Self: Sources of Meaning in Late Life* (Madison: University of Wisconsin Press, 1994); and Richard C. Atchley, "Retirement and Leisure Participation: Continuity or Crisis?" *Gerontologist* 11, no. 1 (1971): 13–17. See also the classic debate between Hochschild, *The Unexpected Community,* 1973, and Elaine Cumming and William Earl Henry, *Growing Old (Aging and Old Age)* (Manchester, NH: Ayer, 1979).

17. As discussed in the sections above, there is an ever-growing body of evidence showing the effect of social circumstances both in aging and health generally. Although sometimes neglected, the way these circumstances and the division of labor shape biology has been a concern of sociologists since the time of Durkheim. For classical statements of this latter point, see Pierre Bourdieu, *Distinction: A Social Critique of the Judgement of Taste* (Cambridge, MA: Harvard University Press, 1984); and Bryan S. Turner, *The Body and Society: Explorations in Social Theory,* 3rd ed. (London: Sage Publications Ltd., 2008). For effects on aging in particular, see Matilda White Riley, "Overview and Highlights of a Sociological Perspective," in *Human Development and the Life Course: Multidisciplinary Perspectives,* eds. Aage B. Sorensen, Franz E. Weinert, and Lonnie R. Sherrod (Hillsdale, NJ: Lawrence Erlbaum, 1986), 153–175; *Sociology of Age Stratification (Aging and Society),* eds. Matilda White Riley, Marilyn E. Johnson, and Anne Foner, 3rd ed. (New York: Russell Sage Foundation, 1972); and Calasanti and Slevin, *Gender, Social Inequalities,* 2001. For a recent synthesis, see Mason, "Stratification and the Body," 2013.

18. Sociologist Charles Tilly famously coined the term "durable inequality" in his book of the same name as a way of referring to persistent categorical distinctions that are reproduced in light of social change (such as race, and, as I argue, age). See Charles Tilly, *Durable Inequality* (Berkeley: University of California Press, 1999). See also Riley, Johnson, and Foner, *Age Stratification,* 1972.

19. See, for instance, James J. Dowd, "Reification of Age: Age Stratification Theory and the Passing of the Autonomous Subject," *Journal of Aging Studies* 1, no. 4 (1987): 317–335.

20. Sociologists have long charted how social forces and institutions—for example, an unequal educational system, health disparities, uneven patterns of law enforcement and incarceration, a lopsided distribution of neighborhood resources, inequalities in people's social networks, residential segregation, and institutional discrimination—produce unequal outcomes. For evidence that substantial inequalities in income, race, and education persist in America, see Douglas S. Massey, *Categorically Unequal: The American Stratification System* (New York: Russell Sage Foundation, 2007). See also Elizabeth A. Armstrong and Laura T. Hamilton, *Paying for the Party: How College Maintains Inequality* (Cambridge, MA: Harvard University Press, 2013). For a review of the changing historical form of persistent inequalities in American society, see Claude S. Fischer and Mike Hout, *Century of Difference: How America Changed in the Last One Hundred Years* (New York: Russell Sage Foundation, 2006). For a general review of the sources and effects of social inequality, see Neckerman, *Social Inequality,* 2004. For a review of the sources and outcomes of stratification, see Grusky, *Social Stratification,* 2001; Stephen J. Rose and Scott Winship, "Ups and Downs: Does the American Economy Still Promote Upward Mobility?" Economic Mobility Project, The Pew Charitable Trusts, 2009; Ronald J. Breiger, "The Social Class Structure of

Occupational Mobility," *American Journal of Sociology* 87 (1981): 578–611; Breen and Jonsson, "Inequality of Opportunity," 2005; Mary Corcoran, "Rags to Rags: Poverty and Mobility in the United States," *Annual Review of Sociology* 21 (1995): 237–267; Gøsta Esping-Andersen, "Unequal Opportunities and the Mechanisms of Social Inheritance," in *Generational Income Mobility in North America and Europe,* ed. Miles Corak (Cambridge: Cambridge University Press, 2004), 289–314; Dalton Conley, *Being Black, Living in the Red: Race, Wealth, and Social Policy in America* (Berkeley: University of California Press, 1999); and Michael Hout and Thomas A. DiPrete, "What We Have Learned: RC28's Contributions to Knowledge about Social Stratification," *Research in Social Stratification and Mobility* 24 (2006): 1–20.

21. See Freese and Lutfey, "Fundamental Causality," 2011, 67. For a general overview of the fundamental causes of health disparity, see Link and Phelan, "Social Conditions," 1995; and Jo C. Phelan and Bruce G. Link, "Controlling Disease and Creating Disparities: A Fundamental Cause Perspective," *Journals of Gerontology, Series B: Psychological Sciences and Social Sciences* 60, no. S2 (2005): S27–S33.

For a general discussion of evidence that substantial inequalities in income, race, and education persist in America, see Massey, *Categorically Unequal,* 2007. For historical information on persistent inequalities in American society see Fischer and Hout, *Century of Difference,* 2006. For information on wealth, jobs, and mobility, as well as their link to health, see Link and Phelan, "Social Conditions," 1995; Conley, *Being Black,* 1999; and Neckerman, *Social Inequality,* 2004. See also George Howard et al., "Race, Socioeconomic Status, and Cause-Specific Mortality," *Annals of Epidemiology* 10, no. 4 (2000): 214–223; and David R. Williams and Chiquita Collins, "US Socioeconomic and Racial Differences in Health: Patterns and Explanations," *Annual Review of Sociology* 21 (1995): 349–386.

22. See Alberto Palloni and Carolina Milesi, "Economic Achievement, Inequalities and Health Disparities: The Intervening Role of Early Health Status," *Research in Social Stratification and Mobility* 24 (2006): 21–40; David R. Williams, "The Health of US Racial and Ethnic Populations," *Journals of Gerontology, Series B: Psychological Sciences and Social Sciences* 60 (2005): S53–S62; and Williams and Collins, "Socioeconomic and Racial Differences," 1995. For a review of mobility and illness, see Nancy E. Adler and Katherine Newman, "Socioeconomic Disparities in Health: Pathways and Policies," *Health Affairs* 21, no. 2 (2002): 60–76.

For information on childhood illness and life trajectory, see Mark D. Hayward and Bridget K. Gorman, "The Long Arm of Childhood: The Influence of Early-Life Social Conditions on Men's Mortality," *Gerontology* 41, no. 1 (2004): 87–107; Jo C. Phelan, Bruce G. Link, and Parisa Tehranifar, "Social Conditions as Fundamental Causes of Health Inequalities: Theory, Evidence, and Policy Implications," *Journal of Health and Social Behavior* 51 Suppl. (2010): S28–S40; and Steven Haas, "Trajectories of Functional Health: The 'Long

Arm' of Childhood Health and Socioeconomic Factors," *Social Science and Medicine* 66, no. 4 (2008): 849–861. See also Roberta Spalter-Roth, Terri Ann Lowenthal, and Mercedes Rubio, "Race, Ethnicity, and the Health of Americans," *ASA Series on How Race and Ethnicity Matter,* ed. Roberta Spalter-Roth (American Sociological Association, 2005): 1–16; and Catherine E. Ross and John Mirowsky, "Neighborhood Socioeconomic Status and Health: Context or Composition?" *City and Community* 7 (2008): 163–179.

23. For information on macrostructural and institutional factors on health, see Fred C. Pampel, Patrick M. Krueger, and Justin T. Denney, "Socioeconomic Disparities in Health Behaviors," *Annual Review of Sociology* 36 (2010): 349–370.

24. See Massey, *Categorically Unequal,* 2007; Fischer and Hout, *Century of Difference,* 2006; and Armstrong and Hamilton, *Paying for the Party,* 2013. See also Paul Farmer, *Infections and Inequalities: The Modern Plague* (Berkeley: University of California Press, 1999); Amartya Sen, *Resources, Values, and Development* (Cambridge, MA: Harvard University Press, 1984); *Unequal Treatment: Confronting Racial and Ethnic Disparities in Health Care,* eds. Brian D. Smedley, Adrienne Y. Stith, and Alan R. Nelson (Washington, DC: National Academies Press, 2002); Bartley, *Health Inequality,* 2004; Kevin Fiscella et al., "Disparities in Health Care by Race, Ethnicity, and Language among the Insured: Findings from a National Sample," *Medical Care* 40, no. 1 (2002): 52–59; and Spalter-Roth, Lowenthal, and Rubio, "Health of Americans," 2005.

On responses to physical issues, see Icek Ajzen, "The Theory of Planned Behavior," *Organizational Behavior and Human Decision Processes* 50 (1991): 179–211; Ronald M. Anderson, "Revisiting the Behavioral Model and Access to Medical Care: Does it Matter?" *Journal of Health and Social Behavior* 36, no. 1 (1995): 1–10; and Seth M. Noar and Rick S. Zimmerman, "Health Behavior Theory and Cumulative Knowledge Regarding Health Behaviors: Are We Moving in the Right Direction?" *Health Education Research* 20, no. 3 (2005): 275–290.

25. See Spalter-Roth, Lowenthal, and Rubio, "Health of Americans," 2005; David R. Williams and Chiquita Collins, "Racial Residential Segregation: A Fundamental Cause of Racial Disparities in Health," *Public Health Reports* 116, no. 5 (2001): 404–417; Massey, *Categorically Unequal,* 2007; and William Julius Wilson, *When Work Disappears: The World of the New Urban Poor* (New York: Vintage Books, 1996). For information on how neighborhoods impact health care, see James B. Kirby and Toshiko Kaneda, "Neighborhood Socioeconomic Disadvantage and Access to Health Care," *Journal of Health and Social Behavior* 46 (2005): 5–31. See also Eric Klinenberg, *Heat Wave: A Social Autopsy of Disaster in Chicago* (Chicago: University of Chicago Press, 2002); and Gary W. Evans and Susan Saegert, "Residential Crowding in the Context of Inner City Poverty," in *Theoretical Perspectives in Environment-Behavior Research,* eds. Seymour Wapner et al. (New York: Kluwer Academic/Plenum, 2000), 320.

On the importance of context, see also Catherine E. Ross and John Mirowsky, "Neighborhood Disadvantage, Disorder, and Health," *Journal of Health and Social Behavior* 42, no. 3 (2001): 258–276; Robert J. Sampson, "Neighborhood-Level Context and Health," in *Neighborhoods and Health*, eds. Ichiro Kawachi and Lisa F. Berkman, (New York: Oxford University Press, 2003), 132–146; and Ross and Mirowsky, "Context or Composition," 2008. On the qualitative side, see Martín Sánchez-Jankowski, *Cracks in the Pavement: Social Change and Resilience in Poor Neighborhoods* (Berkeley: University of California Press, 2008); Robert J. Sampson, *Great American City: Chicago and the Enduring Neighborhood Effect* (Chicago: University of Chicago Press, 2012); Claude S. Fischer, "Showing That Neighborhoods Matter: Review Essay on Sampson, *Great American City*," *City and Community* 12, no. 1 (2013): 7–12; and David J. Harding, *Living the Drama: Community, Conflict, and Culture among Inner-City Boys* (Chicago: University of Chicago Press, 2010).

26. In this book, I use the term "culture" to refer to three connected components: *shared meanings* that make the world comprehensible, *inputs* that direct action toward particular ends (e.g., cognitive orientations, motivations, and values), and *collective tools and strategies* that influence, in conjunction with larger social structures, whether particular ends can be reached. For a fuller treatment of my use of the term, and a model of the structural contingencies under which different elements most strongly influence action and outcomes, see Corey M. Abramson, "From 'Either-Or' to 'When and How': A Context-Dependent Model of Culture in Action," *Journal for the Theory of Social Behaviour* 42, no. 2 (2012): 155–180. See also Herbert J. Gans, "Against Culture versus Structure," *Identities: Global Studies in Culture and Power* 19, no. 2 (2012): 125–134; and William H. Sewell Jr., "A Theory of Structure: Duality, Agency, and Transformation," *American Journal of Sociology* 98, no. 1 (1992): 1–29. For some key examples of how cultural and social aspects of social life are intertwined, see Bourdieu, *In Other Words*, 1990; Ann Swidler, *Talk of Love: How Culture Matters* (Chicago: University of Chicago Press, 2001); and Stephen Vaisey, "Motivation and Justification: Towards a Dual-Process Theory of Culture in Action," *American Journal of Sociology* 114, no. 6 (2009): 1675–1715. For a discussion and admirable attempt at overcoming structure/culture dualisms, see Sewell, "A Theory of Structure," 1992.

For the classic statement of the culture of poverty, see Oscar Lewis, *Five Families: Mexican Case Studies in the Culture of Poverty* (New York: Basic Books, 1975). For a discussion of how the specter of the culture of poverty continues to shape current debate, see also Stephen Vaisey, "What People Want: Rethinking Poverty, Culture, and Educational Attainment," *Annals of the American Academy of Political and Social Science* 629, no. 1 (2010): 75–101; and Michael Jindra, "The Dilemma of Equality and Diversity," *Current Anthropology* 55, no. 3 (2014): 316–334.

27. See Lewis, *Five Families*, 1975; see also the Moynihan report: US Department of Labor, "The Negro Family: The Case for National Action," Office of Policy Planning and Research, Mar. 1965, http://www.blackpast.org /primary/moynihan-report-1965.

   A classic statement of the way culture can function as a resource or tool kit is provided by Swidler in her foundational article "Culture in Action: Symbols and Strategies," *American Sociological Review* 51, no. 2 (1986): 273–386; and expanded in her book *Talk of Love*, 2001. See also Daniel Dohan, *The Price of Poverty: Money, Work, and Culture in the Mexican American Barrio* (Berkeley: University of California Press, 2003); Annette Lareau, *Unequal Childhoods: Class, Race, and Family Life* (Berkeley: University of California Press, 2003); Bourdieu, *Distinction*, 1984; Freidenberg, *El Barrio*, 2000; and Sánchez-Jankowski, *Cracks in the Pavement*, 2008.

28. For the precariousness of seniors living alone, see Klinenberg, *Heat Wave*, 2002; Elena Portacolone, "The Myth of Independence for Older Americans Living Alone in the Bay Area of San Francisco: A Critical Reflection," *Aging and Society* 31 (2011): 803–828; and Portacolone, "Precariousness," 2013.

   Scholars frequently invoke the term "social capital" to highlight the way interpersonal ties function as a resource that varies between people and groups. Social capital has been shown to affect concrete outcomes ranging from the ability to secure health care to whether one gets a job. For more on the various definitions and invocations of this term, see Alejandro Portes, "Social Capital: Its Origins and Applications in Modern Sociology," *Annual Review of Sociology* 24 (1998): 1–24. While this term has a strong following in the social sciences, it has also been criticized for being overly broad and ill-defined in practical terms, as well as thin and "marketizing" in its ability to strip key subjective characteristics from interpersonal relationships. See Claude S. Fischer, "Bowling Alone: What's the Score?" *Social Networks* 27 (2005): 155–167; and Hochschild, *Commercialization*, 2003. For a classic example of social capital, see Emile Durkheim, *Suicide: A Study in Sociology*, Reissue ed. (New York: Free Press, 1997). More recent iterations include Mark S. Granovetter, "The Strength of Weak Ties," *American Journal of Sociology* 78, no. 6 (1973): 1360–1380; and Claude S. Fischer, *America Calling: A Social History of the Telephone to 1940* (Berkeley: University of California Press, 1994). For a summary of new directions, see Jennifer Schultz and Ronald L. Breiger, "The Strength of Weak Culture," *Poetics* 38, no. 6 (2010): 610–624; and Mark A. Pachucki and Ronald L. Breiger, "Cultural Holes: Beyond Relationality in Social Networks and Culture," *Annual Review of Sociology* 36, no. 1 (June 2010): 205–224.

   See also Shari S. Bassuk, Thomas A. Glass, and Lisa F. Berkman, "Social Disengagement and Incident Cognitive Decline in Community-Dwelling Elderly Persons," *Annals of Internal Medicine* 131, no. 3 (1999): 165–173; Robyn A. Findlay, "Interventions to Reduce Social Isolation amongst Older People: Where Is the Evidence?" *Ageing and Society* 23 (2003): 647–658; Joe Tomaka,

Sharon Thompson, and Rebecca Palacios, "The Relation of Social Isolation, Loneliness, and Social Support to Disease Outcomes among the Elderly," *Journal of Aging and Health* 18, no. 3 (2006): 359–384; and Nan Sook Park, "The Relationship of Social Engagement to Psychological Well-Being of Older Adults in Assisted Living Facilities," *Journal of Applied Gerontology* 28, no. 4 (2009): 461–481.

29. More nuanced approaches to social interaction are gaining traction. See for instance Breiger, "Social Class Structure," 1981; Pachucki and Breiger, "Cultural Holes," 2010; and Sandra Susan Smith, "A Test of Sincerity: How Black and Latino Service Workers Make Decisions about Making Referrals," *Annals of the American Academy of Political and Social Sciences* 629, no. 1 (2010): 30–52. For more on the point of the side effects of social interaction, see Fischer, *Still Connected: Family and Friends in America since 1970* (New York: Russell Sage Foundation, 2011), which shows that although the quantity of some forms of social ties may have declined during the last thirty years, the quality has improved in several arenas, and statements about the decline of American community are overblown.

30. Mario Small's ethnographic work provides a notable exception to considerations of linkage by highlighting the importance of context in looking at the development and implementation of social ties. See Mario Luis Small, *Villa Victoria: The Transformation of Social Capital in a Boston Barrio* (Chicago: University of Chicago Press, 2004); and Mario Luis Small, *Unanticipated Gains: Origins of Network Inequality in Everyday Life* (New York: Oxford University Press, 2009). For references to social interaction and health, see Peggy A. Thoits, "Mechanisms Linking Social Ties and Support to Physical and Mental Health," *Journal of Health and Social Behavior* 52, no. 2 (2011): 145–161. The importance of the relationship between context and network structure is also made by Barbara Entwisle et al., "Networks and Contexts: Variation in the Structure of Social Ties," *American Journal of Sociology* 112, no. 5 (2007): 1495–1533, albeit in a more structural sense. Klinenberg's work *Heat Wave,* 2002, makes this point as well. Specifically, Klinenberg shows the importance of context to different levels of social connectedness and consequently different patterns of life and death among Chicago residents. Still, his "social autopsy" was necessarily conducted after the event. We can infer the way the higher level and type of connectedness held by Latinos influenced their behaviors during that heat wave, but we do not have direct observations. My data complement these findings by showing how social connectedness influences everyday life across a variety of settings.

31. As discussed in the section on how to define old age, numeric cutoffs are necessarily arbitrary, and discerning the social boundaries of "old age" in different contexts is a key aspect of this study. Still, the practical issues involved in producing social research typically make including arbitrary chronological cutoffs an unfortunate necessity. Sixty-five, the age at which Medicare takes full effect, is often invoked as the cutoff for old age. My sample is slightly broader. Still, this work is guided by the assumption that

age is not just a number, and field observations included younger individuals. Further, all research protocols were reviewed and approved by the university's institutional review board.

32. I also attempted to address the issue of examining prior inequality by collecting life-history data in interviews.

This strategy parallels that used by Mario Small in *Villa Victoria* (2004) examining the transformation of social capital, and *Unanticipated Gains* (2009) on network inequality. This stands in contrast to the community-focused tradition of urban ethnography often associated with the classic work of scholars such as Herbert J. Gans, *Urban Villagers: Group and Class in the Life of Italian-Americans* (New York: Free Press, 1982); Gerald Suttles, *The Social Order of the Slum: Ethnicity and Territory in the Inner City* (Chicago: University of Chicago Press, 1970); and William Foote Whyte, *Street Corner Society: The Social Structure of an Italian Slum* (Chicago: University of Chicago Press, 1993); and the contemporary approach of scholars such as Sánchez-Jankowski, *Cracks in the Pavement,* 2008.

For examples of sociological studies pointing to the importance of neighborhoods, see Sánchez-Jankowski, *Cracks in the Pavement,* 2008; Fischer, "Neighborhoods Matter," 2013; Sampson, *Great American City,* 2012; Small, *Unanticipated Gains,* 2009; Harding, *Living the Drama,* 2010; and Ross and Mirowsky, "Context or Composition," 2008.

1. "Old Is a Different Animal Altogether"

1. The reader will recall that two of the communities are poor (Rockport and Elm Flats), and two are middle class (Baygardens and Cedar Hills). It is worth reiterating a point made in the introduction: though "James" and "Lila" are pseudonyms used to protect the identities of the seniors involved in this study, they are real people rather than rhetorical composites. Consequently, their cases reflect observed empirical differences rather than hypothetical or literary illustrations of a concept.

2. For more on historical forms of American inequality and their change over time, see Claude S. Fischer and Mike Hout, *Century of Difference: How America Changed in the Last One Hundred Years* (New York: Russell Sage Foundation, 2006); and Douglas S. Massey, *Categorically Unequal: The American Stratification System* (New York: Russell Sage Foundation, 2007).

3. Per standard publisher practices and the analytical focus on behavior and narrative, vocalizations such as *um* and *uh* are left out of transcribed quotations for readability.

4. An overwhelming body of evidence shows that social inequalities shape how long people from different backgrounds and resource levels live. Further, voluminous research has shown that the timing, severity, and concrete manifestation of the physical challenges associated with aging are a function of differences in the resources available to specific individuals and the social groups they constitute (i.e., a part of larger processes of

cumulative disadvantage). See Corey M. Abramson and Martín Sánchez-Jankowski, "Racial Differences in Physician Usage among the Elderly Poor in the United States," *Research in Social Stratification and Mobility* 30, no. 2 (2012): 203–217; Mel Bartley, *Health Inequality: An Introduction to Concepts, Theories and Methods* (Cambridge, Polity Press, 2004); Matthew E. Dupre, "Educational Differences in Age-Related Patterns of Disease: Reconsidering the Cumulative Disadvantage and Age-as-Leveler Hypotheses," *Journal of Health and Social Behavior* 48 (2007): 1–15; James S. House et al., "The Social Stratification of Aging and Health," *Journal of Health and Social Behavior* 35 (1994): 213–234; and Scott M. Lynch, "Explaining Life Course and Cohort Variation in the Relationship between Education and Health: The Role of Income," *Journal of Health and Social Behaviour* 47 (2006): 324–338. See also Jeremy Freese and Karen Lutfey, "Fundamental Causality: Challenges of an Animating Concept for Medical Sociology," in *Handbook of the Sociology of Health, Illness, and Healing: A Blueprint for the 21st Century,* eds. Bernice A. Pescosolido et al. (New York: Springer, 2011), 67–82; Jo C. Phelan, Bruce G Link, and Parisa Tehranifar, "Social Conditions as Fundamental Causes of Health Inequalities: Theory, Evidence, and Policy Implications," supplement, *Journal of Health and Social Behavior* 51 (2010): S28–S40; Lisa F. Berkman et al., "From Social Integration to Health: Durkheim in the New Millennium," *Social Science and Medicine* 51, no. 6 (2000): 843–857; Teresa E. Seeman et al., "Social Relationships, Gender, and Allostatic Load Across Two Age Cohorts," *Psychosomatic Medicine* 64, no. 3 (2002): 395–406; Pamela Herd, Brian Goesling, and James S. House, "Socioeconomic Position and Health: The Differential Effects of Education Versus Income on the Onset Versus Progression of Health Problems," *Journal of Health and Social Behavior* 48 (2007): 223–238; and Debra Umberson, Robert Crosnoe, and Corinne Reczek, "Social Relationships and Health Behavior across Life Course," *Annual Review of Sociology* 36 (2010): 139–157.

5. Even changes on the genetic level make the elderly more vulnerable to diseases such as cancer. For the biology of aging, see Robin Holliday, "Aging Is No Longer an Unsolved Problem in Biology," *Annals of the New York Academy of Sciences* 1067 (2006): 1–9; and Suresh I. S. Rattan, "Theories of Biological Aging: Genes, Proteins, and Free Radicals," *Free Radical Research* 40, no. 12 (2006): 1230–1238. The importance of physical processes in the social experience of aging is seen even in more optimistic accounts of growing old; see, for example, Meika Loe, *Aging Our Way: Lessons for Living from 85 and Beyond* (New York: Oxford University Press, 2011).

6. It is important to acknowledge the complexity of these processes—including how the politics and practices of medical categorization can shape inequality and the ways socially produced notions of health can take on a normative dimension that can marginalize people. My point here is not to endorse biological determinism or reinforce youth and health as unquestioned norms against which all else should be judged, nor is it to attack those who see aging in these terms. Rather, as a scholar of stratification, I simply aim

to show how problems of everyday life connected to physiological changes created concrete behavioral challenges for seniors across the neighborhoods and in the process became a key aspect of stratification in everyday life.

For more on the critiques of biomedicalization, see Carroll L. Estes, Simon Biggs, and Chris Phillipson, *Social Theory, Social Policy, and Ageing: Critical Perspectives* (Berkshire, UK: Open University Press, 2003); Carroll L. Estes and Elizabeth A. Binney, "The Biomedicalization of Aging: Dangers and Dilemmas," *Gerontologist* 29, no. 5 (1989): 587–596; Adele E. Clarke et al., eds., *Biomedicalization: Technoscience, Health, and Illness in the US* (Durham, NC: Duke University Press, 2010); and Adele E. Clarke et al., "Biomedicalization: Technoscientific Transformations of Health, Illness, and US Biomedicine," *American Sociological Review* 68 (2003): 161–194. See Katherine Mason, "Social Stratification and the Body: Gender, Race, and Class," *Sociology Compass* 7/8 (2013): 686–698, for a review of how growing older is inseparable from the physical processes of aging. See also Barbara Hulka and John R. Wheat, "Patterns of Utilization: The Patient Perspective," *Medical Care* 23, no. 5 (1985): 438–460; Marilyn J. Field and Christine K. Cassel eds., *Approaching Death: Improving Care at the End of Life* (Washington, DC: National Academy Press, 1997); and Crystal Dea Moore and Meika Loe, "From Nursing Home to Green House: Changing Contexts of Elder Care in the United States," *Journal of Applied Gerontology* 31, no. 6 (2011): 755–763.

To further clarify, my focus on behavioral challenges and what they allow us to learn about stratification is not meant to suggest that the expansion of Western models of medical categorization are unimportant avenues of inquiry, or even to challenge the notion that they represent a fundamentally new form of power and social control (e.g., Michel Foucault, *The History of Sexuality, Volume 1: An Introduction* [New York: Vintage Books, 1980]). The point is simply to show how physical issues create problems of social action in stratified social systems, even if we can understand them only in terms of cultural-cognitive systems. For a recent critique on the dangers of taking biological deterministic distinctions as normative, see Mason, "Social Stratification and the Body," 2013. See also Estes, Biggs, and Phillipson, *Social Theory, Social Policy*, 2003; Estes and Binney, "Biomedicalization of Aging," 1989; Adele E. Clarke et al., eds., *Biomedicalization: Technoscience, Health, and Illness in the US* (Durham, NC: Duke University Press, 2010); and Clarke et al., "Technoscientific Transformations," 2003.

7. This is due largely to a combination of neuromuscular and circulatory factors. While there are debates about which levels of fatigue are normal versus pathological, like the other biological changes described in this section, there is generally a consensus among scientists and physicians. Of course, as the examples in this chapter show, there is great variability. For a review, see Susan B. Roberts and Irwin Rosenberg, "Nutrition and Aging: Changes in the Regulation of Energy Metabolism with Aging," *American Physiological Review* 86, no. 2 (2006): 651–667.

In a parallel example, a seventy-six-year-old woman who worked full-time (and whose identity was deeply invested in her job) noted, as you get old, "You're a little more tired. You're just a little more tired, that's all. I [still] do everything that I did when I was younger." When I asked her if she had as much energy as she used to, she simply said, "No." Later she told me that over the last year, she had worked fewer days, begun taking naps, and had been compelled to take more time off, because she was too tired to keep up with her former routine.

For relevant findings on the link between retirement, performance, and health, see Stephen E. Snyder and William N. Evans, "The Effect of Income on Mortality: Evidence from the Social Security Notch," *Review of Economics and Statistics* 88 (2006): 482–495; Beverly A. Roberts et al., "Does Retirement Influence Cognitive Performance? The Whitehall II Study," *Journal of Epidemiological Community Health* 65 (2011): 958–963; Markus Jokela et al., "From Midlife to Early Old Age: Health Trajectories Associated with Retirement," *Epidemiology* 21 (2010): 284–290; Mauricio Avendano and Ichiro Kawachi, "Why Do Americans Have Shorter Life Expectancy and Worse Health Than Do People in Other High-Income Countries?" *Annual Review of Public Health* 35 (2014): 307–325; and Ann C. Case and Christina Paxson, "Sex Differences in Morbidity and Mortality," *Demography* 42, no. 2 (2005): 189–214.

8. See, for instance, House et al., "Aging and Health," 1994; Berkman et al., "From Social Integration," 2000; Seeman et al., "Social Relationships," 2002; Katherine S. Newman, *A Different Shade of Gray: Midlife and beyond in the Inner City* (New York: New Press, 2004); Loe, *Aging Our Way*, 2011; and Barbara Myerhoff, *Number Our Days: A Triumph of Continuity and Culture among Jewish Old People in an Urban Ghetto* (New York: Touchstone, 1980).

9. As noted previously, how to conceptualize health has been problematized by sociologists. Biological changes blend together with categories shaped by social institutions. Sociologist Katherine Mason explains this well when she notes that in practice, this means "'health' [functions] as an unmarked, often invisible norm against which people with disabilities, the elderly, and other groups are often unfavorably compared." While acknowledging these issues is important, for the purpose of readability, clarity, and reference to the subjective experiences of the seniors in this study I use the term "health problems." See Mason, "Social Stratification and the Body," 2013. See also John R. Logan, Russell Ward, and Glenna Spitze, "As Old as You Feel: Age Identity in Middle and Later Life, *Social Forces* 71, no. 2 (1992): 451–467; Umberson, Crosnoe, and Reczek, "Social Relationships," 2010; Zheng Wu, Christoph M. Schimmele, and Neena L. Chappell, "Aging and Late-Life Depression," *Journal of Aging and Health* 24, no. 1 (2012): 3–28; and House et al., "Social Stratification," 1994.

10. For many seniors in this study, the weekly (or biweekly) trip to the doctor was the only time they left their homes. For those in nursing homes, trips to the hospital or other medical institutions were often the only time they left the facility. But even for seniors who were younger (i.e., aged seventy-four or

below), more socially active, and not institutionalized, health issues and their effect on organizing activity came up frequently.

For more on illness and identity, see, for instance, Cynthia M. Mathieson and Henderikus J. Stam, "Renegotiating Identity: Cancer Narratives," *Sociology of Health and Illness* 17, no. 3 (1995): 283–306; Crystal L. Park, Ianita Zlateva, and Thomas O. Blank, "Self-Identity after Cancer: 'Survivor,' 'Victim,' 'Patient,' and 'Person with Cancer,'" *Journal of General Internal Medicine* 24, no. S2 (2009): 430–435; and Vicki S. Helgeson, "Survivor Centrality among Breast Cancer Survivors: Implications for Well-Being," *Psychooncology* 20, no. 5 (2011): 517–524.

11. Even steroids used to treat other problems and reduce inflammation could make sleeping difficult, and, although they provide an immediate energy boost, lead to a lack of overall energy. It is worth noting that this is not unique to old age—physical issues, health problems, and the body more generally shape opportunities, behaviors, and outcomes over the life course. This book's concluding chapter relates this to broader sociological theories of stratification. However, as discussed above, seniors become increasingly physiologically vulnerable to these issues as they age.

There is a substantial social psychological literature on the meaning of pain within and across groups. How this plays out in everyday life is discussed in Chapter 3. For a review see Bridgett Rahim-Williams et al., "A Quantitative Review of Ethnic Group Differences in Experimental Pain Response: Do Biology, Psychology and Culture Matter?" *Pain Medicine* 13, no. 4 (2012): 522–540; R. Tyson Smith, "Pain in the Act: The Meanings of Pain among Professional Wrestlers," *Qualitative Sociology* 31 (2008): 129–148; Linda Smith-Lovin and Piotr Winkielman, "The Social Psychologies of Emotion: A Bridge That Is Not Too Far," *Social Psychology Quarterly* 73, no. 4 (2010): 327–332. See also Field and Cassel, *Approaching Death*, 1997.

12. See Loe, *Aging Our Way*, 2011, as well as Claude S. Fischer and Lauren Beresford, "Changes in Support Networks in Late Middle Age: The Extension of Gender and Educational Differences," *Journals of Gerontology, Series B Advance Access: Psychological and Social Sciences,* doi:10.1093/geronb/gbu057.

Some seniors talked about what they gain as they grow older, and examining this is extremely important. See, for instance, Arlie Russell Hochschild, *The Unexpected Community* (Englewood Cliffs, NJ: Prentice Hall, 1973). However, in this study, these instances were both rarer, more contingent, and decisively less linked to the way changes in the human body create cross-contextual issues.

13. Mobility issues varied not only among seniors but also for a given senior over a particular period of time. While shopping, one senior noted, "I hurt, but you have good days and bad days. I have arthritis." I observed that she seemed to be moving well. She said, "Yeah, it is in my shoulders today, so my legs are holding up." See also Corey M. Abramson, "Who Are the Clients? Goal Displacement in an Adult Day Care Center for Elders with Dementia," *International Journal of Aging and Human Development* 68, no. 1 (2009): 65–92.

14. Even when falls were not catastrophic, they had consequences. These consequences became an axis of inequality by shaping how seniors could act in the world as well as how they were perceived by others. Although her work is not about inequality explicitly, Meika Loe has a similar observation: "An ambulatory elder will experience age differently and thus have different needs than a wheelchair bound elder" (Loe, *Aging Our Way*, 2011), 389.

15. As individuals age, they must contend with changes in memory, even if these changes do not become a dominant structuring force in their daily lives. Again, there is a massive empirical literature in psychology, biology, and clinical sciences suggesting that the cognitive and memory declines associated with old age are observable and have a physiological dimension (rather than simply being an artifact of projected stereotypes). These literatures also show, however, that the extent to which aging affects focused versus general tasks may vary. See Shu-Chen Li, "Connecting the Many Levels and Facets of Cognitive Aging," *Current Directions in Psychological Science* 11, no. 1 (2002): 38–43; and Timothy A. Salthouse, "What and When of Cognitive Aging," *Current Directions in Psychological Science* 13, no. 4 (2004): 140–144. Cognitive sociologists have also long pointed out the importance of memory and cognition, and their biological bases for social life more generally. See, for example, Albert J. Bergesen, "Turning Durkheim on His Head: A Reply to Peterson and Bjerre," *Journal for the Theory of Social Behaviour* 42, no. 4 (2012): 485–495; and Aaron V. Cicourel, "Cognitive/Affective Processes, Social Interaction, and Social Structure as Representational Re-Descriptions: Their Contrastive Bandwidths and Spatio-Temporal Foci," *Mind and Society* 5, no. 1 (2006): 39–70.

16. There is an extensive literature that shows how and why sensory changes operate on a biological level. For a basic review see Neil J. Nusbaum, "Aging and Sensory Senescence," *Southern Medical Journal* 92, no. 3 (1999): 267–276.

17. As the chapters that follow show, there was great variability in how the elders in my study dealt with these losses. Some said it made them appreciate life and what they still had, some became preoccupied with preventing future losses, and others become fatalistic and depressed. These responses are underwritten by variation in material and cultural resources, meanings, and dispositions (the subject of Chapter 3). Interestingly, the orientations for dealing with the losses of old age line up closely with the orientations to material scarcity described by urban ethnographers; see, for example, Daniel Dohan, *The Price of Poverty: Money, Work, and Culture in the Mexican-American Barrio* (Berkeley: University of California Press, 2003); and Martín Sánchez-Jankowski, *Cracks in the Pavement: Social Change and Resilience in Poor Neighborhoods* (Berkeley: University of California Press, 2008). Perhaps this is because the structural dilemma of aging involves scarcity, but the resources that become scarce are rooted in the body.

   For more on independence as a value among seniors, see Elena Portacolone, "The Myth of Independence for Older Americans Living Alone in the Bay Area of San Francisco: A Critical Reflection." *Ageing and Society* 31 (2011): 803–828.

18. The effect where seniors were ignored was observed even when I would follow at a distance and/or try to avoid eye contact. This echoes Goffman's work on stigma. See Erving Goffman, *Stigma: Notes on the Management of Spoiled Identity* (Englewood Cliffs, NJ: Prentice Hall, 1963). See also Kenneth A. Root and Rosemarie J. Park, *Forced Out: Older Workers Confront Job Loss* (Boulder, CO: Lynne Rienner, 2008); Lynn M. Shore and Caren B. Goldberg, "Age Discrimination in the Workplace," in *Discrimination at Work: The Psychological and Organizational Bases,* eds. Robert L. Dipboye and Adrienne Colella, (Mahwah, NJ: Lawrence Erlbaum, 2005): 203–226; and Vincent J. Roscigno, Sherry Mong, and Reginald Byron, "Age Discrimination, Social Closure and Employment," *Social Forces* 86, no. 1 (2007): 313–334.

19. Wacquant and Sánchez-Jankowski show how poverty is associated with a very physical existence and habitus in urban America. See Loïc Wacquant, *Body and Soul: Notebooks of an Apprentice Boxer* (New York: Oxford University Press, 2004); and Sánchez-Jankowski, *Cracks in the Pavement,* 2008.

    For more on physical vulnerability and aging, see Eric Klinenberg, *Heat Wave: A Social Autopsy of Disaster in Chicago* (Chicago: University of Chicago Press, 2002); and Newman, *Shade of Gray,* 2004.

20. Although many seniors contested or strategically used the "sick role" in interactions with people and organizations, the classical sociological insight that certain social roles become less viable when the body breaks down was visible among and acknowledged by the seniors in my study. Consequently, seniors who faced social adaptation changes as a result of illness experienced a shared sense of loss in losing their identities as "well" individuals. For more on identity, see Miriam Bernard et al., eds., *Women Ageing: Changing Identities, Challenging Myths* (New York: Routledge, 2001); Kathleen Riach, "'Othering': Older Worker Identity in Recruitment," *Human Relations* 60, no. 11 (2007): 1701–1726; and Root and Park, *Forced Out,* 2008. For a classic reading of role and identity, see Talcott Parsons, *The Social System* (New York: Free Press, 1951).

    Of course, it is also important to recognize physical challenges are not unique to seniors. Illnesses minor and catastrophic can affect the young as well as the old. The challenges faced by those who lack traditional "able bodies" have been well documented. However, the point here is simply that as the people in this study aged, dealing with increasing health problems became a common shared fact of life that was seen as intrinsically tied to growing old. See James L. Charlton, *Nothing about Us without Us: Disability Oppression and Empowerment* (Berkeley: University of California Press, 2000); Lennard J. Davis, ed., *The Disability Studies Reader,* 3rd ed. (New York: Routledge, 2010); and Paul K. Longmore, *Why I Burned My Book and Other Essays on Disability* (Philadelphia: Temple University Press, 2003).

21. Here the physical tools available to seniors are a direct correlate to the cultural tools used to construct lines of action. I expand upon these points in Chapter 3 and this book's conclusion.

22. For similar findings, see Portacolone, "Myth of Independence," 2011.

23. Social scientists have often examined issues of bias and discrimination among seniors, showing how this functions on the macro level as an aspect of distinction and inequality. However, an additional dimension was that seniors often engaged in similar behavior when interacting with one another and negotiating status among themselves. The experiences of the seniors from the four neighborhoods I observed support this point and show how the symbolic aspects of old age combine with physical changes to reinforce distinctions among seniors. See Mason, "Social Stratification and the Body," 2013. See also Laurie Russell Hatch, "Gender and Ageism," *Generations* 29, no. 3 (2005): 19–24; Jon F. Nussbaum et al., "Ageism and Ageist Language across the Life Span: Intimate Relationships and Non-Intimate Interactions," *Journal of Social Issues* 61, no. 2 (2005): 287–305; Elias S. Cohen, "The Complex Nature of Ageism: What Is It? Who Does It? Who Perceives It?" *Gerontologist* 41, no. 5 (2001): 576–577; and Goffman, *Stigma,* 1963.

24. See Ann Swidler, *Talk of Love: How Culture Matters* (Chicago: University of Chicago Press, 2001), 201.

25. See Portacolone, "Myth of Independence," 2011.

26. These questions also precede any questions about health or the body in the interview schedule. The subjects are not primed that this is an interview on physical issues. They are told simply (and correctly) that this project is about what it is like to get older in America. For a complete copy of the interview schedule, see the methodological appendix.

27. For a similar finding on seniors and their reasons for isolation, see Klinenberg, *Heat Wave,* 2002. See also Newman, *Shade of Gray,* 2004.

28. The fact that their understandings of these processes do not necessarily invoke mind-body dualisms is important and telling. However, for the purposes of charting the concrete problems of everyday life that seniors experience, it is useful (at least briefly) to maintain the analytical (but not ontological) distinction between "physical" and "cognitive" slowing. In many ways this parallels Pierre Bourdieu's notion of habitus: socially constituted psychosocial-cognitive dispositions, ingrained through everyday life, that affect how people experience and act in the world. See Pierre Bourdieu, *In Other Words: Essays toward a Reflexive Sociology* (Stanford, CA: Stanford University Press, 1990); and *The Logic of Practice* (Stanford, CA: Stanford University Press, 1992).

29. Of course, some forms of social inquiry, such as ethnomethodology, linguistic anthropology, and cognitive sociology, have long focused on the importance of rules or rule-like invariance in seemingly everyday phenomenon. The point here is not to argue that social science should focus exclusively on these topics, but to acknowledge an often discarded insight that

seemingly mundane phenomena are essential for understanding both the universalities and contingencies of the human condition.

The predicaments experienced by seniors who grow old in America also highlight ongoing problems in contemporary social-scientific understandings of the relationship between the human body and social systems. In disciplines such as sociology and anthropology, which emphasize context and interpretation, it is important to remember that contingency is not without limits. Some aspects of life, such as coming to terms with the body's "breaking down," "wearing out," and stopping, are comparatively universal.

Even if the social solutions and tools brought to bear by different individuals and groups are different, the root problems are similar. Mason, "Social Stratification and the Body," 2013, correctly notes that the importance of the body has long been acknowledged in feminist scholarship and disability studies, but, with a few exceptions (e.g., Bourdieu), embodiment has been underacknowledged in mainstream models of stratification.

2. The Uneven Playing Field

1. For a review of the food desert literature, see Renee E. Walker, Christopher R. Keane, and Jessica G. Burke, "Disparities and Access to Healthy Food in the United States: A Review of Food Deserts Literature," *Health and Place* 16, no. 5 (2010): 876–884.

2. I use the term "context" to refer to the physical and social environments in which people go about their everyday lives. Sociologically, contexts can be thought of as overlapping meso-level social structures, constituted by cultural schemas and resource distributions that operate in a particular historical period. See Corey M. Abramson, "From 'Either-Or' to 'When and How': A Context-Dependent Model of Culture in Action," *Journal for the Theory of Social Behaviour* 42, no. 2 (2012): 155–180; and William H. Sewell Jr., "A Theory of Structure: Duality, Agency, and Transformation," *American Journal of Sociology* 98, no. 1 (1992): 1–29. The subcategories of context (e.g., structures and schemas) reflect important distinctions between characteristics of these structures, but in reality the distinction is analytical rather than ontological, as these components are mutual and overlapping.

3. For a review of the literature on the relationship between inequality, context, and health, see Catherine E. Ross and John Mirowsky, "Neighborhood Socioeconomic Status and Health: Context or Composition?" *City and Community* 7 (2008): 163–179; Brian D. Smedley, Adrienne Y. Stith, and Alan R. Nelson, *Unequal Treatment: Confronting Racial and Ethnic Disparities in Health Care* (Washington, DC: National Academies Press, 2002); and David R. Williams and Chiquita Collins, "Racial Residential Segregation: A Fundamental Cause of Racial Disparities in Health," *Public Health Reports* 116, no. 5 (2001): 404–417. For a review of the literature on access and quality of healthcare, see James B. Kirby and Toshiko Kaneda, "Neighborhood

Socioeconomic Disadvantage and Access to Health Care," *Journal of Health and Social Behavior* 46 (2005): 5–31; and Pamela Herd, Brian Goesling, and James S. House, "Socioeconomic Position and Health: The Differential Effects of Education Versus Income on the Onset Versus Progression of Health Problems," *Journal of Health and Social Behavior* 48 (2007): 223–238. For an overview of the "food deserts" literature, see Renee E. Walker, Christopher R. Keane, and Jessica G. Burke, "Disparities and Access to Healthy Food in the United States: A Review of Food Deserts Literature," *Health and Place* 16, no. 5 (2010): 876–884. For a general review of the relationship between the housing environment and health, see Mary Shaw, "Housing and Public Health," *Annual Review of Public Health* 25, no. 1 (2004): 397–418. For an example of how environmental hazards can affect everyday life, see Javier Auyero and Debora Alejandra Swistun, *Flammable: Environmental Suffering in an Argentine Shantytown* (New York: Oxford University Press, 2009).

4. For more on people processing, see Prottas, Jeffrey Manditch, *People Processing: The Street-Level Bureaucrat in Public Service Bureaucracies* (Lexington, MA: Lexington Books, 1979); and Yeheske Hasenfeld, "People Processing Organizations: An Exchange Approach," *American Sociological Review* 37 (1972): 256–263.

For more on spillover and socioeconomic status disadvantage, see Jeremy Freese and Karen Lutfey, "Fundamental Causality: Challenges of an Animating Concept for Medical Sociology," in *Handbook of the Sociology of Health, Illness, and Healing: A Blueprint for the 21st Century*, edited by Bernice A. Pescosolido et al. (New York: Springer, 2011), 67–82. For the cocontributing roles of context and composition, see Ross and Mirowsky, "Context or Composition," 2008; and Mario Luis Small, *Unanticipated Gains: Origins of Network Inequality in Everyday Life* (New York: Oxford University Press, 2009). For convergent hardships in old age, see Katherine S. Newman, *A Different Shade of Gray: Midlife and beyond in the Inner City* (New York: New Press, 2004).

5. For a prominent example of discussion of the declining significance of space, see David Harvey, *The Condition of Postmodernity* (Hoboken, NJ: Wiley-Blackwell, 1991). See also Robert D. Atkinson, "Technological Change and Cities," *Cityscape* 3, no. 3 (1998): 129–170; and Stephen Graham and Simon Marvin, *Telecommunications and City: Electronic Spaces, Urban Places* (New York: Routledge, 1996).

6. A similar phenomenon is seen with respect to jobs after "postindustrialization." See William Julius Wilson, *When Work Disappears: The World of the New Urban Poor* (New York: Vintage Books, 1996). For more on the aging population specifically, see Eric Klinenberg, *Heat Wave: A Social Autopsy of Disaster in Chicago* (Chicago: University of Chicago Press, 2002); and Elena Portacolone, "The Myth of Independence for Older Americans Living Alone in the Bay Area of San Francisco: A Critical Reflection," *Ageing and Society* 31 (2011): 803–828.

7. It is hard to overstate the importance of the environmental pathway. Researchers in the social and biological sciences have shown that the greater physiological stresses they encounter, the toxicity of the environments in which they live, the lack of access to quality care, and their behavioral adaptations to everyday circumstances lead the bodies of the poor and marginalized to "wear out" and "break down" faster. This is discussed in more depth in Chapters 1 and 2. For a review see Nancy E. Adler and Katherine S. Newman, "Socioeconomic Disparities in Health: Pathways and Policies," *Health Affairs* 21, no. 2 (2002): 60–76; Smedley et al., *Unequal Treatment*, 2002; and Roberta Spalter-Roth, Terri Ann Lowenthal, and Mercedes Rubio, "Race, Ethnicity, and the Health of Americans," in *ASA Series on How Race and Ethnicity Matter,* edited by Roberta Spalter-Roth (American Sociological Association, 2005): 1-16, http://www2.asanet.org/centennial/race_ethnicity _health.pdf. For a review of this well-documented trend, see Raynard S. Kington and James P. Smith, "Socioeconomic and Ethnic Differences in Functional Status Associated with Chronic Diseases," *American Journal of Public Health* 87, no. 5 (1997): 805–810; and Sandra Y. Moody-Ayers et al., "Black-White Disparities in Functional Decline in Older Persons: The Role of Cognitive Function," *Journals of Gerontology, Series A: Biological Sciences and Medical Sciences* 60, no. 7 (2005): 933–939. See also Adler and Newman, "Socioeconomic Disparities," 2002.
8. See Debra Umberson, Robert Crosnoe, and Corinne Reczek, "Social Relationships and Health Behavior across Life Course," *Annual Review of Sociology* 36 (2010): 139–157, as well as Freese and Lutfey, "Fundamental Causality," 2011, for a discussion of the "spillover" effects of socioeconomic status.
9. I discuss only buses here, as there was no functional rail system serving these neighborhoods. Still, the challenges are similar. The urban–rural divide is an important aspect of inequality but was not directly investigated in this study. For a discussion of these, as well as other burdens associated with public transit in California (and how to measure them), see Hiroyuki Iseki et al., "Evaluating Transit Stops and Stations from the Perspective of Transit Users" (Sacramento, CA: California Department of Transportation, 2007).
10. Independence is a normative historical concept, rooted in a particular Western ideology, which seniors use to make sense of this dilemma. For a discussion about how this ties into the deeply rooted power of the notion of independence, see Portacolone, "Myth of Independence," 2011. For a historical perspective on the continuing importance of "competence" and personal efficacy, see Claude S. Fischer, *Made in America: A Social History of American Culture and Character* (Chicago: University of Chicago Press, 2010). For a theory of how capacities for action, cultural and otherwise, shape longitudinal strategies of behavior, see Ann Swidler, *Talk of Love: How Culture Matters* (Chicago: University of Chicago Press, 2001).

11. For parallel findings on the centrality of independence, see Portacolone, "Myth of Independence," 2011.

12. I discussed some of the issues this can create on the organizational end in my 2009 article on adult day care. Just as individual seniors were often left stranded, the inconsistency of the service created logistical issues for the adult day care center I observed. See Corey M. Abramson, "Who Are the Clients? Goal Displacement in an Adult Day Care Center for Elders with Dementia," *International Journal of Aging and Human Development* 68, no. 1 (2009): 65–92.

13. When I was observing specific seniors, I would often drive them around, so I did not always have the opportunity to be there when they were left by the transit agency. However, the facts that seniors are left places and that the transit program is inconsistent are commonly acknowledged—confirmed by myriad seniors and the organizations that deal with them. I have observed this in my past work (e.g., Abramson, "Who Are the Clients," 2009) and during my time at various senior organizations for this study.

14. This is consistent with an emerging criticism of the food desert literature that argues that while poor areas do provide access to more unhealthy food, they also provide substantial access to healthy food, and access alone cannot explain differences in epidemiological outcomes such as obesity. These studies also raise questions about which metrics are reasonable for measuring food deserts. For a recent example, see Helen Lee, "The Role of Local Food Availability in Explaining Obesity Risk among Young School-Aged Children," *Social Science and Medicine* 74, no. 8 (2012): 1193–1203. However, given the structure of this study, it is important to acknowledge that the level of access to food and the presence of farmers' markets could also be a function of the Bay Area context.

15. As in the senior centers, the delivered meals in general were quite large. They generally consisted of a piece of fruit, some vegetables, starches such as rice, and a large serving of meat. The agencies involved would also accommodate seniors' dietary needs. These meals were provided on a sliding scale, so affordability was not a major issue. Further, the ability to socialize with the volunteer driver was a major part of the social life, and a key lifeline, for seniors who were more isolated.

16. There are a number of reports, however, that indicate that food security is a major aspect of inequality earlier in life—particularly for people under sixty-five with health problems, who may be unable to get the subsidized food available to these seniors. Many of the senior centers did not provide food for those under fifty-five (although they sometimes made exceptions). Likewise, the mobile food programs typically had similar age restrictions but had exceptions for those with disabilities. This was also the case in other cities. Although Rockport is poor, and Elm Flats is both poor and segregated, these neighborhoods are less physically isolated than some of those in Detroit or the South Side of Chicago. See Christine M. Olson, "Nutrition and Health Outcomes Associated with Food Insecurity and

Hunger," *Journal of Nutrition* 129, no. 2 (1999): 5215–5245; and Donald Rose, "Economic Determinants and Dietary Consequences of Food Insecurity in the United States," *Journal of Nutrition* 129, no. 2 (1999): 5175–5205.

17. For more on the historical angle, see James T. Patterson, *America's Struggle against Poverty in the Twentieth Century,* 4th ed. (Cambridge, MA: Harvard University Press, 2000); and Jill Quadagno, *The Transformation of Old Age Security: Class and Politics in the American Welfare State* (Chicago: University of Chicago Press, 1988). I volunteered at several of these agencies for a number of years and was able to observe their operations.

18. The one notable exception was an informal organization that provided services to Latino seniors in Rockport. This organization was run by a local neighborhood group and was not directly tied to a church, senior center, or service organization. However, despite repeated attempts, I was never able to gain entry into this organization—in part because my Spanish is poor, and many of the individuals involved spoke no English.

19. Many accounts of social disorganization are also plagued by measurement problems (e.g., the assumption measures of efficacious organizations focus only on organizations that are effective in nonpoor areas). See Mitchell Duneier, *Sidewalk* (New York: Farrar Straus Giroux, 1999); Martín Sánchez-Jankowski, *Cracks in the Pavement: Social Change and Resilience in Poor Neighborhoods* (Berkeley: University of California Press, 2008); Herbert J. Gans, *Urban Villagers: Group and Class in the Life of Italian-Americans.* (New York: Free Press, 1982); Mario Luis Small, *Villa Victoria: The Transformation of Social Capital in a Boston Barrio* (Chicago: University of Chicago Press, 2004); Gerald D. Suttles, *The Social Order of the Slum: Ethnicity and Territory in the Inner City* (Chicago: University of Chicago Press, 1970); and William Foote Whyte, *Street Corner Society: The Social Structure of an Italian Slum* (Chicago: University of Chicago Press, 1993).

I have argued this is part of a more general analytical error whereby critics make assumptions based on aesthetics and decontextualized meanings, rather than examining what happens on the ground. See Corey M. Abramson and Darren Modzelewski, "Caged Morality: Moral Worlds, Subculture, and Stratification among Middle-Class Cage-Fighters," *Qualitative Sociology* 34, no. 1 (2011): 143–175. Still, social life takes place in physical settings, and the allocation of spatial resources is a key aspect of the contexts of aging.

20. For more on caretakers in poor areas, see Sánchez-Jankowski, *Cracks in the Pavement,* 2008. For more on brokering and network inequality, see Small 2004 and 2009.

21. It would be possible to write an entire paper on the way people adapt to the combination of their environment and physiological problems—but the point here is simply that those living in more affluent areas generally have environments that are easier to navigate.

22. Whether this sort of concentration is beneficial earlier in the life course is much less clear. For instance, the debate around the role of housing projects

is contentious; see Sudhir Alladi Venkatesh, *American Project: The Rise and Fall of a Modern Ghetto* (Cambridge, MA: Harvard University Press, 2002); and Sánchez-Jankowski, *Cracks in the Pavement,* 2008. There is also growing debate around whether living alone is actually negative in the earlier years: see Eric Klinenberg, *Going Solo: The Extraordinary Rise and Surprising Appeal of Living Alone* (New York: Penguin Books, 2013). However, the literature on seniors in particular emphasizes the way being in proximity and connection with others is beneficial. See Arlie Russell Hochschild, *The Unexpected Community* (Englewood Cliffs, NJ: Prentice Hall, 1973); Meika Loe, *Aging Our Way: Lessons for Living from 85 and Beyond* (New York: Oxford University Press, 2011); and Klinenberg, *Heat Wave,* 2002. Hochschild (1973) presents similar findings in her ethnography of a senior community: seniors being in the presence of other seniors facilitated sociability and engagement. However, since Hochschild's study lacked a comparative axis, it is unclear whether that finding was the result of the specific community she studied. As I show in the chapter on social networks, while, in general, proximity to other seniors enhanced sociability, the extent to which people helped one another was not just a function of concentration but also of cultural understandings of when and how much people should help each other. This feature was especially noticeable in the communal settings of nursing homes, where many seniors were often tightly packed together.

23. Further, when an organization won a multiyear grant, they were compelled to spend the money so as to avoid having their funding cut in future years. Not spending the money signaled to granting agencies that the organization was allotted more money than it needed, thereby justifying these cuts. Spending the money was therefore seen as part of successful grant management.

24. See Karen Lutfey and Jeremy Freese, "Toward Some Fundamentals of Fundamental Causality: Socioeconomic Status and Health in the Routine Clinic Visit for Diabetes," *American Journal of Sociology* 110 (2005): 1326–1372.

25. For a review of the demographic leveling versus cumulative disadvantage debate, see Matthew E. Dupre, "Educational Differences in Age-Related Patterns of Disease: Reconsidering the Cumulative Disadvantage and Age-as-Leveler Hypotheses," *Journal of Health and Social Behaviour* 48 (2007): 1–15.

26. For a similar finding see Newman, *Shade of Gray,* 2004.

27. Whether this is simply a justification is impossible to discern. However, having a market creates additional choices that can be problematic—such as whether to keep one's oxycodone or sell it on the street to someone for a hundred dollars or more per bottle. Some seniors from middle-class backgrounds also used marijuana, often acquired through friends with medical cannabis cards (or their own cards).

28. See Dalton Conley, *Being Black, Living in the Red: Race, Wealth, and Social Policy in America* (Berkeley: University of California Press, 1999); Kenneth T.

Jackson, *Crabgrass Frontier: The Suburbanization of the United States* (New York: Oxford University Press, 1987); Douglas S. Massey and Nancy A. Denton, *American Apartheid: Segregation and the Making of the Underclass* (Cambridge, MA: Harvard University Press, 1993); and William M. Rohe and Harry L. Watson, eds., *Chasing the American Dream: New Perspectives on Affordable Homeownership* (Ithaca, NY: Cornell University Press, 2007).

29. This was not only observed in this study but also has been documented more broadly. See, for instance, Christine Loignon et al., "What Makes Primary Care Effective for People in Poverty Living with Multiple Chronic Conditions? Study Protocol," *BMC Health Services Research* 10 (2010): 320.

30. The fact that more affluent areas are associated with better care is well documented. For reviews see Smedley et al., *Unequal Treatment*, 2002; and Kevin Fiscella et al., "Disparities in Health Care by Race, Ethnicity, and Language among the Insured: Findings from a National Sample," *Medical Care* 40, no. 1 (2002): 52–59. For literature on patient load in public versus private clinics and care facilities, see Warren Davidson et al., "Relation between Physician Characteristics and Prescribing for Elderly People in New Brunswick," *Canadian Medical Association Journal* 150, no. 6 (1994): 917–921; Peifeng Hu and David B. Reuben, "Effects of Managed Care on the Length of Time That Elderly Patients Spend with Physicians during Ambulatory Visits: National Ambulatory Medical Care Survey," *Medical Care* 40, no. 7 (2002): 606–613; and David C. Dugdale, Ronald Epstein, and Steven Z. Pantilat, "Time and the Patient-Physician Relationship," *Journal of General Internal Medicine* 14, no. S1 (1999): S34–S40.

31. Those who were proactive in taking care of health and managing illness would often go to senior clinics or free clinics. Those who did not often waited until a problem required them to go to the emergency department. These differences in strategies are discussed in the next chapter. For a more in-depth discussion of how "street-level bureaucrats" engage in gate-keeping, see Jeffrey Manditch Prottas, *People Processing: The Street-Level Bureaucrat in Public Service Bureaucracies* (Lexington, MA: Lexington Books, 1979).

32. It is also possible—although I was not able to observe this due to the structure of this study—that service providers make implicit or explicit assumptions about who is really worth helping, which affected the way they provided care. See, for instance, Abramson, "Who Are the Clients," 2009; Charles L. Bosk, *Forgive and Remember: Managing Medical Failure* (Chicago: University of Chicago Press, 2003); and Stefan Timmermans, "When Death Isn't Dead: Implicit Social Rationing during Resuscitative Efforts," *Sociological Inquiry* 69, no. 1 (1999): 51–75. Negative past experiences with health care were also a major factor that affected seniors' orientations toward the body, an issue discussed in the next chapter.

33. Many seniors were hesitant around me as well, until it became clear that I was a "student" rather than a "spy" or state agent. For an interesting discussion of how research subjects categorize the researcher, see Sudhir Alladi

Venkatesh, "'Doin' the Hustle': Constructing the Ethnographer in the American Ghetto," *Ethnography* 3, no. 1 (2002): 91–111.

Seniors orientations toward these gatekeepers are also likely related to earlier negative experiences with "state agents" and surveillance over the life course. See, for instance, Alice Goffman, "On the Run: Wanted Men in a Philadelphia Ghetto," *American Sociological Review* 74, no. 3 (2009): 339–357; and Loïc Wacquant, *Punishing the Poor: The Neoliberal Government of Social Insecurity* (Durham, NC: Duke University Press, 2009). Further, a number of seniors in Elm Flats and Rockport had been incarcerated previously, and even more had some form of previous legal problems. This likely added to their hesitancy. In a sense this supports the literature on surveillance in poverty (e.g., Goffman, "On the Run," 2009), or, at the very least, that service provisions are seen that way by residents. The presence of desirable resources accords with the notion of the state as simultaneously generative and constraining, which fits the Foucaultian model of biopower: see Michel Foucault, *The History of Sexuality: An Introduction,* vol. 1 (New York: Vintage Books, 1980). However, unlike in the Foucaultian model, not only does subjective experience matter, but also it affects strategic and calculated action. See, for instance, Sylvia Pasquetti, "Legal Emotions: An Ethnography of Distrust and Fear in the Arab Districts of an Israeli City," *Law and Society Review* 47, no. 3 (2013): 461–492.

34. For a more thorough discussion of this "precariousness," see Elena Portacolone, "The Notion of Precariousness among Older Adults Living Alone in the US," *Journal of Aging Studies* 27, no. 2 (2013): 166–174.

3. Game-Day Strategies

1. The connections between these cultural elements are discussed in Corey M. Abramson, "From 'Either-Or' to 'When and How': A Context-Dependent Model of Culture in Action," *Journal for the Theory of Social Behaviour* 42, no. 2 (2012): 155–180, and elaborated in the conclusion of this book. For a sociological explanation of motivations, see Stephen Vaisey, "Motivation and Justification: Towards a Dual-Process Theory of Culture in Action," *American Journal of Sociology.* 114, no. 6 (2009): 1975–1715. For orientations see Pierre Bourdieu, *Distinction: A Social Critique of the Judgement of Taste* (Cambridge, MA: Harvard University Press, 1984); Clifford Geertz, "Religion as a Cultural System," in *The Interpretation of Cultures: Selected Essays* (New York: Basic Books, 2000), 87–125; and David D. Laitin, *Hegemony and Culture: Politics and Religious Change among the Yoruba* (Chicago: University of Chicago Press, 1986). For tools and strategies, see Ann Swidler, *Talk of Love: How Culture Matters* (Chicago: University of Chicago Press, 2001). For group cultures and styles, see Nina Eliasoph and Paul Lichterman, "Culture in Interaction," *American Journal of Sociology* 108 (2003): 735–794.

2. With respect to end-of-life planning and the physical issues of aging more generally, see Deborah Carr, "The Social Stratification of Adults' Preparations

for End-of-Life Health Care," *Journal of Health and Social Behavior* 53, no. 3 (2012): 297–312; and Jung Kwak and William E. Haley. "Current Research Findings on End-of-Life Decision Making Among Racially or Ethnically Diverse Groups," *Gerontologist* 45, no. 5 (2005): 634–641. For gender effects, even within class strata, see Kristen W. Springer and Dawne M. Mouzon, "'Macho Men' and Preventative Health Care," *Journal of Health and Social Behavior* 52, no. 2 (2011): 212–227. For findings on seniors in poverty and a brief review of this literature, see Corey M. Abramson and Martín Sánchez-Jankowski, "Racial Differences in Physician Usage among the Elderly Poor in the United States," *Research in Social Stratification and Mobility* 30, no. 2 (2012): 203–217. For more on this operationalization of culture, see Abramson, "Either-Or," 2012, as well as Chapter 6.

3. For a general review of these literatures, see Swidler, *Talk of Love,* 2001; Vaisey, "Motivation and Justification," 2009; and Abramson, "Either-Or," 2012. For recent attempts to reconcile the various aspects of culture, see Abramson, "Either-Or," 2012; and Margaret Frye, "Bright Futures in Malawi's New Dawn: Educational Aspirations as Assertions of Identity," *American Journal of Sociology* 117, no. 6 (2012): 1565–1624.

For classic descriptions, see Max Weber, "The Social Psychology of the World Religions," in *Max Weber: Essays in Sociology,* eds. Hans Heinrich Gerth and C. Wright Mills (New York: Oxford University Press, 1946); Talcott Parsons, *The Structure of Social Action* (New York: Free Press, 1937); Talcott Parsons and Edward Shils, *Toward a General Theory of Action* (New York: Harper and Row, 1951); and Clyde Kluckhohm, "Values and Value-Orientations," in *Toward a General Theory of Action,* eds. T. Parsons and E. A. Shils (New York: Harper & Row, 1951), 388–433. With a few exceptions, even seemingly more open-ended notions such as Kluckhohn's "conceptions of the desirable" are often dismissed as part of the values paradigm. See also Ann Swidler, "Culture in Action: Symbols and Strategies," *American Sociological Review* 51, no. 2 (1986): 273–386; Charles A. Valentine, *Culture and Poverty: Critique and Counterproposals* (Chicago: University of Chicago Press, 1967); and Michèle Lamont and Mario Luis Small, "How Culture Matters: Enriching Our Understandings of Poverty," in *The Colors of Poverty:Why Racial and Ethnic Disparities Persist,* eds. David Harris and Ann Lin (New York: Russell Sage Foundation, 2008), 76–102. Empirical evidence of the importance of examining cultural motivations is seen in fields such as sociology, psychology, cognitive science, psychology, and political science. See Stephen Vaisey, "What People Want: Rethinking Poverty, Culture, and Educational Attainment," *Annals of the American Academy of Political and Social Science* 629, no. 1 (2010): 75–101, for a brief review.

For an empirical application that explicitly argues for the continuing salience of coherent "value-orientations," see Martín Sánchez-Jankowski, *Cracks in the Pavement: Social Change and Resilience in Poor Neighborhoods* (Berkeley: University of California Press, 2008). For an important discussion of the relationship between wants, social inequality, and academic politics after the misappropriation of the "culture of poverty," see Vaisey, "What People Want," 2010; Sánchez-Jankowski, *Cracks in the Pavement*, 2008; and Michael Jindra, "The Dilemma of Equality and Diversity," *Current Anthropology* 55, no. 3 (2014): 316–334.

For important conceptual critiques of the classical notion of values as inadequately predictive, see Swidler, "Culture in Action," 1986; Valentine, *Culture and Poverty*, 1967; and Lamont and Small, "How Culture Matters," 2008. See also Paul DiMaggio, "Culture and Cognition," *Annual Review of Sociology* 23 (1997): 263–287. For a criticism of classical sociologies' tendency to look at value internalization without examining the biosocial roots, see Albert J. Bergesen, "Turning Durkheim on His Head: A Reply to Peterson and Bjerre," *Journal for the Theory of Social Behaviour* 42, no. 4 (2012): 485–495. For more on the criticism that values fail as a stand-alone model of culture but can be integrated into a more holistic model, see Abramson, "Either-Or," 2012. For a contemporary example of empirical work that directly employs the concept of values as predictive of behavior, see Sánchez-Jankowski, *Cracks in the Pavement*, 2008.

Although recent sociological inquiries into health and illness have begun to take the relationship between culture and health more seriously— for example, Janet K. Shim, "Cultural Health Capital: A Theoretical Approach to Understanding Health Care Interactions and the Dynamics of Unequal Treatment," *Journal of Health and Social Behavior* 51, no. 1 (2010): 1–15—as Bernice A. Pescosolido and Sigrum Olafsdottir note in "The Cultural Turn in Sociology: Can It Help Us Resolve an Age-Old Problem in Understanding Decision Making for Health Care?" *Sociological Forum* 25, no. 4 (2010): 655–676, these concepts remain poorly measured in quantitative inquiry. Likewise, systematic comparative direct observation studies such as this one are essentially nonexistent, and economic models that discount the importance of culture a-priori abound (see Abramson and Sánchez-Jankowski, "Racial Differences," 2012). See also Katherine S. Newman, *A Different Shade of Gray: Midlife and beyond in the Inner City* (New York: New Press, 2004). For a more specific application to health and health behavior, see Janet K. Shim, "Cultural Health Capital," *Journal of Health and Social Behavior* 51, no. 1 (2010): 1–15.

4. See Abramson, "Either-Or," 2012, 157. More technically, as I note in the article, "I introduce the concept of a cultural *input* to refer to those aspects of culture that determine the valued ends of action. I do not enter this term into the already crowded vocabulary of cultural theory haphazardly. Rather, there is an essential (if subtle) distinction to maintain. The term "motivation" seemingly emphasizes the impetus to act. The term "input" is deliberately more inclusive. It refers to a wider set of attributions that point action toward particular ends on the biosocial, subconscious, and conscious levels. While the function of inputs may be most pronounced in determining the motivational force for specific behaviors, an input functions through the complete sequence of actions while still pointing toward

a preferred end or outcome." Examining points of maximization has been an important topic for social scientists. For a model of how these points are connected to "universal" values, see Shalom H. Schwartz, "Are There Universal Aspects in the Structure and Contents of Human Values?" *Journal of Social Issues* 50, no. 4 (1994): 19–45. For an application of how value-centered differences in maximization affect how people live in urban poverty, see Sánchez-Jankowski, *Cracks in the Pavement,* 2008.

Also, note that while points of maximization are often presented as contradictory, and are even treated as such by seniors, the dichotomy may not be as hard and fast. Rather, it is more accurate to think of the degree to which enjoyment or security is maximized as an individual trait that could be represented by a continuous psychometric measure. However, this does not mean that the trait is evenly distributed among the seniors I observed. Rather, it was clustered around the two types described as *preserving the body* and *maximizing enjoyment.*

5. See Elena Portacolone, "The Myth of Independence for Older Americans Living Alone in the Bay Area of San Francisco: A Critical Reflection." *Ageing and Society* 31 (2011): 803–828. The phrase on home safety was presented by a member of the Baygardens Fire Department at a special event for "living independently." This phrase was also found in the brochures passed out and is a typical party line for many organizations that provide in-home services to seniors. For a criticism of the gerontological literature on "aging successfully," see Meika Loe, *Aging Our Way: Lessons for Living from 85 and Beyond* (New York: Oxford University Press, 2011). Ironically, however, in her discussion of how conscientiousness and comfortable aging coincide, Loe replaces an overt normative framework with a slightly more subtle one.

6. For more on security maximization, see Schwartz, "Universal Aspects," 1994. For a parallel finding in responses to material scarcity and persistent poverty, see Sánchez-Jankowski, *Cracks in the Pavement,* 2008. For seniors' attempts to create continuity as they age, see Loe, *Aging Our Way,* 2011, and Sharon R. Kaufman, *The Ageless Self: Sources of Meaning in Late Life* (Madison: University of Wisconsin Press, 1994).

7. The interview schedule and vignettes are provided in the methodological appendix.

8. For congruent responses to the challenges and uncertainties of urban poverty, see Sánchez-Jankowski, *Cracks in the Pavement,* 2008.

9. Each of these behaviors was observed, or, in the case of sexual activity, independently verified verbally. The subject noted that the type of chemotherapy Jane was undergoing causes people to lose their nails, or the nails get sickly and black.

10. I use the term "suggest," which implies imputed association rather than direct observation, since I did not directly observe the seniors prior to old age. However, although this link is not directly observed, the claim is grounded in speech behaviors and life history information collected during interviews. For a discussion of motivations, see Vaisey, "Motivation and

Justification," 2009; and Vaisey, "What People Want," 2010. This finding is also consistent with recent developments in the psychological literature on aging, which emphasizes behavioral continuity and declining cognitive and emotive flexibility in old age. For a discussion see Wendy Berry Mendes, "Weakened Links between Mind and Body in Older Age: The Case for Maturational Dualism in the Experience of Emotion," *Emotion Review* 2, no. 3 (2010): 240–244. The issue of orientation change was more prevalent. This also lines up with the life-course approaches found in sociological and anthropological work emphasizing continuity in longitudinal strategies of approaching life and aging. See Loe, *Aging Our Way,* 2011, and Kaufman, *The Ageless Self,* 1994.

11. For a discussion of the body and distinction topic, see Bourdieu, *Distinction,* 1984, 92–93; and Katherine Mason, "Social Stratification and the Body: Gender, Race, and Class," *Sociology Compass* 7/8 (2013): 686–698. On the issue of variation in what people maximize, psychologists have long looked at value orientations across national contexts and found similar continuities. For example, see macro-level findings in Schwartz, "Universal Aspects," 1994.

12. The term "moral boundary" in contemporary sociology is fruitfully employed in the work of Lamont, who articulates the concept and describes the different ways working-class men draw distinctions to maintain a sense of dignity in light of socioeconomic inequalities. See Michèle Lamont, *The Dignity of Working Men: Morality and the Boundaries of Race, Class, and Immigration* (Cambridge, MA: Harvard University Press, 2000). The broader notion of social boundaries separating good people from bad, sacred from profane, and so on has deep roots in both classical sociology (i.e., Durkheim) and structuralist anthropology (Lévi-Strauss). See Emile Durkheim, *The Elementary Forms of Religious Life* (New York: Free Press, 1995); and Claude Lévi-Strauss, *Structural Anthropology* (New York: Basic Books, 1974).

13. Many seniors had ready access to narcotic medications through their doctors and clinics.

14. The next chapter turns to the issue of how these boundaries, and even underlying motivations, are connected to social networks and the normative expectations they place on seniors. See also Debra Umberson, Robert Crosnoe, and Corinne Reczek, "Social Relationships and Health Behavior across Life Course," *Annual Review of Sociology* 36 (2010): 139–157.

15. For a broader discussion of how orientations differ from attitudes, motivations, and values, drawing on Geertz and Bourdieu, see Abramson, "Either-Or," 2012. The term "attitude" alone is inadequate. Orientations can be understood only as clusters of ideas that hold a nominal degree of internal coherence that points people toward viewing particular behaviors and outcomes as reasonable. As used here, orientations differ from the somewhat more nebulous concept of a "cognitive frame" in that they have a specifically defined object, a moral/evaluative component, and can operate on a discursive as well as automatic level. See Erving Goffman, *Frame Analysis: An Essay on the Organization of Experience* (Boston: Northeastern

Press, 1986); Mario Luis Small, *Unanticipated Gains: Origins of Network Inequality in Everyday Life* (New York: Oxford University Press, 2009); and David J. Harding, *Living the Drama: Community, Conflict, and Culture among Inner-City Boys* (Chicago: University of Chicago Press, 2010).

16. Bourdieu uses the term "natural body" as well, although in a slightly different sense. The emphasis here is less on the symbolic and moral ramification of pursuing a set of practices related to class position and more on how a category that can occur across class boundaries orients action as an input. In a Bourdieusian conception, the natural body as used here would likely be folded into the umbrella of "habitus."

17. For a review, see Brian D. Smedley et al., *Unequal Treatment: Confronting Racial and Ethnic Disparities in Health Care* (Washington, DC: National Academies Press, 2003).

18. Metaphysics refers to a broad set of philosophies around existence frequently connected to the "new age" movement.

19. For more on how the categories seniors employ do not necessarily map onto those of the medical establishment, see Judith Noemi Freidenberg, *Growing Old in El Barrio* (New York: New York University Press, 2000).

20. These two orientations bear a resemblance to parenting strategies of "fostering natural growth" among working-class children, in contrast to middle-class "concerted cultivation" among the middle class observed by Annette Lareau, *Unequal Childhoods: Class, Race, and Family Life* (Berkeley: University of California Press, 2003). For a discussion of how networks shape behavior, see Carr, "End-of-Life," 2012.

21. Tricholitis, also referred to as diverticulitis, is a sometimes painful gastrointestinal ailment.

22. For similar findings on networks, see Carr, "End-of-Life," 2012; Portacolone, "Myth of Independence," 2011; and Abramson and Sánchez-Jankowski, "Racial Differences," 2012.

23. For more on the moral connotations of these bodily practices and their moral signification, see Bourdieu, *Distinction*, 1984; Mason, "Stratification and the Body," 2013; Erving Goffman, *The Presentation of Self in Everyday Life* (New York: Anchor Books, 1959); Natalie C. Boero, *Killer Fat: Media, Medicine, and Morals in the American "Obesity Epidemic"* (New Brunswick, NJ: Rutgers University Press, 2013); and Abigail C. Saguy, *What's Wrong with Fat?* (Oxford: Oxford University Press, 2013).

24. For a critical discussion of health and aging, see Carroll L. Estes, Simon Biggs, and Chris Phillipson, *Social Theory, Social Policy, and Ageing: Critical Perspectives* (Berkshire, UK: Open University Press, 2003); Carroll L. Estes and Elizabeth A. Binney, "The Biomedicalization of Aging: Dangers and Dilemmas," *Gerontologist* 29, no. 5 (1989): 587–596; and Adele E. Clarke et al., "Biomedicalization: Technoscientific Transformations of Health, Illness, and U.S. Biomedicine," *American Sociological Review* 68 (2003): 161–194.

25. For a finding where women are more likely to seek care at a given level of health and illness generally, see Kristen W. Springer and Dawne M. Mouzon, "'Macho Men' and Preventative Health Care," *Journal of Health and Social*

Behavior, 52 no. 2 (2011): 212–227. Even among seniors living in poverty (Abramson and Sánchez-Jankowski, "Racial Differences," 2012), this finding occurs in quantitative research as well. The point here is not to make a distributional claim about the prevalence of this attitude or orientation in a wider population, but to describe its content and effect on everyday life among the seniors in this study.

26. I saw this status ritual play out numerous times at various senior centers, clinics, health fairs, and apartment common areas. For a corresponding example earlier in life, see the popular movement toward quantified selves: Quantified Self Labs, *Quantified Self: Self-Knowledge through Numbers,* http://quantifiedself.com. For a powerful articulation of the notion that culture can be both incoherent and powerful, see Swidler, *Talk of Love,* 2001. For the classic examples of the approach being criticized, see Parsons, *The Social System* (New York: Free Press, 1951), and Geertz, "Religion as a Cultural System," 2000.

27. See Mark P. Doescher et al., "Racial and Ethnic Disparities in Perceptions of Physician Style and Trust," *Archives of Family Medicine* 9, no. 10 (2000): 1156–1163; Vicki S. Freimuth et al., "African Americans' Views on Research and the Tuskegee Syphilis Study," *Social Science and Medicine* 52 (2001): 797–808; Alexander M. McBean and Marian E. Gornick, "Differences by Race in the Rates of Procedures Performed in Hospitals for Medicare Beneficiaries," *Health Financing Review* 15, no. 4 (1994): 77–90; and Carr, "End-of-Life," 2012.

28. For the importance of behavioral pathways in health disparities, see Nancy E. Adler and Katherine S. Newman, "Socioeconomic Disparities in Health: Pathways and Policies," *Health Affairs* 21, no. 2 (2002): 60–76.

29. See Swidler, "Culture in Action," 1986, 277; Bourdieu, *Distinction,* 1984; and Pierre Bourdieu, "The Forms of Capital," in *Handbook for Theory and Research for the Sociology of Education,* ed. John Richardson (Westport, CT: Greenwood): 241–258. For an empirical examination in youth, see Lareau, *Unequal Childhoods,* 2003.

30. See also John R. Hall, "The Capital(s) of Cultures: A Nonholistic Approach to Status Situations, Class, Gender, and Ethnicity," in *Cultivating Boundaries: Symbolic Boundaries and the Making of Inequality,* eds. Michéle Lamont and Marcel Fournier (Chicago and London: University of Chicago Press., 1992): 257–285.

31. For an example of resilience in the context of persistent poverty, see Sánchez-Jankowski, *Cracks in the Pavement,* 2008. For an examination of how older working-class African American men in Chicago create a meaningful social space with relatively few financial resources, see Mitchell Duneier, *Slim's Table: Race, Respectability, and Masculinity* (Chicago: University of Chicago Press, 1994). See also Elliot Liebow, *Tally's Corner: A Study of Negro Streetcorner Men,* (Lanham, MD: Rowman and Littlefield, 2003).

32. See Swidler, "Culture in Action," 1986, 277; and *Talk of Love,* 2001, for a more thorough formulation of strategies of action.

33. For a review of the role of culture in inequality, see Bourdieu, *Distinction,* 1984, 12; *In Other Words: Essays toward a Reflexive Sociology* (Stanford, CA: Stanford University Press, 1990); and *The Logic of Practice* (Stanford, CA: Stanford University Press, 1992). For other examples and reviews, see Jeffrey J. Sallaz and Jane Zavisca, "Bourdieu in American Sociology, 1980-2004," *Annual Review of Sociology* 33, no. 1 (2007): 21–41; Lareau, *Unequal Childhoods,* 2003; Jeffrey J. Sallaz, "The Making of the Global Gambling Industry: An Application and Extension of Field Theory," *Theory and Society* 35, no. 3 (2006): 265–297; Sánchez-Jankowski, *Cracks in the Pavement,* 2008; Shim, "Cultural Health Capital," 2010; Vaisey, "What People Want," 2010; and Mario Luis Small, David J. Harding, and Michèle Lamont, "Reconsidering Culture and Poverty," *Annals of the American Academy of Political and Social Science* 629, no. 1 (2010): 6–27.

4. Team Dynamics

1. For a review see Alejandro Portes, "Social Capital: Its Origins and Applications in Modern Sociology," *Annual Review of Sociology* 24 (1998): 1–24; Alejandro Portes and Erik Vickstrom, "Diversity, Social Capital, and Cohesion," *Annual Review of Sociology* 37 (2011): 461–479; and Mario Luis Small, *Villa Victoria: The Transformation of Social Capital in a Boston Barrio* (Chicago: University of Chicago Press, 2004). For the relationship to health and biosocial issues in general, see Mel Bartley, *Health Inequality: An Intro- duction to Concepts, Theories and Methods* (Cambridge, MA: Polity Press, 2004); Lisa F. Berkman, "The Health Divide," *Contexts* 4 (2004): 38–51; Lisa F. Berkman et al., "From Social Integration to Health: Durkheim in the New Millennium," *Social Science and Medicine* 51, no. 6 (2000): 843–857; Bernice A. Pescosolido, "Beyond Rational Choice: The Social Dynamics of How People Seek Help," *American Journal of Sociology* 97, no. 4 (1992): 1096–1138; and Peggy A. Thoits, "Mechanisms Linking Social Ties and Support to Physical and Mental Health," *Journal of Health and Social Behavior* 52, no. 2 (2011): 145–161.

2. The events below were directly observed during the first phase of this project, which involved the observation of individual and group behavior in public settings. They are presented in a way that uses counterfactual logic for com- parable events to evaluate the plausibility of a proposition (i.e., the notion that if social connectedness is not contextual, there should be no behavioral differences). For more on counterfactual modeling generally, see Stephen L. Morgan and Christopher Winship, *Counterfactuals and Causal Inference: Methods and Principles for Social Research Analytical Methods for Social Research* (New York: Cambridge University Press, 2007). For its application to eth- nography, as in the case below, see Robert Courtney Smith, "Ethnography, Epistemology, and Counterfactual Causality," working paper, *American Journal of Sociology Conference on Causal Thinking and Ethnographic Research,* https://sites.google.com/site/ajs2012conference/2011-ieee-ss.

3. All the Jewish individuals observed in this study would generally be considered white, although they often saw themselves as ethnically distinct.

4. The point is not that connection versus isolation is irrelevant. Voluminous works show that even within a racial group, those who are more connected tend to be better off, on average, with regard to health. As I have shown in past work using this measure (e.g., Corey M. Abramson and Martín Sánchez-Jankowski, "Racial Differences in Physician Usage among the Elderly Poor in the United States," *Research in Social Stratification and Mobility* 30, no. 2 [2012]: 203–217), even among poor seniors of the same racial group, whether or not one is connected matters for health and health behavior. Still, the effect is not homogenous, and ethnography is well suited to showing why.

5. See, for instance, Mark S. Granovetter, "The Strength of Weak Ties: A Network Theory Revisited," *Sociological Theory* 1 (1983): 201–233; Nan Lin, *Social Capital: A Theory of Social Structure and Action* (Cambridge: Cambridge University Press, 2001); and Portes, "Social Capital," 1998. For a relevant review of the relationship between social ties and health, see Peggy A. Thoits, "Mechanisms Linking Social Ties and Support to Physical and Mental Health," *Journal of Health and Social Behavior* 52, no. 2 (2011): 145–161; and Debra Umberson, Robert Crosnoe, and Corinne Reczek, "Social Relationships and Health Behavior across Life Course," *Annual Review of Sociology* 36 (2010): 139–157. For a review of research on social ties, see Claude S. Fischer, "Bowling Alone: What's the Score?" *Social Networks* 27 (2005): 155–167. Though the term "social capital" can be found throughout sociology, the recent resurgence is most closely associated with popular works by James S. Coleman, "Social Capital in the Creation of Human Capital," *American Journal of Sociology* 94, no. S1 (1988): S95–S120; and Robert D. Putnam, *Bowling Alone: The Collapse and Revival of American Community* (New York: Touchstone, 2001). For a representative example of the relationship between social capital and neighborhood effects, see Robert J. Sampson and Corina Graif, "Neighborhood Social Capital as Differential Social Organization: Resident and Leadership Dimensions," *American Behavioral Scientist* 52, no. 11 (2009): 1579–1605; Robert J. Sampson, Jeffrey D. Morenoff, and Thomas Gannon-Rowley, "Assessing 'Neighborhood Effects': Social Processes and New Directions in Research," *Annual Review of Sociology* 28 (2002): 443–478; William Julius Wilson, *When Work Disappears: The World of the New Urban Poor* (New York: Vintage Books, 1996); and Robert J. Bursik Jr. and Harold G. Grasmick, *Neighborhoods and Crime: The Dimensions of Effective Community Control* (New York: Lexington Books, 1993).

While this framing of social capital has a strong following in the social sciences in general, and the literature on health in particular, it has also been criticized for being overly broad, ill-defined in practical terms, an artifact of poor measure selection, thin, marketizing, and inattentive to meaning (e.g., Corey M. Abramson and Darren Modzelewski, "Caged Morality: Moral Worlds, Subculture, and Stratification among Middle-Class Cage-Fighters," *Qualitative Sociology* 34, no. 1 (2011): 143–175; Fischer, "What's the Score," 2005; and Arlie Russell Hochschild, *The Commercialization of Intimate*

Life: Notes from Home and Work (Berkeley: University of California Press, 2003).

6. For a recent discussion of social connectedness, see also Elena Portacolone, "The Myth of Independence for Older Americans Living Alone in the Bay Area of San Francisco: A Critical Reflection," *Ageing and Society* 31 (2011): 803–828; Arlie Russell Hochschild, *The Unexpected Community* (Englewood Cliffs, NJ: Prentice Hall, 1973); and Eric Klinenberg, *Heat Wave: A Social Autopsy of Disaster in Chicago* (Chicago: University of Chicago Press, 2002).

7. For a discussion of networks and connectedness, see Barbara Entwisle et al., "Networks and Contexts: Variation in the Structure of Social Ties," *American Journal of Sociology* 112, no. 5 (2007): 1495–1533; and Claude S. Fischer, *Still Connected: Family and Friends in America since 1970* (New York: Russell Sage Foundation, 2011). For a discussion of the cultural underpinnings of networks, see Pescosolido, "Beyond Rational Choice," 1992; and Bernice Pescosolido et al., "Under the Influence of Genetics: How Transdisciplinarity Leads Us to Rethink Social Pathways to Illness," *American Journal of Sociology* 114, no. S1 (2008): S171–S201. See also Stephen Vaisey and Omar Lizardo, "Can Cultural Worldviews Influence Network Composition?" *Social Forces* 88, no. 4 (2010): 1595–1618; and Berkman et al., "Social Integration," 2000. For the potential downsides of connectedness, see, for instance, Toni C. Antonucci, Hiroko Akiyama, and Jennifer E. Lansford, "Negative Effects of Close Social Relations," *Family Relations* 47, no. 4 (1998): 379–384; and Karen Rook, "Positive and Negative Social Exchanges: Weighing Their Effects in Later Life," *Journals of Gerontology, Series B: Psychological Sciences and Social Sciences* 52 (1997): S167–S169. For a detailed ethnographic examination of the net effects of social ties, see Small, *Villa Victoria,* 2004.

8. As social psychologists have long noted, forms of reciprocity and identity are key to exchange. See Linda D. Molm, Monica M. Whitham, and David Melamed, "Forms of Exchange and Integrative Bonds: Effects of History and Embeddedness," *American Sociological Review* 77, no. 1 (2012): 141–165. See also Andrew Miles, "Addressing the Problem of Cultural Anchoring: An Identity-Based Model of Culture in Action," *Social Psychology Quarterly* 77, no. 2 (2014): 210–227. For more on networks and health behavior specifically, see Pescosolido, "Beyond Rational Choice," 1992. For classic statements see Marcel Mauss, *The Gift: The Form and Reason for Exchange in Archaic Societies* (New York: W. W. Norton, 2000); Alan P. Fiske, "The Four Elementary Forms of Sociality: Framework for a Unified Theory of Social Relations," *Psychological Review* 99, no. 4 (1992): 689–723; and Barry Schwartz, "The Social Psychology of the Gift," *American Journal of Sociology* 73, no. 1 (1967): 1–11.

9. For a classic statement on norms, see Max Weber, *Economy and Society* (Berkeley: University of California Press, 1978); and Martin E. Spencer, "Weber on Legitimate Norms and Authority," *British Journal of Sociology* 21, no. 2 (1970): 123–134, which offers a useful explication. For a discussion of cultural schemas more generally, see Roy G. D'Andrade, "Cultural Meaning Systems," in *Culture Theory: Essays on Mind, Self, and Emotion,* eds. Richard A.

Schweder and Robert A. Levine (Cambridge: Cambridge University Press, 1984); and William H. Sewell Jr., "A Theory of Structure: Duality, Agency, and Transformation," *American Journal of Sociology* 98, no. 1 (1992): 1–29. I define normative schemas as cultural frameworks that "are institutionally reinforced (codified and supported by laws, funding requirements, etc.) and take on normative significance. They prescribe what is seen as the correct course of action for individuals and organizations." See Corey M. Abramson, "Who Are the Clients? Goal Displacement in an Adult Day Care Center for Elders with Dementia," *International Journal of Aging and Human Development* 68, no 1. (2009): 65–92, 86. Although norms and the schemas that underwrite them can be internalized in the classic Parsonian sense, the possibility of sanctions allows them to function without commanding belief; see, for example, Steve Derné, "Cultural Conceptions of Human Motivation and Their Significance for Culture Theory," in *The Sociology of Culture,* ed. Diana Crane (Cambridge: Blackwell, 1994): 267–287; and Ann Swidler, *Talk of Love: How Culture Matters* (Chicago: University of Chicago Press, 2001). In this way normative schemas are different from worldviews. They are also different in that they can be more limited in scope. For more on how culture can affect action in this way—that is, without requiring belief—see Corey M. Abramson, "From 'Either-Or' to 'When and How': A Context-Dependent Model of Culture in Action," *Journal for the Theory of Social Behaviour* 42, no. 2 (2012): 155–180; and Stephen Vaisey, "Motivation and Justification: Towards a Dual-Process Theory of Culture in Action," *American Journal of Sociology* 114, no. 6 (2009): 1675–1715.

10. This is closely related to the literature showing that formal ties generally improve health and shape bodily behaviors, even net of other factors. See Umberson, Crosnoe, and Reczek, "Social Relationships," 2010, for a review. See also Pescosolido, "Beyond Rational Choice," 1992. Although Jews share religion, often these organizations are broader and include individuals with various levels of religiosity. For many, being a Jew was a broader identity not reducible to religion. This did not preclude participation in religious organizations such as synagogues, but participation with a general Jewish community organization and religious participation were not the same. Recent survey evidence suggests that this pattern, where religion is not necessarily the "tie that binds" American Jews, goes beyond this study. See Pew Research Center, "A Portrait of American Jews," Religion and Public Life Project, http://www.pewforum.org/2013/10/01/jewish-american-beliefs-attitudes-culture-survey/.

11. Interestingly, this senior was not only close in age to the Filipino woman, but also she was the oldest and, growing up, was expected to take care of her sisters.

12. This also raises the question of what constitutes "family." In practice, although typically this involved some sort of blood relation, the relationship worked because the social tie was strong. Therefore, this relationship could exist with "fictive kin" or other nonblood relations. The key

distinction is that these people were not just casual friends or neighbors. Responsibility for elder care was often a source of major contention among families. Those who cared for the seniors felt that they were fulfilling their obligations at substantial cost while their siblings were shirking theirs. This sometimes translated into feuds after seniors died or were institutionalized, as seemingly tight-knit families competed over the incapacitated or dead seniors' assets.

The financial aspects of receiving public support were often quite complex—as more affluent seniors would have to "spend down" to use certain services such as Medicare. A complete discussion of this is outside the scope of this book; the point, however, is that the families provided both logistical and instrumental support.

13. In a recent article, Elena Portacolone refers to these individuals who chose to leave the household as the "gated elite": individuals with great resources, who live in age-segregated service. See Elena Portacolone, "Older Americans Living Alone: The Influence of Resources and Intergenerational Integration on Inequality," *Journal of Contemporary Ethnography* 43, no. 2 (2014): 123–147. Two factors, dementia and incontinence, provided the greatest logistical difficulties and often led to seniors being removed from the program. These same criteria were operative in the adult day care study I observed during a previous study (Abramson, "Who Are the Clients," 2009).

14. In this case, the senior was referring to companionship. She noted, "In reality you want the companionship and support more than anything. I don't need the money or anything. It's the love and companionship of a friend that really matters."

15. James, the African American man in Chapter 2, made a similar point about how asking for help signals vulnerability when he noted, "A man has a certain image to project. And that image, it don't include doctors." For theoretical background on gift exchange, see Mauss, *The Gift*, 2000.

16. Claude S. Fischer, *Made in America: A Social History of American Culture and Character* (Chicago: University of Chicago Press, 2010), talks about how the notion of independence and competence is central to American character. Portacolone, "Myth of Independence," 2011, explains how this "myth of independence" increases the vulnerability of seniors. For an interesting discussion of how American notions of individualism permeate organizations that are often placed as contrary to American ideals, see Martín Sánchez-Jankowski, *Islands in the Street: Gangs and American Urban Society* (Berkeley: University of California Press, 1991) for a discussion of individualism among gang members. See also Sandra Susan Smith, *Lone Pursuit: Distrust and Defensive Individualism among the Black Poor* (New York: Russell Sage Foundation, 2007), regarding individualism among African Americans, although her explanation differs in that it emphasizes instrumentality rather than ideology.

17. For more on informal economies generally, see Sudhir Alladi Venkatesh, *Off the Books: The Underground Economy of the Urban Poor* (Cambridge, MA:

Harvard University Press, 2009); *American Project: The Rise and Fall of a Modern Ghetto* (Cambridge, MA: Harvard University Press, 2002); and *Floating City: A Rogue Sociologist Lost and Found in New York's Underground Economy* (New York: Penguin Press HC, 2013). See also Sánchez-Jankowski, *Islands in the Street,* 1991.

18. For a review see Claude S. Fischer and Lauren Beresford, "Changes in Support Networks in Late Middle Age: The Extension of Gender and Educational Differences," *Journals of Gerontology, Series B Advance Access: Psychological Sciences and Social Sciences* (2014). See also Mario Luis Small, *Unanticipated Gains: Origins of Network Inequality in Everyday Life* (New York: Oxford University Press, 2009).

19. Similarly, in her otherwise comparatively optimistic work on the "oldest old" (that is, those over eighty-five), sociologist Meika Loe notes, "Most of the participants [in the study] went out of their way to tell me that living into old age means watching your contemporaries die. All were affected by this, and in this context of loss, isolation can be magnified." See Loe, *Aging Our Way: Lessons for Living from 85 and Beyond* (New York: Oxford University Press, 2011), 547. See also Fischer and Beresford, "Changes in Support Networks," 2014.

20. Loe argues that seniors' abilities to come to terms with the end of life are a major predictor of their ability to "age comfortably" (Loe, *Aging Our Way,* 2011). For more on pets, see Judith M. Siegel, "Stressful Life Events and Use of Physician Services among the Elderly: The Moderating Role of Pet Ownership," *Journal of Personality and Social Psychology* 58, no. 6 (1990): 1081–1086; Dan Labo, Mary Delaney, Melody Miller, and Claire Grill, "Companion Animals, Attitudes toward Pets, and Health Outcomes among the Elderly: A Long-Term Follow-Up," *Anthrozoos* 3, no. 1 (1989): 25–34; and Marian R. Banks and William A. Banks, "The Effects of Animal-Assisted Therapy on Loneliness in an Elderly Population in Long-Term Care Facilities," *Journals of Gerontology, Series A: Biological Sciences and Medical Sciences* 57A, no. 7 (2002): M428–M432.

21. For seniors living in institutions such as nursing homes, this was such a common occurrence that it bordered on the mundane for residents. During a regular visit to a nursing home in Baygardens, I asked one man what had happened to his bedbound roommate, who was absent. He nonchalantly commented, "He died . . . This is the fourth one to die on me." Psychiatrists and gerontologists often refer to the increasing volume of loss, corresponding strain, and potential desensitization as "bereavement overload." Once more, this is a trend that is well documented as an aggregate pattern. See Robert J. Kastenbaum, *Death, Society, and Human Experience* (Boston: Allyn and Bacon, 2008). For similar findings see Loe, *Aging Our Way,* 2011; and Katherine S. Newman, *A Different Shade of Gray: Midlife and beyond in the Inner City* (New York: New Press, 2004).

22. For more on isolation, see Portacolone, "Myth of Independence," 2011; and Klinenberg, *Heat Wave,* 2002.

In addition to the instrumental issues created by loss, patterns and routines were often a very important coping strategy for seniors who lacked the energy, and physical and cognitive flexibility, of youth. Even seemingly small disruptions could be experienced as powerful or distressing events.

23. Sociologist Arlie Russell Hochschild notes the growth of outsourced care and the net effect on families both in the United States and abroad is a larger moral issue we must engage with as the population ages. However, the simpler point here is that, despite the provision of government entitlements, differences in wealth continued to affect older people's options for dealing with everyday challenges. See Hochschild, *Commercialization of Intimate Life,* 2003.

The importance of ties with respect to health outcomes among seniors and others is particularly well documented. See, for instance, Umberson, Crosnoe, and Reczek, "Social Relationships," 2010; Peter S. Bearman and James Moody, "Suicide and Friendships among American Adolescents," *American Journal of Public Health* 94, no. 1 (2004): 89–95; Teresa E. Seeman et al., "Social Relationships, Gender, and Allostatic Load across Two Age Cohorts," *Psychosomatic Medicine* 64, no. 3 (2002): 395–406; Portacolone, "Myth of Independence," 2011; and Klinenberg, *Heat Wave,* 2002.

24. See Umberson, Crosnoe, and Reczek, "Social Relationships," 2010, for more on how this works generally; and Debra Umberson, "Gender, Marital Status and the Social Control of Health Behavior," *Social Science and Medicine* 34, no. 8 (1992): 907–917, for the role of spouses specifically.

25. For a discussion of neighborhood groupings, motivations, and networks, see Martín Sánchez-Jankowski, *Cracks in the Pavement: Social Change and Resilience in Poor Neighborhoods* (Berkeley: University of California Press, 2008). Sánchez-Jankowski also finds motivational variation within families, even among those living in poverty. For the broader debate on the extent to which culture is contextual versus internal, see Vaisey and Lizardo, "Cultural Worldviews," 2010; Stephen Vaisey, "Is Interviewing Compatible with the Dual-Process Model of Culture?" *American Journal of Cultural Sociology* (forthcoming); see also Mario Luis Small, Erin M. Jacobs, and Rebekah Peeples Massengill, "Why Organizational Ties Matter for Neighborhood Effects: Resource Access through Childcare Centers," *Social Forces* 87, no. 1 (2008): 387–414; Sánchez-Jankowski, *Islands in the Street,* 1991; and Ruth E. Malone and Daniel Dohan, "Emergency Department Closures: Policy Issues," *Journal of Emergency Nursing* 26, no. 4 (2000): 380–383. More theoretically, Giddens refers to the dual nature of social systems, or the "duality of structure," in which social systems reflect both human volition and shape the range of volitional behaviors available to us. See Anthony Giddens, *The Constitution of Society: Outline of the Theory of Structuration* (Berkeley: University of California Press, 1986).

26. For more on stress and its relationship to health, see Sheldon Cohen, "Social Relationships and Health," *American Psychologist* 59 (2004): 676–684.

While it is important to move away from seeing networks as universally "good or bad," it is equally important to avoid doing the same thing with norms. Norms, and the schemas that underlie them, result from complex sociohistorical processes that reflect inequalities past and present. The question for social science is not to superimpose our own moral frameworks to decide which set of norms is "good" or "bad," but to examine how these norms shape the behavior of people and organizations—and to what effects. The divergent motivations individuals hold, and the moral connotation of these, lead people to select into friendship networks with those who share their views, consequently reinforcing the operation of both.

27. Whether and how urban ethnographers impose their own moral frameworks on their subjects is a point of assiduous debate—which usually takes place among other urban ethnographers. For example, see Loïc Wacquant, "Scrutinizing the Street: Poverty, Morality, and the Pitfalls of Urban Ethnography," *American Journal of Sociology* 107, no. 6 (2002): 1468–1532, for criticisms and responses.

Conclusion

1. Although there are other mechanisms of inequality that could be included, these five are the pivotal components most closely related to the empirical observations and theoretical questions driving this book.

2. As discussed previously, research in sociology, medicine, and epidemiology has continually shown that ethnic and racial minorities and those of lower socioeconomic status live shorter lives on average, have access to lower quality health care, receive worse treatment for the same conditions, are exposed to higher levels of psychosocial and physical stresses, receive less preventative care, and are more likely to suffer from a host of medical conditions. For a review, see Chapter 1, as well as Nancy E. Adler and Katherine Newman, "Socioeconomic Disparities in Health: Pathways and Policies," *Health Affairs* 21, no. 2 (2002): 60–76; Brian D. Smedley, Adrienne Y. Stith, and Alan R. Nelson, eds. *Unequal Treatment: Confronting Racial and Ethnic Disparities in Health Care* (Washington, DC: National Academies Press, 2003); Roberta Spalter-Roth, Terri Ann Lowenthal, and Mercedes Rubio, "Race, Ethnicity, and the Health of Americans," in *ASA Series on How Race and Ethnicity Matter,* ed. Roberta Spalter-Roth (American Sociological Association, 2005), 1–16, http://www2.asanet.org/centennial/race_ethnicity_health.pdf.

3. See Charles Tilly, *Durable Inequality* (Berkeley: University of California Press, 1999); and Erving Goffman, *Stigma: Notes on the Management of Spoiled Identity* (Englewood Cliffs, NJ: Prentice Hall, 1963).

4. Although her model does not focus on physical resources, once the body is integrated, Swidler's conceptualization of a structural dilemmas becomes a powerful lens for examining the predicaments of growing old in America. See Ann Swidler, *Talk of Love: How Culture Matters* (Chicago: University of Chicago Press, 2001), 201.

5. See Pierre Bourdieu, *Distinction: A Social Critique of the Judgement of Taste* (Cambridge, MA: Harvard University Press, 1984); and Bryan S. Turner, *The Body and Society: Explorations in Social Theory,* 3rd ed. (London: Sage Publications, 2008). For a classic look at labeling and signification, see Goffman, *Stigma,* 1963. For recent examples within the context of poverty and middle-class neighborhoods, see Loïc Wacquant, *Body and Soul: Notebooks of an Apprentice Boxer* (New York: Oxford University Press, 2004); and Martín Sánchez-Jankowski, *Cracks in the Pavement: Social Change and Resilience in Poor Neighborhoods* (Berkeley: University of California Press, 2008). See also Chris Shilling, *The Body and Social Theory* (New York: Sage Publications, 2012); and Loïc Wacquant, "The Pugilistic Point of View: How Boxers Think and Feel about Their Trade," *Theory and Society* 24, no. 4 (1995): 489–535.

    In Jason's case, he lacked the physical resources for pursuing the cultural ends he desired. On a related but more philosophical level, many have argued that the human body is a necessary *precursor* to social structure, as it provides the raw material for social actions and cultural-cognitive constructs that are the foundations of higher-level structures. Shared meanings do not exist without a biologically grounded cognitive system, and physical action cannot take place without an instrument. Although physical traces such as artifacts can exist after our deaths, societies cannot exist without living inhabitants, and at present these agents are still biological beings. See, for instance, Albert J. Bergesen, "Turning Durkheim on His Head: A Reply to Peterson and Bjerre," *Journal for the Theory of Social Behaviour* 42, no. 4 (2012): 485–495; Turner, *Body and Society,* 2008; Bourdieu, *Distinction,* 1984; Aaron V. Cicourel, "Cognitive/Affective Processes, Social Interaction, and Social Structure as Representational Re-Descriptions: Their Contrastive Bandwidths and Spatio-Temporal Foci," *Mind and Society* 5, no. 1 (2006): 39–70; and Stephen Vaisey, "Motivation and Justification: Towards a Dual-Process Theory of Culture in Action," *American Journal of Sociology* 114, no. 6 (2009): 1675–1715.

6. For spillover effects and health, see Jeremy Freese and Karen Lutfey, "Fundamental Causality: Challenges of an Animating Concept for Medical Sociology," in *Handbook of the Sociology of Health, Illness, and Healing: A Blueprint for the 21st Century,* eds. Bernice A. Pescosolido et al. (New York: Springer, 2011), 67–82. See also Alberto Palloni and Carolina Milesi, "Economic Achievement, Inequalities and Health Disparities: The Intervening Role of Early Health Status," *Research in Social Stratification and Mobility* 24 (2006): 21–40.

    For the role of neighborhoods more generally, see Claude S. Fischer, "Showing That Neighborhoods Matter: Review Essay on Sampson, *Great American City,*" *City and Community* 12, no. 1 (2013): 7–12; Robert J. Sampson, *Great American City: Chicago and the Enduring Neighborhood Effect* (Chicago: University of Chicago Press, 2012); and Catherine E. Ross and John Mirowsky, "Neighborhood Socioeconomic Status and Health: Context or Composition?" *City and Community* 7 (2008): 163–179.

7. This is discussed in the introduction. For a review see James S. House et al., "The Social Stratification of Aging and Health," *Journal of Health and Social Behavior* 35 (1994): 213–234; Diane S. Lauderdale, "Education and Survival: Birth Cohort, Period, and Age Effects," *Demography* 38, no. 4 (2001): 551–561; Pamela Herd, "Do Functional Health Inequalities Decrease in Old Age? Educational Status and Functional Decline among the 1931–1941 Birth Cohort," *Research on Aging* 28, no. 3 (2006): 375–392; Jinyoung Kim and Richard Miech, "The Black-White Difference in Age Trajectories of Functional Health over the Life Course," *Social Science and Medicine* 68, no. 4 (2009): 717–725; Timothy J. Owens and Richard Settersten Jr., "New Frontiers in Socialization: An Introduction," in *Advances in Life Course Research: New Frontiers in Socialization,* eds. Richard Settersten Jr. and Timothy Owens, vol. 7 (Oxford: Elsevier, 2002), 3–11; Andrea E. Willson and Kim M. Shuey, "Cumulative Advantage Processes as Mechanisms of Inequality in Life Course Health," *American Journal of Sociology* 112, no. 6 (2007): 1886–1924; Scott M. Lynch, "Explaining Life Course and Cohort Variation in the Relationship between Education and Health: The Role of Income," *Journal of Health and Social Behavior* 47 (2006): 324–338; and Kim M. Shuey and Andrea E. Willson, "Cumulative Disadvantage and Black-White Disparities in Life-Course Health Trajectories," *Research on Aging* 30, no. 2 (2008): 200–225.
8. Although in everyday life the boundaries are fuzzier and overlapping, for analytical clarity and summation, I have separated two categories of resources (columns): individually held resources and contextual resources (those that operate at the level of the group, neighborhood, or community). The resources are further broken into three broad types (rows): material, cultural (i.e., related to shared understandings and symbolic capacities), and physical. The nonmaterial resources are discussed in the sections that follow.
9. In recent decades, a great deal of contemporary scholarship on the relationship between culture and behavior in unequal contexts has focused on how culture can serve as a resource that is unequally distributed across different groups of people. Culture in this sense forms the "tool kits," "repertoires," and "cultural capital" that can influence how people act net of the *inputs* that shape what they find desirable, reasonable, and sensible. I use the term "cultural resource" to group these facets of culture—to emphasize the way culture enables and constrains action not so much by individual belief or motivation but by its social capacity to enable and constrain certain paths of action. For foundational statements see Bourdieu, *Distinction,* 1984; and Swidler, *Culture in Action,* 1986. For a review see Corey M. Abramson, "From 'Either-Or' to 'When and How': A Context-Dependent Model of Culture in Action," *Journal for the Theory of Social Behaviour* 42, no. 2 (2012): 155–180.

   In the larger context-dependent theory of culture, different components of culture lead to the adoption of divergent strategies in different times and places. The implication is that the connection between culture and action is largely context dependent. *Cultural inputs* shape action most directly when all else was equal—that is, they better explain intrastrata variation. *Cultural resources* affect which options can ultimately be pursued—that is, interstrata possibilities and variation. Shared *cultural meanings* (discussed in the next section) form the "raw material" for both social structures and other facets of culture but connect to action most concretely when elaborated, codified, and sanctioned—that is, they better explain behavior in contexts where they are translated into enforceable norms, laws, or customs. See Abramson, "Either-Or," 2012.

10. Max Weber made a similar point when he claimed that sociology is a "science which is concerned with the subjective meaning of action, explanation requires a grasp of the complex of meaning in which an actual course of understandable action thus interpreted belongs." See Max Weber, *Economy and Society* (Berkeley: University of California Press, 1978), 9. See also Abramson, "Either-Or," 2012.

    Throughout this book, and in my formal theoretical work, I have used the term "cultural inputs" to refer to those facets of culture that most directly influence action by shaping what people desire and notice in the world (i.e., motivations and orientations). See Abramson, "Either-Or," 2012. See also Vaisey, "Motivation and Justification," 2009; Sánchez-Jankowski, *Cracks in the Pavement*, 2008; and Ann Swidler, "Culture in Action: Symbols and Strategies," *American Sociological Review* 51, no. 2 (1986): 273–386; and *Talk of Love*, 2001.

11. These understandings about what being connected means shaped how networks functioned and influenced the utility of both strong and weak ties. Cultural meanings, including those around reciprocity, can organize ties through belief (e.g., "I will help a tripping senior, since I should help") or a calculation of sanctions and rewards (e.g., "I will help because if I don't, people will think less of me"). Aiding a senior who trips and falls in the lunchroom can be seen as fulfilling an obligation to a community or disrespecting the foundering individual by highlighting his or her lost independence. In either case, when enforced and codified, these meanings become norms that shape "team dynamics"; they become frameworks that shape what is seen as acceptable or justifiable behavior, whether particular individuals agree with them or not. In other words, they shape action by influencing how action is read. See Abramson, "Either-Or," 2012; Steve Derné, "Cultural Conceptions of Human Motivation and Their Significance for Culture Theory," in *The Sociology of Culture*, ed. Diana Crane (Cambridge: Blackwell, 1994), 267–287; Mario Luis Small, *Unanticipated Gains: Origins of Network Inequality in Everyday Life* (New York: Oxford University Press, 2009); and Swidler, *Talk of Love*, 2001.

12. I am indebted to my colleague Lane Kenworthy, who convincingly argued this point at a recent town hall meeting on better addressing the needs of the working poor in Tucson, Arizona.

13. Smedley et al., *Unequal Treatment*, 2003; and Corey M. Abramson and Martín Sánchez-Jankowski, "Racial Differences in Physician Usage among the

Elderly Poor in the United States," *Research in Social Stratification and Mobility* 30, no. 2 (2012): 203–217.

Methodological Appendix

1. For a classical definition, see Howard Becker, "Problems of Inference and Proof in Participant Observation" *American Sociological Review* 23, no. 6 (1958): 652–660. For a modern take that corresponds to the way it is used in this study, see Martín Sánchez-Jankowski, "Representation, Responsibility and Reliability in Participant Observation" in *Qualitative Research in Action*, ed. Tim May (London: Sage Publications, 2002): 144–159.

2. See Mario Luis Small, "Culture, Cohorts, and Social Organization Theory: Understanding Local Participation in a Latino Housing Project," *American Journal of Sociology* 108, no.1 (2002): 1–54, 9.

3. "A Profile of Older Americans," (Washington DC: U.S. Administration on Aging, 2009); U.S. Census Bureau: California State and County Quickfacts 2013: http://quickfacts.census.gov/qfd/states/06000.html; and Barrett A. Lee, John Iceland, and Gregory Sharp,"Racial and Ethnic Diversity Goes Local: Charting Change in American Communities over Three Decades" (US2010 Project, 2012): http://www.s4.brown.edu/us2010/Data/Report/report08292012.pdf.

4. See Eric Klinenberg, *Heat Wave: A Social Autopsy of Disaster in Chicago* (Chicago: University of Chicago Press, 2002). While these events are rare, the point is they are possible in less temperate regions. See, for example, Susan Candiotti, "Michigan Senior's Freezing Death Preventable, Relative Says" 9*CNN.com/US.*, 2009): http://edition.cnn.com/2009/US/01/29/michigan.freezing.death/index.html.

5. For an example of ethnographic representation using composites, see Nancy Scheper-Hughes, *Saints, Scholars, and Schizophrenics* (Berkeley: University of California Press, 2001).

6. Annette Lareau, *Unequal Childhoods: Class, Race, and Family Life.* (Berkeley: University of California Press, 2003).

7. For more on the topic of CAQDAS and its contribution to ethnographic work, see Daniel Dohan and Martín Sánchez-Jankowski, "Using Computers to Analyze Ethnographic Field Data: Theoretical and Practical Considerations," *Annual Review of Sociology* 24 (1998): 477–498. My general philosophy on examining code associations, which revolves around using codes as an orienting tool to help recognize patterns and deviations, is described in detail elsewhere. For a nontechnical explanation, see Corey M. Abramson, "Qualitative Research in the Positivist-Behavioral Tradition Resources for Addressing Type I and Type II Errors in Code Associations Using ATLAS.ti," *QDA Newsletter* 3 (2011): 5–9. perhttp://cer.berkeley.edu/research-associates-0?

8. Emile Durkheim, *The Division of Labor in Society* (New York: Free Press, 1984), xxvii.

REFERENCES

Abel, Emily K., and Margaret K. Nelson, eds. 1990. *Circles of Care: Work and Identity in Women's Lives*. New York: State University of New York Press.

Abramson, Corey M. 2009. "Who Are the Clients? Goal Displacement in an Adult Day Care Center for Elders with Dementia." *International Journal of Aging and Human Development* 68 (1): 65–92.

———. 2011. "Qualitative Research in the Positivist-Behavioral Tradition: Resources for Addressing Type I and Type II Errors in Code Associations Using ATLAS.ti." *QDA Newsletter* 3: 5–9.

———. 2012. "From 'Either-Or' to 'When and How': A Context-Dependent Model of Culture in Action." *Journal for the Theory of Social Behaviour* 42 (2): 155–180.

Abramson, Corey M., and Darren Modzelewski. 2011. "Caged Morality: Moral Worlds, Subculture, and Stratification among Middle-Class Cage-Fighters." *Qualitative Sociology* 34 (1): 143–175.

Abramson, Corey M., and Martín Sánchez-Jankowski. "Inequality, Race, and Emergency Room Use among Older Americans Living in Poverty" (working paper, Faculty of Sociology, University of Arizona, Tucson).

———. 2012. "Racial Differences in Physician Usage among the Elderly Poor in the United States." *Research in Social Stratification and Mobility* 30 (2): 203–217.

Achenbaum, W. Andrew. 2009. "A Metahistorical Perspective on Theories of Aging." In *Handbook of Theories of Aging*, edited by Vern L. Bengtson, Daphna Gans, Norella M. Putney, and Merril Silverstein, 2nd ed., 25–38. New York: Springer.

Adler, Nancy E., and Katherine S. Newman. 2002. "Socioeconomic Disparities in Health: Pathways and Policies." *Health Affairs* 21 (2): 60–76.

Ajzen, Icek. 1991. "The Theory of Planned Behavior." *Organizational Behavior and Human Decision Processes* 50: 179–211.

Andersen, Ronald M. 1995. "Revisiting the Behavioral Model and Access to Medical Care: Does It Matter?" *Journal of Health and Social Behavior* 36 (1): 1–10.

Antonucci, Toni C., Hiroko Akiyama, and Jennifer E. Lansford. 1998. "Negative Effects of Close Social Relations." *Family Relations* 47 (4): 379–384.

Armstrong, Elizabeth A., and Laura T. Hamilton. 2013. *Paying for the Party: How College Maintains Inequality.* Cambridge, MA: Harvard University Press.

Atchley, Robert C. 1971. "Retirement and Leisure Participation: Continuity or Crisis?" *Gerontologist* 11 (1): 13–17.

Atkinson, Robert D. 1998. "Technological Change and Cities." *Cityscape* 3 (3): 129–170.

Aubert, Geraldine, and Peter M. Landsdorp. 2008. "Telomeres and Aging." *Physiological Review* 88 (2): 557–579.

Auyero, Javier, and Debora Alejandra Swistun. 2009. *Flammable: Environmental Suffering in an Argentine Shantytown.* New York: Oxford University Press.

Avendano, Mauricio, and Ichiro Kawachi. 2014. "Why Do Americans Have Shorter Life Expectancy and Worse Health Than Do People in Other High-Income Countries?" *Annual Review of Public Health* 35: 307–325.

Banks, Marian R., and William A. Banks. 2002. "The Effects of Animal-Assisted Therapy on Loneliness in an Elderly Population in Long-Term Care Facilities." *Journals of Gerontology, Series A: Biological Sciences and Medical Sciences* 57A (7): M428–M432.

Bartley, Mel. 2004. *Health Inequality: An Introduction to Concepts, Theories and Methods.* Cambridge, MA: Polity.

Bassuk, Shari S., Thomas A. Glass, and Lisa F. Berkman. 1999. "Social Disengagement and Incident Cognitive Decline in Community-Dwelling Elderly Persons." *Annals of Internal Medicine* 131 (3): 165–173.

Bearman, Peter S., and James Moody. 2004. "Suicide and Friendships among American Adolescents." *American Journal of Public Health* 94 (1): 89–95.

Becker, Howard. 1958. "Problems of Inference and Proof in Participant Observation." *American Sociological Review* 23 (6): 652–660.

Benetos, Athanase, Koji Okuda, Malika Lajemi, Masayuki Kimura, Frederique Thomas, Joan Skurnick, Carlos Labat, Kathryn Bean, and Abraham Aviv. 2001. "Telomere Length as an Indicator of Biological Aging: The Gender Effect and Relation with Pulse Pressure and Pulse Wave Velocity." *Hypertension* 37: 381–385.

Bergesen, Albert J. 2012. "Turning Durkheim on His Head: A Reply to Peterson and Bjerre." *Journal for the Theory of Social Behaviour* 42 (4): 485–495.

Berkman, Lisa F. 2004. "The Health Divide." *Contexts* 4: 38–51.

Berkman, Lisa F., Thomas Glass, Ian Brissette, and Teresa E. Seeman. 2000. "From Social Integration to Health: Durkheim in the New Millennium." *Social Science and Medicine* 51 (6): 843–857.

Bernard, Miriam, Val Harding Davies, Linda Machin, and Judith Phillips, eds. 2001. *Women Ageing: Changing Identities, Challenging Myths.* New York: Routledge.

Best, Rachel Kahn, Lauren B. Edelman, Linda Hamilton Krieger, and Scott R. Eliason. 2011. "Multiple Disadvantages: An Empirical Test of Intersectionality Theory in EEO Litigation." *Law and Society Review* 45 (4): 991–1025.

Binstock, Robert H., and Linda K. George, eds. 2010. *Handbook of Aging and the Social Sciences.* 7th ed. London: Academic Press.

Boero, Natalie. 2013. *Killer Fat: Media, Medicine, and Morals in the American "Obesity Epidemic."* New Brunswick, NJ: Rutgers University Press.

Bosk, Charles L. 2003. *Forgive and Remember: Managing Medical Failure.* Chicago: University of Chicago Press.

Bourdieu, Pierre. 1984. *Distinction: A Social Critique of the Judgement of Taste.* Cambridge, MA: Harvard University Press.

——. 1986. "The Forms of Capital." In *Handbook for Theory and Research for the Sociology of Education,* edited by John Richardson, 241–258. Westport, CT: Greenwood.

——. 1990. *In Other Words: Essays toward a Reflexive Sociology.* Stanford, CA: Stanford University Press.

——. 1992. *The Logic of Practice.* Stanford, CA: Stanford University Press.

Breen, Richard, and Jan O. Jonsson. 2005. "Inequality of Opportunity in Comparative Perspective: Recent Research on Educational Attainment and Social Mobility." *Annual Review of Sociology* 31: 223–243.

Breiger, Ronald L. 1981. "The Social Class Structure of Occupational Mobility." *American Journal of Sociology* 87: 578–611.

Bursik Jr., Robert J., and Harold G. Grasmick. 1993. *Neighborhoods and Crime: The Dimensions of Effective Community Control.* New York: Lexington Books.

Calasanti, Toni M., and Kathleen F. Slevin. 2001. *Gender, Social Inequalities, and Aging.* New York: AltaMira.

Candiotti, Susan. 2009. "Michigan Senior's Freezing Death Preventable, Relative Says." *CNN.com/US.* http://edition.cnn.com/2009/US/01/29/michigan.freezing.death/index.html.

Carr, Deborah. 2012. "The Social Stratification of Older Adults' Preparations for End-of-Life Health Care." *Journal of Health and Social Behavior* 53 (3): 297–312.

Case, Ann C., and Christina Paxson. 2005. "Sex Differences in Morbidity and Mortality." *Demography* 42 (2): 189–214.

Charlton, James L. 2000. *Nothing about Us without Us: Disability Oppression and Empowerment.* Berkeley: University of California Press.

Christensen, Kaare, Gabriele Doblhammer, Roland Rau, and James W. Vaupel. 2009. "Ageing Populations: The Challenges Ahead." *Lancet* 374: 1196–1208.

Cicourel, Aaron V. 2006. "Cognitive/Affective Processes, Social Interaction, and Social Structure as Representational Re-Descriptions: Their Contrastive Bandwidths and Spatio-Temporal Foci." *Mind and Society* 5 (1): 39–70.

Clarke, Adele E., Laura Mamo, Jennifer Ruth Fosket, Jennifer R. Fishman, and Janet K. Shim, eds. 2010. *Biomedicalization: Technoscience, Health, and Illness in the US.* Durham, NC: Duke University Press.

Clarke, Adele E., Janet K. Shim, Laura Mamo, Jennifer Ruth Fosket, and Jennifer R. Fishman. 2003. "Biomedicalization: Technoscientific Transformations of Health, Illness, and US Biomedicine." *American Sociological Review* 68: 161–194.

Cohen, Elias S. 2001. "The Complex Nature of Ageism: What Is It? Who Does It? Who Perceives It?" *Gerontologist* 41 (5): 576–577.

Cohen, Sheldon. 2004. "Social Relationships and Health." *American Psychologist* 59: 676–684.

Coleman, James S. 1988. "Social Capital in the Creation of Human Capital." In "Organizations and Institutions: Sociological and Economic Approaches to the Analysis of Social Structure," supplement, *American Journal of Sociology* 94 (S1): S95–S120.

Collins, Patricia Hill. 2000. *Black Feminist Thought.* 2nd ed. New York: Routledge.

Conley, Dalton. 1999. *Being Black, Living in the Red: Race, Wealth, and Social Policy in America.* Berkeley: University of California Press.

Corcoran, Mary. 1995. "Rags to Rags: Poverty and Mobility in the United States." *Annual Review of Sociology* 21: 237–267.

Crenshaw, Kimberle. 1989. "Demarginalizing the Intersection of Race and Sex: A Black Feminist Critique of Antidiscrimination Doctrine, Feminist Theory, and Antiracist Politics." *University of Chicago Legal Forum* 140: 139–167.

———. 1991. "Mapping the Margins: Intersectionality, Identity Politics, and Violence against Women of Color." *Stanford Law Review* 43 (6): 1241–1299.

Cumming, Elaine, and William Earl Henry. 1979. *Growing Old (Aging and Old Age).* Manchester, NH: Ayer.

Davidson, Warren, D. William Molloy, George Somers, and Michel Bedard. 1994. "Relation between Physician Characteristics and Prescribing for Elderly People in New Brunswick." *Canadian Medical Association Journal* 150 (6): 917–921.

Davis, Lennard J., ed. 2010. *The Disability Studies Reader.* 3rd ed. New York: Routledge.

Derné, Steve. 1994. "Cultural Conceptions of Human Motivation and Their Significance for Culture Theory." In *The Sociology of Culture,* edited by Diana Crane, 267–287. Cambridge: Blackwell.

Doescher, Mark P., Barry G. Saver, Peter Franks, and Kevin Fiscella. 2000. "Racial and Ethnic Disparities in Perceptions of Physician Style and Trust." *Archives of Family Medicine* 9 (10): 1156–1163.

Dohan, Daniel. 2003. *The Price of Poverty: Money, Work, and Culture in the Mexican-American Barrios.* Berkeley: University of California Press.

Dohan, Daniel, and Martín Sánchez-Jankowski. 1998. "Using Computers to Analyze Ethnographic Field Data: Theoretical and Practical Considerations." *Annual Review of Sociology* 24: 477–498.

Dowd, James J. 1987. "Reification of Age: Age Stratification Theory and the Passing of the Autonomous Subject." *Journal of Aging Studies* 1 (4): 317–335.

Dugdale, David C., Ronald Epstein, and Steven Z. Pantilat. 1999. "Time and the Patient–Physician Relationship." *Journal of General Internal Medicine* 14 (S1): S34–S40.

Duneier, Mitchell. 1994. *Slim's Table: Race, Respectability, and Masculinity.* American Studies Collection. Chicago: University of Chicago Press.

———. 1999. *Sidewalk.* New York: Farrar Straus Giroux.

Dupre, Matthew E. 2007. "Educational Differences in Age-Related Patterns of Disease: Reconsidering the Cumulative Disadvantage and Age-as-Leveler Hypotheses." *Journal of Health and Social Behavior* 48: 1–15.

Durkheim, Emile. 1995. *The Elementary Forms of Religious Life.* New York: Free Press.

———. 1997a. *Suicide: A Study in Sociology.* Reissue ed. New York: Free Press.

———. 1997b. *The Division of Labor in Society.* New York: Free Press.

Elder, Glen H., Monica Kirkpatrick Johnson, and Robert Crosnoe. 2003. "The Emergence and Development of Life Course Theory." In *Handbook of the Life Course,* edited by Jeylan T. Mortimer and Michael J. Shanahan, 3–19. New York: Springer.

Eliasoph, Nina, and Paul Lichterman. 2003. "Culture in Interaction." *American Journal of Sociology* 108: 735–794.

Entwisle, Barbara, Katherine Faust, Ronald R. Rindfuss, and Toshiko Kaneda. 2007. "Networks and Contexts: Variation in the Structure of Social Ties." *American Journal of Sociology* 112 (5): 1495–1533.

Esping-Andersen, Gøsta. 2004. "Unequal Opportunities and the Mechanisms of Social Inheritance." In *Generational Income Mobility in North America and Europe,* edited by Miles Corak, 289–314. Cambridge: Cambridge University Press.

Estes, Carroll L., Simon Biggs, and Chris Phillipson. 2003. *Social Theory, Social Policy, and Ageing: Critical Perspectives.* Berkshire, UK: Open University Press.

Estes, Carroll L., and Elizabeth A. Binney. 1989. "The Biomedicalization of Aging: Dangers and Dilemmas." *Gerontologist* 29 (5): 587–596.

Evans, Gary W., and Susan Saegert. 2000. "Residential Crowding in the Context of Inner City Poverty." In *Theoretical Perspectives in Environment-Behavior Research,* edited by Seymour Wapner, Jack Demick, Takiji Yamamoto, and Hirofumi Minami, 320. New York: Kluwer Academic/Plenum.

Farmer, Paul. 1999. *Infections and Inequalities: The Modern Plagues.* Berkeley: University of California Press.

Field, Marilyn J., and Christine K. Cassel, eds. 1997. *Approaching Death: Improving Care at the End of Life.* Washington, DC: National Academy Press.

Findlay, Robyn A. 2003. "Interventions to Reduce Social Isolation amongst Older People: Where Is the Evidence?" *Ageing and Society* 23: 647–658.

Fiscella, Kevin, Peter Franks, Mark P. Doescher, and Barry G. Saver. 2002. "Disparities in Health Care by Race, Ethnicity, and Language among the Insured: Findings from a National Sample." *Medical Care* 40 (1): 52–59.

Fischer, Claude S. 1994. *America Calling: A Social History of the Telephone to 1940.* Berkeley: University of California Press.

———. 2005. "Bowling Alone: What's the Score?" *Social Networks* 27: 155–167.

———. 2010. *Made in America: A Social History of American Culture and Character.* Chicago: University of Chicago Press.

———. 2011. *Still Connected: Family and Friends in America since 1970.* New York: Russell Sage Foundation.

———. 2013. "Showing That Neighborhoods Matter: Review Essay on Sampson, *Great American City.*" *City and Community* 12 (1): 7–12.

Fischer, Claude S., and Lauren Beresford. 2014. "Changes in Support Networks in Late Middle Age: The Extension of Gender and Educational Differences." *Journals of Gerontology, Series B Advance Access: Psychological Sciences and Social Sciences.* doi: 10.1093/geronb/gbu057.

Fischer, Claude S., and Michael Hout. 2006. *Century of Difference: How America Changed in the Last One Hundred Years.* New York: Russell Sage Foundation.

Foucault, Michel. 1980. *The History of Sexuality: An Introduction,* vol. 1. New York: Vintage Books.

Freese, Jeremy, and Karen Lutfey. 2011. "Fundamental Causality: Challenges of an Animating Concept for Medical Sociology." In *Handbook of the Sociology of Health, Illness, and Healing: A Blueprint for the 21st Century,* edited by Bernice A. Pescosolido, Jack K. Martin, Jane D. McLeod, and Anne Rogers, 67–82. New York: Springer.

Freidenberg, Judith Noemi. 2000. *Growing Old in El Barrio.* New York: New York University Press.

Freimuth, Vicki S., Sandra Crouse Quinn, Stephen B. Thomas, Galen Cole, Eric Zook, and Ted Duncan. 2001. "African Americans' Views on Research and the Tuskegee Syphilis Study." *Social Science and Medicine* 52: 797–808.

Frye, Margaret. 2012. "Bright Futures in Malawi's New Dawn: Educational Aspirations as Assertions of Identity." *American Journal of Sociology* 117 (6): 1565–1624.

Gans, Herbert J. 1982. *Urban Villagers: Group and Class in the Life of Italian-Americans.* New York: Free Press.

———. 2012. "Against Culture Versus Structure." *Identities: Global Studies in Culture and Power* 19 (2): 125–134.

Geertz, Clifford. 2000. "Religion as a Cultural System." In *The Interpretation of Cultures: Selected Essays,* 87–125. New York: Basic Books.

Giddens, Anthony. 1986. *The Constitution of Society: Outline of the Theory of Structuration.* Berkeley: University of California Press.

Goesling, Brian. 2007. "The Rising Significance of Education for Health?" *Social Forces* 85 (4): 1622–1644.

Goffman, Alice. 2009. "On the Run: Wanted Men in a Philadelphia Ghetto." *American Sociological Review* 74 (3): 339–357.

Goffman, Erving. 1959. *The Presentation of Self in Everyday Life.* New York: Anchor Books.

———. 1963. *Stigma: Notes on the Management of Spoiled Identity.* Englewood Cliffs, NJ: Prentice Hall.

Graham, Stephen, and Simon Marvin. 1996. *Telecommunications and City: Electronic Spaces, Urban Places*. New York: Routledge.

Granovetter, Mark S. 1973. "The Strength of Weak Ties." *American Journal of Sociology* 78 (6): 1360–1380.

———. 1983. "The Strength of Weak Ties: A Network Theory Revisited." *Sociological Theory* 1: 201–233.

Grusky, David B., ed. 2001. *Social Stratification: Class, Race, and Gender in Sociological Perspective*. 2nd ed. Boulder, CO: Westview.

Haas, Steven. 2008. "Trajectories of Functional Health: The 'Long Arm' of Childhood Health and Socioeconomic Factors." *Social Science and Medicine* 66 (4): 849–861.

Hall, John R. 1992. "The Capital(s) of Cultures: A Nonholistic Approach to Status Situations, Class, Gender, and Ethnicity." In *Cultivating Boundaries: Symbolic Boundaries and the Making of Inequality*, edited by Michéle Lamont and Marcel Fournier, 257–285. Chicago and London: University of Chicago Press.

Harding, David J. 2010. *Living the Drama: Community, Conflict, and Culture among Inner-City Boys*. Chicago: University of Chicago Press.

Harvey, David. 1991. *The Condition of Postmodernity*. Hoboken, NJ: Wiley-Blackwell.

Hasenfeld, Yeheskel. 1972. "People Processing Organizations: An Exchange Approach." *American Sociological Review* 37: 256–263.

Hatch, Laurie Russell. 2005. "Gender and Ageism." *Generations* 29 (3): 19–24.

Hayes-Bautista, David E., Paul Hsu, Aide Perez, and Christina Gamboa. 2002. "The 'Browning' of the Graying of America: Diversity in the Elderly Population and Policy Implications." *Generations* 26 (3): 15–24.

Hayward, Mark D., and Bridget K. Gorman. 2004. "The Long Arm of Childhood: The Influence of Early-Life Social Conditions on Men's Mortality." *Demography* 41 (1): 87–107.

Hedström, Peter. 2005. *Dissecting the Social: On the Principles of Analytical Sociology*. Cambridge: Cambridge University Press.

Hedström, Peter, and Richard Swedberg. 1998. "Social Mechanisms: An Introductory Essay." In *Social Mechanisms: An Analytical Approach to Social Theory*, edited by Peter Hedström and Richard Swedberg, 1–31. Cambridge: Cambridge University Press.

Hedström, Peter, and Petri Ylikoski. 2010. "Causal Mechanisms in the Social Sciences." *Annual Review of Sociology* 26: 49–67.

Helgeson, Vicki S. 2011. "Survivor Centrality among Breast Cancer Survivors: Implications for Well-Being." *Psychooncology* 20 (5): 517–524.

Herd, Pamela. 2006. "Do Functional Health Inequalities Decrease in Old Age? Educational Status and Functional Decline among the 1931–1941 Birth Cohort." *Research on Aging* 28 (3): 375–392.

Herd, Pamela, Brian Goesling, and James S. House. 2007. "Socioeconomic Position and Health: The Differential Effects of Education Versus Income on the Onset Versus Progression of Health Problems." *Journal of Health and Social Behavior* 48: 223–238.

Hochschild, Arlie Russell. 1973. *The Unexpected Community.* Englewood Cliffs, NJ: Prentice Hall.

———. 2003. *The Commercialization of Intimate Life: Notes from Home and Work.* Berkeley: University of California Press.

Holliday, Robin. 2006. "Aging Is No Longer an Unsolved Problem in Biology." *Annals of the New York Academy of Sciences* 1067: 1–9.

House, James S., Paula M. Lantz, and Pamela Herd. 2005. "Continuity and Change in the Social Stratification of Aging and Health over the Life Course: Evidence from a Nationally Representative Longitudinal Study from 1986 to 2001/2002 (Americans' Changing Lives Study)," special issue, *Journals of Gerontology, Series B: Psychological Sciences and Social Sciences* 60 (SI2): 15–26.

House, James S., James M. Lepkowski, Ann M. Kinney, Richard P. Mero, Ronald C. Kessler, and A. Regula Herzog. 1994. "The Social Stratification of Aging and Health." *Journal of Health and Social Behavior* 35: 213–234.

Hout, Michael, and Thomas A. DiPrete. 2006. "What We Have Learned: RC28's Contributions to Knowledge about Social Stratification." *Research in Social Stratification and Mobility* 24: 1–20.

Howard, George, Roger T. Anderson, Gregory Russell, Virginia J. Howard, and Gregory L. Burke. 2000. "Race, Socioeconomic Status, and Cause-Specific Mortality." *Annals of Epidemiology* 10 (4): 214–223.

Hoyert, Donna L., and Jiaquan Xu. 2012. "Deaths: Preliminary Data for 2011." *National Vital Statistics Reports* 61 (6): 1–52.

Hu, Peifeng, and David B. Reuben. 2002. "Effects of Managed Care on the Length of Time That Elderly Patients Spend with Physicians during Ambulatory Visits: National Ambulatory Medical Care Survey." *Medical Care* 40 (7): 606–613.

Hulka, Barbara, and John R. Wheat. 1985. "Patterns of Utilization: The Patient Perspective." *Medical Care* 23 (5): 438–460.

Iseki, Hiroyuki, Adina Ringler, Brian D. Taylor, Mark Miller, and Michael Smart. 2007. "Evaluating Transit Stops and Stations from the Perspective of Transit Users." Sacramento, CA: California Department of Transportation.

Jackson, Kenneth T. 1987. *Crabgrass Frontier: The Suburbanization of the United States.* New York: Oxford University Press.

Jindra, Michael. 2014. "The Dilemma of Equality and Diversity." *Current Anthropology* 55 (3): 316–334.

Jokela, Markus, Jane E. Ferrie, David Gimeno, Tarani Chandola, Martin J. Shipley, Jenny Head, Jussi Vahtera, Hugo Westerlund, Michael G. Marmot, and Mika Kivimaki. 2010. "From Midlife to Early Old Age: Health Trajectories Associated with Retirement." *Epidemiology* 21: 284–290.

Kastenbaum, Robert J. 2008. *Death, Society, and Human Experience.* Boston: Allyn and Bacon.

Kaufman, Sharon R. 1994. *The Ageless Self: Sources of Meaning in Late Life*. Madison: University of Wisconsin Press.

Kim, Jinyoung. 2008. "Intercohort Trends in the Relationship between Education and Health." *Journal of Aging and Health* 20 (6): 671–693.

Kim, Jinyoung, and Richard Miech. 2009. "The Black-White Difference in Age Trajectories of Functional Health over the Life Course." *Social Science and Medicine* 68 (4): 717–725.

Kington, Raynard S., and James P. Smith. 1997. "Socioeconomic and Ethnic Differences in Functional Status Associated with Chronic Diseases." *American Journal of Public Health* 87 (5): 805–810.

Kirby, James B., and Toshiko Kaneda. 2005. "Neighborhood Socioeconomic Disadvantage and Access to Health Care." *Journal of Health and Social Behavior* 46: 5–31.

Klinenberg, Eric. 2002. *Heat Wave: A Social Autopsy of Disaster in Chicago*. Chicago: University of Chicago Press.

———. 2013. *Going Solo: The Extraordinary Rise and Surprising Appeal of Living Alone*. New York: Penguin Books.

Kuhn, Thomas S. 1996. *The Structure of Scientific Revolutions*. 3rd ed. Chicago: University of Chicago Press.

Kwak, Jung, and William E. Haley. 2005. "Current Research Findings on End-of-Life Decision Making among Racially or Ethnically Diverse Groups." *Gerontologist* 45 (5): 634–641.

Labo, Dan, Mary Delaney, Melody Miller, and Claire Grill. 1989. "Companion Animals, Attitudes toward Pets, and Health Outcomes among the Elderly: A Long-Term Follow-Up." *Anthrozoos* 3 (1): 25–34.

Laitin, David D. 1986. *Hegemony and Culture: Politics and Religious Change among the Yoruba*. Chicago: University of Chicago Press.

Lamont, Michèle. 2000. *The Dignity of Working Men: Morality and the Boundaries of Race, Class, and Immigration*. Cambridge, MA: Harvard University Press.

Lamont, Michèle, and Mario Luis Small. 2008. "How Culture Matters: Enriching Our Understandings of Poverty." In *The Colors of Poverty: Why Racial and Ethnic Disparities Persist,* edited by David Harris and Ann Lin, 76–102. New York: Russell Sage Foundation.

Lareau, Annette. 2003. *Unequal Childhoods: Class, Race, and Family Life*. Berkeley: University of California Press.

Lauderdale, Diane S. 2001. "Education and Survival: Birth Cohort, Period, and Age Effects." *Demography* 38 (4): 551–561.

Lee, Barrett A., John Iceland, and Gregory Sharp. 2012. "Racial and Ethnic Diversity Goes Local: Charting Change in American Communities over Three Decades." US2010 Project. http://www.s4.brown.edu/us2010/Data/Report/report08292012.pdf.

Lee, Helen. 2012. "The Role of Local Food Availability in Explaining Obesity Risk among Young School-Aged Children." *Social Science and Medicine* 74 (8): 1193–1203.

Lévi-Strauss, Claude. 1974. *Structural Anthropology*. New York: Basic Books.

Lewis, Oscar. 1975. *Five Families: Mexican Case Studies in the Culture of Poverty.* New York: Basic Books.

Li, Shu-Chen. 2002. "Connecting the Many Levels and Facets of Cognitive Aging." *Current Directions in Physiological Science* 11 (1): 38–43.

Liebow, Elliot. 2003. *Tally's Corner: A Study of Negro Streetcorner Men.* Legacies of Social Thought Series. Lanham, MD: Rowman and Littlefield.

Lin, Nan. 2001. *Social Capital: A Theory of Social Structure and Action.* Cambridge: Cambridge University Press.

Link, Bruce G., and Jo C. Phelan. 1995. "Social Conditions as Fundamental Causes of Disease." *Journal of Health and Social Behavior* 35: 80–94.

Lizardo, Omar. 2004. "The Cognitive Origins of Bourdieu's Habitus." *Journal for the Theory of Social Behaviour* 34 (4): 375–401.

Loe, Meika. 2011. *Aging Our Way: Lessons for Living from 85 and Beyond.* New York: Oxford University Press.

Logan, John R., Russell Ward, and Glenna Spitze. 1992. "As Old as You Feel: Age Identity in Middle and Later Life." *Social Forces* 71 (2): 451–467.

Loignon, Christine, Jeannie L. Haggerty, Martin Fortin, Christophe P. Bedos, David Barbeau, and Dawn Allen. 2010. "What Makes Primary Care Effective for People in Poverty Living with Multiple Chronic Conditions? Study Protocol." *BMC Health Services Research* 10: 320.

Longmore, Paul K. 2003. *Why I Burned My Book and Other Essays on Disability.* Philadelphia: Temple University Press.

Lutfey, Karen, and Jeremy Freese. 2005. "Toward Some Fundamentals of Fundamental Causality: Socioeconomic Status and Health in the Routine Clinic Visit for Diabetes." *American Journal of Sociology* 110: 1326–1372.

Lynch, Scott M. 2003. "Cohort and Life-Course Patterns in the Relationship between Education and Health: A Hierarchical Approach." *Demography* 40: 309–331.

———. 2006. "Explaining Life Course and Cohort Variation in the Relationship between Education and Health: The Role of Income." *Journal of Health and Social Behavior* 47: 324–338.

Malone, Ruth E., and Daniel Dohan. 2000. "Emergency Department Closures: Policy Issues." *Journal of Emergency Nursing* 26 (4): 380–383.

Mason, Katherine. 2013. "Social Stratification and the Body: Gender, Race, and Class." *Sociology Compass* 7/8: 686–698.

Massey, Douglas S. 2007. *Categorically Unequal: The American Stratification System.* New York: Russell Sage Foundation.

Massey, Douglas S., and Nancy A. Denton. 1993. *American Apartheid: Segregation and the Making of the Underclass.* Cambridge, MA: Harvard University Press.

Masters, Ryan K. 2012. "Uncrossing the US Black-White Mortality Crossover: The Role of Cohort Forces in Life Course Mortality Risk." *Demography* 49 (3): 773–796.

Mathieson, Cynthia M., and Henderikus J. Stam. 1995. "Renegotiating Identity: Cancer Narratives." *Sociology of Health and Illness* 17 (3): 283–306.

Mauss, Marcel. 2000. *The Gift: The Form and Reason for Exchange in Archaic Societies.* New York: W. W. Norton.

McBean, Alexander M., and Marian E. Gornick. 1994. "Differences by Race in the Rates of Procedures Performed in Hospitals for Medicare Beneficiaries." *Health Financing Review* 15 (4): 77–90.

Mendes, Wendy Berry. 2010. "Weakened Links between Mind and Body in Older Age: The Case for Maturational Dualism in the Experience of Emotion." *Emotion Review* 2 (3): 240–244.

Mintz, Steven. 2006. *Huck's Raft: A History of American Childhood*. Cambridge, MA: Belknap.

Mirowsky, John, and Catherine E. Ross. 2008. "Education and Self-Rated Health: Cumulative Advantage and Its Rising Importance." *Research on Aging* 30 (1): 93–122.

Molm, Linda D., Monica M. Whitham, and David Melamed. 2012. "Forms of Exchange and Integrative Bonds: Effects of History and Embeddedness." *American Sociological Review* 77 (1): 141–165.

Moody-Ayers, Sandra Y., Kala M. Mehta, Karla Lindquist, Laura Sands, and Kenneth E. Covinsky. 2005. "Black-White Disparities in Functional Decline in Older Persons: The Role of Cognitive Function." *Journals of Gerontology, Series A: Biological Sciences and Medical Sciences* 60 (7): 933–939.

Moore, Crystal Dea, and Meika Loe. 2011. "From Nursing Home to Green House: Changing Contexts of Elder Care in the United States." *Journal of Applied Gerontology* 31 (6): 755–763.

Morgan, Stephen L., and Christopher Winship. 2007. *Counterfactuals and Causal Inference: Methods and Principles for Social Research Analytical Methods for Social Research*. Cambridge: Cambridge University Press.

Murray, Christopher J. L., Sandeep C. Kulkarni, Catherine Michaud, Niels Tomijima, Maria T. Bulzacchelli, Terrell J. Iandiorio, and Majid Ezzati. 2006. "Eight Americas: Investigating Mortality Disparities across Races, Counties, and Race-Counties in the United States." *PLoS Medicine* 3 (9): 1513–1524.

Myerhoff, Barbara. 1980. *Number Our Days: A Triumph of Continuity and Culture among Jewish Old People in an Urban Ghetto*. New York: Touchstone.

Neckerman, Kathryn M., ed. 2004. *Social Inequality*. New York: Russell Sage Foundation.

Newman, Katherine S. 2004. *A Different Shade of Gray: Midlife and beyond in the Inner City*. New York: New Press.

Noar, Seth M., and Rick S. Zimmerman. 2005. "Health Behavior Theory and Cumulative Knowledge Regarding Health Behaviors: Are We Moving in the Right Direction?" *Health Education Research* 20 (3): 275–290.

Nusbaum, Neil J. 1999. "Aging and Sensory Senescence." *Southern Medical Journal* 92 (3): 267–276.

Nussbaum, Jon F., Margaret J. Pitts, Frances N. Huber, Janice L. Raup Krieger, and Jennifer E. Ohs. 2005. "Ageism and Ageist Language across the Life Span: Intimate Relationships and Non-Intimate Interactions." *Journal of Social Issues* 61 (2): 287–305.

Olshansky, S. Jay, Toni Antonucci, Lisa Berkman, Robert H. Binstock, Axel Boersch-Supan, John T. Cacioppo, Bruce A. Carnes, Laura L. Carstensen,

Linda P. Fried, Dana P. Goldman, James Jackson, Martin Kohli, John Rother, Yuhui Zheng, and John Rowe. 2012. "Differences in Life Expectancy Due to Race and Educational Differences Are Widening, and Many May Not Catch Up." *Health Affairs* 31 (8): 1803–1813.

Olson, Christine M. 1999. "Nutrition and Health Outcomes Associated with Food Insecurity and Hunger." *Journal of Nutrition* 129 (2): 521S–524S.

Owens, Timothy J., and Richard A. Settersten Jr. 2002. "New Frontiers in Socialization: An Introduction." In *Advances in Life Course Research: New Frontiers in Socialization,* edited by Richard A. Settersten Jr. and Timothy J. Owens, vol. 7, 3–11. Oxford: Elsevier.

Pachucki, Mark A., and Ronald L. Breiger. 2010. "Cultural Holes: Beyond Relationality in Social Networks and Culture." *Annual Review of Sociology* 36 (1): 205–224.

Palloni, Alberto, and Carolina Milesi. 2006. "Economic Achievement, Inequalities and Health Disparities: The Intervening Role of Early Health Status." *Research in Social Stratification and Mobility* 24: 21–40.

Pampel, Fred C., Patrick M. Krueger, and Justin T. Denney. 2010. "Socioeconomic Disparities in Health Behaviors." *Annual Review of Sociology* 36: 349–370.

Park, Crystal L., Ianita Zlateva, and Thomas O. Blank. 2009. "Self-Identity after Cancer: 'Survivor,' 'Victim,' 'Patient,' and 'Person with Cancer,'" *Journal of General Internal Medicine* 24 (S2): 430–435.

Park, Nan Sook. 2009. "The Relationship of Social Engagement to Psychological Well-Being of Older Adults in Assisted Living Facilities." *Journal of Applied Gerontology* 28 (4): 461–481.

Parsons, Talcott. 1937. *The Structure of Social Action.* New York: Free Press.

———. 1951. *The Social System.* New York: Free Press.

Pasquetti, Sylvia. 2013. "Legal Emotions: An Ethnography of Distrust and Fear in the Arab Districts of an Israeli City." *Law and Society Review* 47 (3): 461–492.

Patterson, James T. 2000. *America's Struggle against Poverty in the Twentieth Century.* 4th ed. Cambridge, MA: Harvard University Press.

Pescosolido, Bernice A. 1992. "Beyond Rational Choice: The Social Dynamics of How People Seek Help." *American Journal of Sociology* 97 (4): 1096–1138.

Pescosolido, Bernice A., and Sigrum Olafsdottir. 2010. "The Cultural Turn in Sociology: Can It Help Us Resolve an Age-Old Problem in Understanding Decision Making for Health Care?" *Sociological Forum* 25 (4): 655–676.

Pescosolido, Bernice A., Brea L. Perry, Scott Long, Jack K. Martin, John I. Nurnberger, and Victor Hesselbrock. 2008. "Under the Influence of Genetics: How Transdisciplinarity Leads Us to Rethink Social Pathways to Illness." *American Journal of Sociology* 114 (S1): S171–S201.

Pew Research Center. "A Portrait of American Jews." 2013. Religion and Public Life Project. http://www.pewforum.org/2013/10/01/jewish-american-beliefs -attitudes-culture-survey/.

Phelan, Jo C., and Bruce G. Link. 2005. "Controlling Disease and Creating Disparities: A Fundamental Cause Perspective," special issue, *Journals of Gerontology, Series B: Psychological Sciences and Social Sciences* 60 (SI2): S27–S33.

Phelan, Jo C., Bruce G. Link, and Parisa Tehranifar. 2010. "Social Conditions as Fundamental Causes of Health Inequalities: Theory, Evidence, and Policy Implications," supplement, *Journal of Health and Social Behavior* 51 (S1): S28–S40.

Portacolone, Elena. 2014. "Older Americans Living Alone: The Influence of Resources and Intergenerational Integration on Inequality." *Journal of Contemporary Ethnography*. doi: 10.1177/0891241614528709: 1–26.

——. 2011. "The Myth of Independence for Older Americans Living Alone in the Bay Area of San Francisco: A Critical Reflection." *Ageing and Society* 31: 803–828.

——. 2013. "The Notion of Precariousness among Older Adults Living Alone in the US" *Journal of Aging Studies* 27 (2): 166–174.

Portes, Alejandro. 1998. "Social Capital: Its Origins and Applications in Modern Sociology." *Annual Review of Sociology* 24: 1–24.

Portes, Alejandro, and Erik Vickstrom. 2011. "Diversity, Social Capital, and Cohesion." *Annual Review of Sociology* 37: 461–479.

Prottas, Jeffrey Manditch. 1979. *People Processing: The Street-Level Bureaucrat in Public Service Bureaucracies*. Lexington, MA: Lexington Books.

Putnam, Robert D. 2001. *Bowling Alone: The Collapse and Revival of American Community*. New York: Touchstone.

Quadagno, Jill. 1988. *The Transformation of Old Age Security: Class and Politics in the American Welfare State*. Chicago: University of Chicago Press.

Quadagno, Jill, and JoEllen Pederson. 2012. "Has Support for Social Security Declined? Attitudes toward the Public Pension Scheme in the USA, 2000 and 2010," supplement, *International Journal of Social Welfare* 21 (S1): S88–S100.

Quantified Self Labs, *Quantified Self: Self-Knowledge through Numbers:* http://quantifiedself.com

Rahim-Williams, Bridgett, Joseph L. Riley III, Ameenah K. K. Williams, and Roger B. Fillingim. 2012. "A Quantitative Review of Ethnic Group Differences in Experimental Pain Response: Do Biology, Psychology and Culture Matter?" *Pain Medicine* 13 (4): 522–540.

Rattan, Suresh I. S. 2006. "Theories of Biological Aging: Genes, Proteins, and Free Radicals." *Free Radical Research* 40 (12): 1230–1238.

Riach, Kathleen. 2007. "'Othering': Older Worker Identity in Recruitment." *Human Relations* 60 (11): 1701–1726.

Riley, Matilda White. 1986. "Overview and Highlights of a Sociological Perspective." In *Human Development and the Life Course: Multidisciplinary Perspectives,* edited by Aage B. Sorensen, Franz E. Weinert, and Lonnie R. Sherrod, 153–175. Hillsdale, NJ: Lawrence Erlbaum.

Riley, Matilda White, Marilyn E. Johnson, and Anne Foner, eds. 1972. *A Sociology of Age Stratification.* Aging and Society, vol. 3. 3rd ed. New York: Russell Sage Foundation.

Roberts, Beverly A., Rebecca Fuhrer, Michael Marmot, and Marcus Richards. 2011. "Does Retirement Influence Cognitive Performance? The Whitehall II Study." *Journal of Epidemiological Community Health* 65: 958–963.

Roberts, Susan B., and Irwin Rosenberg. 2006. "Nutrition and Aging: Changes in the Regulation of Energy Metabolism with Aging." *American Physiological Review* 86 (2): 651–667.

Rohe, William M., and Harry L. Watson, eds. 2007. *Chasing the American Dream: New Perspectives on Affordable Homeownership.* Ithaca, NY: Cornell University Press.

Rook, Karen. 1997. "Positive and Negative Social Exchanges: Weighing Their Effects in Later Life." *Journals of Gerontology, Series B: Psychological Sciences and Social Sciences* 52: S167–S169.

Root, Kenneth A., and Rosemarie J. Park. 2008. *Forced Out: Older Workers Confront Job Loss.* Boulder, CO: Lynne Rienner.

Roscigno, Vincent J., Sherry Mong, and Reginald Byron. 2007. "Age Discrimination, Social Closure and Employment." *Social Forces* 86 (1): 313–334.

Rose, Donald. 1999. "Economic Determinants and Dietary Consequences of Food Insecurity in the United States." *Journal of Nutrition* 129 (2): 5175–5205.

Rose, Stephen J., and Scott Winship. 2009. "Ups and Downs: Does the American Economy Still Promote Upward Mobility?" Economic Mobility Project, Pew Charitable Trusts.

Ross, Catherine E., and John Mirowsky. 2001. "Neighborhood Disadvantage, Disorder, and Health." *Journal of Health and Social Behavior* 42 (3): 258–276.

———. 2008. "Neighborhood Socioeconomic Status and Health: Context or Composition?" *City and Community* 7: 163–179.

Saguy, Abigail C. 2013. *What's Wrong with Fat?* Oxford: Oxford University Press.

Sallaz, Jeffrey J. 2006. "The Making of the Global Gambling Industry: An Application and Extension of Field Theory." *Theory and Society* 35 (3): 265–297.

Sallaz, Jeffrey J., and Jane Zavisca. 2007. "Bourdieu in American Sociology, 1980–2004." *Annual Review of Sociology* 33 (1): 21–41.

Salthouse, Timothy A. 2004. "What and When of Cognitive Aging." *Current Directions in Physiological Science* 13 (4): 140–144.

Sampson, Robert J. 2003. "Neighborhood-Level Context and Health." In *Neighborhoods and Health,* edited by Ichiro Kawachi and Lisa F. Berkman, 132–146. New York: Oxford University Press.

———. 2012. *Great American City: Chicago and the Enduring Neighborhood Effect.* Chicago: University of Chicago Press.

Sampson, Robert J., and Corina Graif. 2009. "Neighborhood Social Capital as Differential Social Organization: Resident and Leadership Dimensions." *American Behavioral Scientist* 52 (11): 1579–1605.

Sampson, Robert J., Jeffrey D. Morenoff, and Thomas Gannon-Rowley. 2002. "Assessing 'Neighborhood Effects': Social Processes and New Directions in Research." *Annual Review of Sociology* 28: 443–478.

Sánchez-Jankowski, Martín. 1991. *Islands in the Street: Gangs and American Urban Society.* Berkeley: University of California Press.

——. 2002. "Representation, Responsibility and Reliability in Participant Observation." In *Qualitative Research in Action*, edited by Tim May, 144–159. London: Sage Publications.

——. 2008. *Cracks in the Pavement: Social Change and Resilience in Poor Neighborhoods*. Berkeley: University of California Press.

Martín Sánchez-Jankowski and Corey M. Abramson, "Direct Observation and Causal Inference: The Function and Practice of Participant Observation in the Positivist-Behavioral Tradition," working paper, *American Journal of Sociology Conference on Causal Thinking and Ethnographic Research*, https://sites .google.com/site/ajs2012conference/2011-ieee-ss.

Sautter, Jessica M., Patricia A. Thomas, Matthew E. Dupre, and Linda K. George. 2012. "Socioeconomic Status and the Black–White Mortality Crossover." *American Journal of Public Health* 102 (8): 1566–1571.

Scheper-Hughes, Nancy. 2001. *Saints, Scholars, and Schizophrenics*. Berkeley: University of California Press.

Schultz, Jennifer, and Ronald L. Breiger. 2010. "The Strength of Weak Culture." *Poetics* 38 (6): 610–624.

Schwartz, Shalom H. 1994. "Are There Universal Aspects in the Structure and Contents of Human Values?" *Journal of Social Issues* 50 (4): 19–45.

Seeman, Teresa E., Burton H. Singer, Carol D. Ryff, Gayle Dienberg Love, and Lene Levy-Storms. 2002. "Social Relationships, Gender, and Allostatic Load across Two Age Cohorts." *Psychosomatic Medicine* 64 (3): 395–406.

Sen, Amartya. 1984. *Resources, Values, and Development*. Cambridge, MA: Harvard University Press.

Sewell Jr., William H. 1992. "A Theory of Structure: Duality, Agency, and Transformation." *American Journal of Sociology* 98 (1): 1–29.

Shaw, Mary. 2004. "Housing and Public Health." *Annual Review of Public Health* 25 (1): 397–418.

Shilling, Chris. 2012. *The Body and Social Theory*. 3rd ed. New York: Sage Publications.

Shim, Janet K. 2010. "Cultural Health Capital: A Theoretical Approach to Understanding Health Care Interactions and the Dynamics of Unequal Treatment." *Journal of Health and Social Behavior* 51 (1): 1–15.

Shore, Lynn M., and Caren B. Goldberg. 2005. "Age Discrimination in the Workplace." In *Discrimination at Work: The Psychological and Organizational Bases*, edited by Robert L. Dipboye and Adrienne Colella, 203–226. Mahwah, NJ: Lawrence Erlbaum.

Shrestha, Laura B., ed. 2006. *Life Expectancy in the United States*. Washington, DC: Congressional Research Service: Library of Congress.

Shuey, Kim M., and Andrea E. Willson. 2008. "Cumulative Disadvantage and Black-White Disparities in Life-Course Health Trajectories." *Research on Aging* 30 (2): 200–225.

Siegel, Judith M. 1990. "Stressful Life Events and Use of Physician Services among the Elderly: The Moderating Role of Pet Ownership." *Journal of Personality and Social Psychology* 58 (6): 1081–1086.

Small, Mario Luis. 2002. "Culture, Cohorts, and Social Organization Theory: Understanding Local Participation in a Latino Housing Project." *American Journal of Sociology* 108 (1): 1–54.

———. 2004. *Villa Victoria: The Transformation of Social Capital in a Boston Barrio.* Chicago: University of Chicago Press.

———. 2009. *Unanticipated Gains: Origins of Network Inequality in Everyday Life.* New York: Oxford University Press.

Small, Mario Luis, David J. Harding, and Michèle Lamont. 2010. "Reconsidering Culture and Poverty." *Annals of the American Academy of Political and Social Science* 629 (1): 6–27.

Small, Mario Luis, Erin M. Jacobs, and Rebekah Peeples Massengill. 2008. "Why Organizational Ties Matter for Neighborhood Effects: Resource Access through Childcare Centers." *Social Forces* 87 (1): 387–414.

Smedley, Brian D., Adrienne Y. Stith, and Alan R. Nelson, eds. 2003. *Unequal Treatment: Confronting Racial and Ethnic Disparities in Health Care.* Washington, DC: National Academies Press.

Smith, R. Tyson. 2008. "Pain in the Act: The Meanings of Pain among Professional Wrestlers." *Qualitative Sociology* 31: 129–148.

Smith, Robert Courtney. 2012. "Ethnography, Epistemology, and Counterfactual Causality," working paper, *American Journal of Sociology Conference on Causal Thinking and Ethnographic Research,* https://sites.google.com/site/ajs2012conference/2011-ieee-ss.

Smith, Sandra Susan. 2007. *Lone Pursuit: Distrust and Defensive Individualism among the Black Poor.* New York: Russell Sage Foundation.

———. 2010. "A Test of Sincerity: How Black and Latino Service Workers Make Decisions about Making Referrals." *Annals of the American Academy of Political and Social Science* 629 (1): 30–52.

Smith-Lovin, Linda, and Piotr Winkielman. 2010. "The Social Psychologies of Emotion: A Bridge That Is Not Too Far." *Social Psychology Quarterly* 73 (4): 327–332.

Snyder, Stephen E., and William N. Evans. 2006. "The Effect of Income on Mortality: Evidence from the Social Security Notch." *Review of Economics and Statistics* 88: 482–495.

Spalter-Roth, Roberta, Terri Ann Lowenthal, and Mercedes Rubio. 2005. "Race, Ethnicity, and the Health of Americans." In *ASA Series on How Race and Ethnicity Matter,* edited by Roberta Spalter-Roth, 1–16. American Sociological Association. http://www2.asanet.org/centennial/race_ethnicity_health.pdf.

Spencer, Martin E. 1970. "Weber on Legitimate Norms and Authority." *British Journal of Sociology* 21 (2): 123–124.

Springer, Kristen W., and Dawne M. Mouzon. 2011. "'Macho Men' and Preventative Health Care." *Journal of Health and Social Behavior* 52 (2): 212–227.

Suttles, Gerald D. 1970. *The Social Order of the Slum: Ethnicity and Territory in the Inner City.* Chicago: University of Chicago Press.

Swidler, Ann. 1986. "Culture in Action: Symbols and Strategies." *American Sociological Review* 51 (2): 273–386.

———. 2001. *Talk of Love: How Culture Matters.* Chicago: University of Chicago Press.

Thoits, Peggy A. 2011. "Mechanisms Linking Social Ties and Support to Physical and Mental Health." *Journal of Health and Social Behavior* 52 (2): 145–161.

Tilly, Charles. 1999. *Durable Inequality.* Berkeley: University of California Press.

Timmermans, Stefan. 1999. "When Death Isn't Dead: Implicit Social Rationing during Resuscitative Efforts." *Sociological Inquiry* 69 (1): 51–75.

Tomaka, Joe, Sharon Thompson, and Rebecca Palacios. 2006. "The Relation of Social Isolation, Loneliness, and Social Support to Disease Outcomes among the Elderly." *Journal of Aging and Health* 18 (3): 359–384.

Turkle, Sherry. 2012. *Alone Together: Why We Expect More from Technology and Less from Each Other.* New York: Basic Books.

Turner, Bryan S. 2008. *The Body and Society: Explorations in Social Theory.* 3rd ed. London: Sage Publications.

Umberson, Debra. 1992. "Gender, Marital Status and the Social Control of Health Behavior." *Social Science and Medicine* 34 (8): 907–917.

Umberson, Debra, Robert Crosnoe, and Corinne Reczek. 2010. "Social Relationships and Health Behavior across Life Course." *Annual Review of Sociology* 36: 139–157.

US Census Bureau. 2013. "California State and County Quickfacts 2013." http://quickfacts.census.gov/qfd/states/06000.html.

US Administration on Aging. 2009. "A Profile of Older Americans." Washington, DC: US Department of Health and Human Services. http://www.aoa.acl. gov/Aging_Statistics/Profile/2009/index.aspx

US Department of Labor. 1965. "The Negro Family: The Case for National Action." [The Monyihan Report.] Washington, DC: Office of Policy Planning and Research.

Vaisey, Stephen. "Is Interviewing Compatible with the Dual-Process Model of Culture?" (*American Journal of Cultural Sociology,* forthcoming).

———. 2009. "Motivation and Justification: Towards a Dual-Process Theory of Culture in Action." *American Journal of Sociology* 114 (6): 1675–1715.

———. 2010. "What People Want: Rethinking Poverty, Culture, and Educational Attainment." *Annals of the American Academy of Political and Social Science* 629 (1): 75–101.

Vaisey, Stephen, and Omar Lizardo. 2010. "Can Cultural Worldviews Influence Network Composition?" *Social Forces* 88 (4): 1595–1618.

Valentine, Charles A. 1967. *Culture and Poverty: Critique and Counterproposals.* Chicago: University of Chicago Press.

Venkatesh, Sudhir Alladi. 2002a. *American Project: The Rise and Fall of a Modern Ghetto.* Cambridge, MA: Harvard University Press.

———. 2002b. "'Doin' the Hustle': Constructing the Ethnographer in the American Ghetto." *Ethnography* 3 (1): 91–111.

———. 2009. *Off the Books: The Underground Economy of the Urban Poor.* Cambridge, MA: Harvard University Press.

——. 2013. *Floating City: A Rogue Sociologist Lost and Found in New York's Underground Economy*. New York: Penguin Press HC.

Vincent, John A. 2006. "Ageing Contested: Anti-Ageing Science and the Cultural Construction of Old Age." *Sociology* 40 (4): 681–698.

Vincent, John A., Chris Phillippson, and Murna Downs, eds. 2006. *The Futures of Old Age*. London: Sage Publications.

Wacquant, Loïc. 1995. "The Pugilistic Point of View: How Boxers Think and Feel about Their Trade." *Theory and Society* 24 (4): 489–535.

——. 2002. "Scrutinizing the Street: Poverty, Morality, and the Pitfalls of Urban Ethnography." *American Journal of Sociology* 107 (6): 1468–1532.

——. 2004. *Body and Soul: Notebooks of an Apprentice Boxer*. New York: Oxford University Press.

——. 2009. *Punishing the Poor: The Neoliberal Government of Social Insecurity*. Durham, NC: Duke University Press.

Walker, Renee E., Christopher R. Keane, and Jessica G. Burke. 2010. "Disparities and Access to Healthy Food in the United States: A Review of Food Deserts Literature." *Health and Place* 16 (5): 876–884.

Warner, David F., and Mark D. Hayward. 2006. "Early-Life Origins of the Race Gap in Men's Mortality." *Journal of Health and Social Behavior* 47 (3): 209–226.

Weber, Max. 1946. "The Social Psychology of the World Religions." In *Max Weber: Essays in Sociology,* edited by Hans Heinrich Gerth and C. Wright Mills, 267–363. New York: Oxford University Press.

——. 1978. *Economy and Society*. Berkeley: University of California Press.

Whyte, William Foote. 1993. *Street Corner Society: The Social Structure of an Italian Slum*. Chicago: University of Chicago Press.

Williams, David R. 2005. "The Health of US Racial and Ethnic Populations," special issue, *Journals of Gerontology, Series B: Psychological Sciences and Social Sciences* 60 (SI2): S53–S62.

Williams, David R., and Chiquita Collins. 1995. "US Socioeconomic and Racial Differences in Health: Patterns and Explanations." *Annual Review of Sociology* 21: 349–386.

——. 2001. "Racial Residential Segregation: A Fundamental Cause of Racial Disparities in Health." *Public Health Reports* 116 (5): 404–417.

Willson, Andrea E., and Kim M. Shuey. 2007. "Cumulative Advantage Processes as Mechanisms of Inequality in Life Course Health." *American Journal of Sociology* 112 (6): 1886–1924.

Wilson, William Julius. 1996. *When Work Disappears: The World of the New Urban Poor*. New York: Vintage Books.

Wu, Zheng, Christoph M. Schimmele, and Neena L. Chappell. 2012. "Aging and Late-Life Depression." *Journal of Aging and Health* 24 (1): 3–28.

ACKNOWLEDGMENTS

The notion that a book manuscript is the work of a single individual, rather than a collective effort that takes place in a larger community of scholars, friends, and family, is misguided. The "lone scholar" framing not only obscures the nature of the research enterprise (doubly so for ethnographic research), but it also robs credit from those who often deserve it most. These acknowledgments are a cursory nod to this fact—an opportunity to briefly thank people who deserve more credit and praise than I can fit into a book.

Foremost among them are my mentors. Martín Sánchez-Jankowski has been a mentor to me since I took his field-methods course as an undergraduate at the University of California–Berkeley. Over the past decade he has invested an incredible amount of time and energy in my intellectual, professional, and personal development. Martín has always challenged me to push myself, even when I protested, and shown remarkable patience in the process. Claude Fischer has also been a mentor to me since the very beginning of my career as a social scientist. Claude has continually worked with me to improve my writing and hone my analytical skills and has provided candid feedback on nearly all my projects, both large and small. Both Claude and Martín have read more rough drafts than anyone ought to be subjected to. Each commented on the various iterations of this manuscript and provided important substantive comments from the very beginning of the project through the final revisions.

Ann Swidler has been a formative influence on me and has provided intellectual guidance, encouragement, and often-needed professional advice on this project and others. Mike Hout has been essential in the development of my interest in inequality and methodology and has provided valuable advice at key points in this project and those before it. Dan Dohan has invested a great deal of time and energy in mentoring me on this project and others, and in the process has challenged me to expand my understandings of what sociologists can do with their methodological tools and how they might relate to policy. Aaron

Cicourel has encouraged me to think critically about the role of ethnographic research in social science and has helped me hone my methodological approach. Aaron has also continually pushed me to consider the role of cognition in my understanding of culture and social action. Steve Vaisey's work has not only helped shape my understanding of culture, but also his detailed feedback allowed me to improve upon this manuscript. David Montejano provided useful feedback, skepticism, and commentary that helped this project take form. Several anonymous reviewers contributed comments that helped improve the manuscript. My editor at Harvard University Press, Michael Aronson, not only provided useful substantive commentary but also showed great patience during the process of producing this manuscript. Editorial assistant Kathleen Drummy was also extremely helpful during the production process.

While conducting field research, the Institute for the Study of Societal Issues (ISSI), the Center for Research on Social Change (CRSC), and the Center for Urban Ethnography (CUE) at UC Berkeley each provided me with physical and intellectual homes. At CRSC, Christine Trost, Deborah Lustig, and David Minkus provided feedback, encouragement, and mentorship on many projects, this one included. Their excellent training program helped expose me to interdisciplinary approaches to social research and public engagement that have shaped this project and broadened my views of social science and its possibilities. The graduate fellows at CUE and CRSC served as a source of support, feedback, and intellectual development while I was collecting data and initially preparing this project as a dissertation. Phillip Fucella has not only been a friend but also has provided commentary on many iterations of many projects. Darren Modzelewski has worked with and encouraged me on various projects, and also has the dubious distinction of being the only person on this list to have given me a concussion. Greggor Mattson, Manata Hashemi, Katie Marker, and Silvia Pasquetti are friends and longtime members of my writing group who provided valuable feedback early in this project. Cynthia Schairer and Eyal Oren provided useful comments on several chapters. My colleagues at the University of Arizona were instrumental in creating a supportive intellectual environment in which to complete this work. The Jacob K. Javits program, the Center for the Study of Social Change (UCB), the Center for Latino Policy Research (UCB), the Department of Sociology at UC Berkeley and the University of California–Berkeley more generally, the School of Sociology at the University of Arizona, the College of Social and Behavioral Sciences at the University of Arizona, and the Office of the Vice President for Research at the University of Arizona each provided funding during various phases of this project.

I was lucky to have a number of exceptional research assistants. Neil Gong has been not only an engaging student and a talented research assistant who contributed to this project in many ways, but also a friend and colleague. Kelsey Hoff contributed an immense amount of time and energy to this project during her tenure as an undergraduate at Berkeley. Laureen Kay Obrien helped in the preparation of the manuscript and made useful substantive suggestions that contributed to its final form. Several other research assistants and interns, including Katherine Hood, Johanna Lee, and Tiffany Abramson, helped with vital tasks at various phases of this project.

My family has provided more support and inspiration than I can ever put into words, both during this project and over the course of my life; so, rather than try and fail, I can only acknowledge that I hope to eventually "make good" on their support and sacrifices.

Finally, although confidentiality requires that they not be named directly, I would like to thank the many seniors who participated in this project and allowed me to be part of their world, as well as the leaders and members of the organizations I observed. Their insights and friendship have profoundly altered the way I approach the world, and it is my sincerest hope that something in this book will be useful for helping to address the challenges they face in their everyday lives.

INDEX

Better safe than sorry (cultural strategy), 100, 141
Bible-study groups, 118
Biological age, 10
Biological imperative, 21
Biology, 6
Biomedicalization, 22
Block grants, 58
Bodily breakdown, 35
Body: moral dimension of, 82; natural, 86–91, 100–101, 104, 141; medical, 91–94, 100, 104, 141; social stratification and, 137
Body preservation, 75–78, 92, 104, 127, 141; alcohol and, 76; pain and, 83
Bourdieu, Pierre, 71, 82, 102, 131; logic of the game and, 2; similarly shaped problems and, 4; cultural capital and, 96
Breast cancer, 5, 24–25, 72–73, 77, 80
Broken windows model, of social disorganization, 56
Brown, William, 1
Burroughs, John, 133
Buses: coverage by, 45; free, 47, 59

Cancer, 31; breast, 5, 24–25, 72–73, 77, 80
Capacities for action, 47
Capital: cultural, 14, 74, 81, 96, 97, 140; financial, 60–63, 139; physical, 31, 137; social, 109, 127; spatial, 42, 138
CAQDAS. See Computer assisted qualitative data analysis software
Cars, 44–45
Catastrophic medical problems, 37, 76
Categorical inequalities, 135–137
Chicago heat wave (1995), 14, 109
China, 113
Chronological age, 9
Churches, 51
Classical anthropology, 93
Cliques, 127
Code switching, 94
Cognitive change, 28–30

Cognitive degeneration, 28
Common sense, 38
Communal orientation, 113
Communities: urban, 16; institutions, 54–55; religious, 112–113
Comparative sampling, 16, 151
Compensatory inversion, 59
Complementary medicine, 101
Computer assisted qualitative data analysis software (CAQDAS), 156
Confidentiality, 154
Conley, Dalton, 61
Constipation, 90
Context-dependence, of cultural resources, 98–99
Contextual inequalities. See Neighborhood resource disparities
Conversion experience, 79
County meal programs, 52–54
Crime, 31, 37
Crossover effect, 8
Cultural adaptations, 113
Cultural capital, 14, 74, 81, 96, 97, 140
Cultural expectations, 13
Cultural inputs, 74, 85; social ties and, 126–130
Cultural resources, 95–99, 141; in contexts, 96–98; context-dependence of, 98–99; identity and, 98–99; resilience and, 98–99
Cultural responses, to inequality, 140–142
Cultural schemas, 110
Cultural skills, 101
Cultural strategies, 99–102; better safe than sorry, 100, 141; fix for fun, 100–101, 141; be healthy, get help if sick, 101, 141; damn the torpedoes, 102, 141
Cultural tools, 74
Culture, 6, 95–96, 102; of poverty, 13; social stratification and, 13–14, 141–142; values and, 74; social ties and, 110–111
Cumulative advantage, 8

Responsible responses to aging, 73–85; body preservation and, 75–78; enjoyment maximization and, 78–82; pain and, 82–85
Risk, 76
Rugged individualism, 31

Safety net services, 70, 138
Sánchez-Jankowski, Martín, 127
Schemas: cultural, 110; normative, 111
Security maximization, 76
Selective mortality, 7, 8, 21, 138–139
Self-neglect, 69
Self-regulation, 83, 86
Self-sufficiency, 33
Semistructured interviews, 155
Senior centers, 54–55, 118; meals at, 50
Senior housing, 55–58; public, 17, 19; subsidized, 17, 55, 58
Senior resource guides, 54
Senior transportation system, 40, 47–48
Sensory change, 28–30
Service hubs, local, 54–58
Shared predicaments, 19–21; everyday life organization, 21–30; physical changes, 21–30; practical predicaments, 30–34; symbolic predicaments, 30–34; structural dilemmas, 34–38; conclusion to, 38
Shuttles, 47–49
Sight problems, 29
Site selection, 150
Small, Mario, 127, 150
Smith, Logan Pearsal, 39
Sobriety, 84
Sociability, 26–28; senior transportation systems and, 48
Social capital, 109, 127
Social connectedness, 14–15, 107–110, 142, 161–163
Social contexts, 137–140
Social independence, 33
Social insurance programs, 8
Social mobility, 10

Social networks, 6, 98, 104, 142–144; historically contingent structure of, 110; inequalities in, 122. *See also* Network shrinkage
Social order, 16
Social organization, 56, 109
Social science, 6
Social Security, 2, 5, 7, 8, 42, 148
Social stratification, 3, 4, 7, 17, 38, 136; catchall pathways of, 6; mechanisms of, 6, 10–15, 133–134, 144; health disparities and, 11–12; structural inequalities and, 12–13; culture and, 13–14, 141–142; social connectedness and, 14–15; body and, 137
Social ties, 53, 142–144; efficacy of, 105, 108; meanings of, 105, 108–121; mobility and, 106–107; context and, 110–111, 126–130; culture and, 110–111; justifiable action and, 110–111; generalized reciprocity and, 111–118; strong, 114–116, 125–126; weak, 116–117; earned reciprocity and, 118–121; differential vulnerability and, 121–126; network shrinkage and, 121–126; ambiguity of, 126–130; cultural inputs and, 126–130; conclusion to, 130–132
Social uncertainty, 136
Social withdrawal, 123–124
Social workers, 41, 43, 49, 66, 69
Socioeconomic status, 60
Space, as structural inequality, 42, 43
Spillover effects, 42, 139
Stamina: decline of, 22–24; pain and, 25
State support, 115
Stigma, 34, 119; money and, 63
Street-level bureaucrats, 64, 70, 139
Stroke, 31, 37
Strong ties, 114–116, 125–126
Structural dilemmas, 34–38, 135–137
Structural inequalities, 12–13, 42, 71, 95
Study design, 15–17, 149–167